THE CAUCASUS

THE CAUCASUS

AN INTRODUCTION

Thomas de Waal

OXFORD
UNIVERSITY PRESS

OXFORD

UNIVERSITY PRESS

Oxford University Press is a department of the University of Oxford. It furthers
the University's objective of excellence in research, scholarship, and education
by publishing worldwide. Oxford is a registered trade mark of Oxford University
Press in the UK and certain other countries.

Published in the United States of America by Oxford University Press
198 Madison Avenue, New York, NY 10016, United States of America.

© Oxford University Press 2019

Library of Congress Cataloging-in-Publication Data
Names: De Waal, Thomas, author.
Title: The Caucasus : an introduction / Thomas de Waal.
Description: Second edition. | New York : Oxford University Press, 2018. |
Identifiers: LCCN 2018042733 | ISBN 9780190683092 (paperback) |
ISBN 9780190683085 (hardcover)
Subjects: LCSH: Caucasus—Politics and government. | Caucasus—History. |
Caucasus—Relations—Russia. | Russia—Relations—Caucasus. |
Caucasus—Relations—Soviet Union. | Soviet Union—Relations—Caucasus. |
BISAC: POLITICAL SCIENCE / History & Theory. | POLITICAL SCIENCE /
Public Policy / Regional Planning.
Classification: LCC DK509 .D33 2018 | DDC 947.5—dc23
LC record available at https://lccn.loc.gov/2018042733

Printed in Canada by Marquis Book Printing

To Zoe

Contents

Author's Note

Such is the complexity of the South Caucasus that this small book has taken more time than it should. For generous supply of comments, expertise, corrections, and support I offer heartfelt thanks to Margarita Akhvlediani, Laurence Broers, Sopho Bukia, Jonathan Cohen, Magdalena Frichova, George Hewitt, Seda Muradian, Donald Rayfield, Laurent Ruseckas, Shahin Rzayev, Larisa Sotieva, Ronald Suny, and Maka Tsnobiladze; for photographs and more to Halid Askerov, Leli Blagonravova, (the late) Zaal Kikodze, Gia Kraveishvili, (the late) Ruben Mangasarian, and Vladimir Valishvili; for elegant and informative maps to Chris Robinson; for making the book possible to my agent David Miller and editors Dave McBride and Alexandra Dauler; for putting up with the book in their midst to my dearest wife and daughter Georgina Wilson and Zoe de Waal.

A brief word about definitions and language. I tread carefully here but will inevitably end up offending some people. I use the word "Caucasian" literally to describe people from the Caucasus region. The old-fashioned usage of the word, still encountered in the United States, to denote white-skinned people of European descent is the legacy of a discredited racial theory devised by the eighteenth-century German anthropologist Johann Friedrich Blumenbach. The Caucasus is a region where different nationalities have called places by different names at different times. I take a pragmatic approach of calling places by the name that was most accepted at a certain historical moment. So I write "Tiflis" for Georgia's main city until the early twentieth century, when it was called by its Georgian version, "Tbilisi"; and I write "Shusha" and "Stepanakert" for the two main towns of Nagorny Karabakh. For the region as a whole, I use the term "Transcaucasus" when talking about it in a Russian historical context but otherwise stick to the more neutral "South Caucasus." Sometimes I will risk offending people from the North Caucasus—which is outside the scope of this book—by writing "Caucasus" when I mean only the area south of the mountains. The North Caucasus is a separate world, equally fascinating and complex, far more within Russia's sphere of influence. The South Caucasus is complex and demanding enough for a small book.

THE CAUCASUS

Introduction

The countries of the South Caucasus have always been the "lands in-between." In between the Black and Caspian seas, Europe and Asia, Russia and the Middle East, Christianity and Islam, and, more recently, democracy and dictatorship. Armenia, Azerbaijan, and Georgia and the territories around them have the mixed blessing of being at the crossing-place of different cultures and political systems. These fault lines have made their region a geopolitical seismic zone. The kind of local shock that might be muffled elsewhere in the world reverberates more loudly here. That was what happened in August 2008, in the tiny territory of South Ossetia, a place with barely 50,000 inhabitants: an exchange of fire between villages escalated into a war between Georgia and Russia and then into a grave crisis in relations between Moscow and the West.

The war over South Ossetia was an extreme illustration of the principle that "all politics is local." The people on the ground were at fault only inasmuch as they called for help from their big outside patrons. A chain of response went from Georgian villagers to the Georgian government in Tbilisi to Georgia's friends in the West; the Ossetian villagers called for help on their own government, which looked to its protector in Moscow.

For such a small region—it has a population of just fifteen million people and the area of a large American state—the South Caucasus has attracted a lot of Western interest since the end of the Soviet Union in 1991. A series of political agendas coincide here. There is a desire to resolve the three

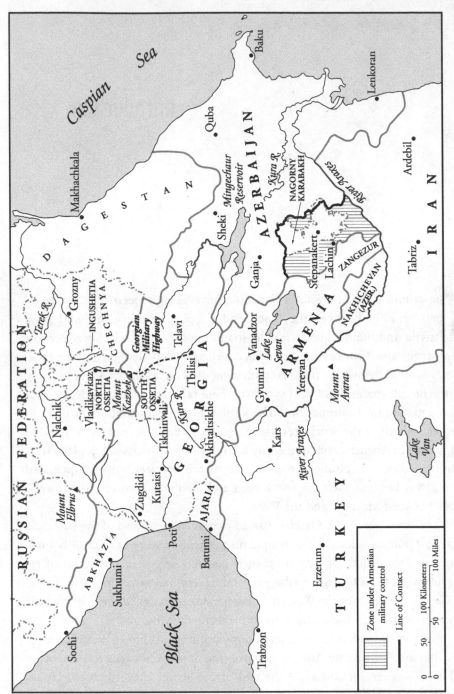

The Caucasus in 2010

ethnoterritorial disputes over Abkhazia, Nagorny Karabakh, and South Ossetia and calm a potential area of instability—the crisis in South Ossetia was in fact the smallest of the three conflicts. There is continued commercial and political interest in the energy resources of the Caspian Sea, which may contain 5 percent of the world's oil and is likely to have a role to play in Europe's future gas supplies. There is support by the large Armenian diaspora in the United States, France, and other countries for the newly independent Republic of Armenia. There has been political investment in Georgia's ambitions to be a model of post-Soviet reform. There is also the challenge of the South Caucasus as an arena of engagement and, more often, confrontation with Russia.

The United States in particular has discovered the South Caucasus. Over the last decade, a number of very senior figures in Washington have taken an interest in the region. In May 2005, President George W. Bush stood in Freedom Square in the Georgian capital, Tbilisi, and told Georgians, "Your courage is inspiring democratic reformers and sending a message across the world—freedom will be a future of each nation and every people on earth." A year later, Senator John McCain was presented with a Georgian sword on his seventieth birthday and told Georgians, "You are America's best friends." Azerbaijan, the largest and wealthiest of the three countries of the region, drew a steady stream of high-level political and commercial visitors from the United States. In the U.S. Congress, a powerful Armenian lobby ensured that Armenia was for a while the largest per capita recipient of U.S. aid money of any country in the world—aid to Georgia would soon match that level. The danger of these kinds of interventions is that they are too narrow and focus on one part of the picture and not the whole. Yet the whole picture is deeply complex and makes the Balkans seem simple by comparison. In the past its multiple local politics have defeated the strategists of the Great Powers of the day. In 1918 British general Lionel Dunsterville tried to sum up the situation he was supposed to be sorting out:

> There are so many situations here, that it is difficult to give
> a full appreciation of each. There is the local situation,
> the all-Persia situation, the Jangali situation, the Persian-
> Russian situation, the Turkish-advance-on-Tabriz situation,
> the question of liquidating Russian debts, the Baku situ-
> ation, the South Caucasus situation, the North Caucasus
> situation, the Bolshevik situation and the Russian situation

as a whole. And each of these subdivides into smaller and
acuter situations for there is no real Caucasian or even
North or South Caucasian point of view, there is no unity
of thought or action, nothing but mutual jealousy and mis-
trust. Thus the Georgians of Tiflis regard the problem from
a Georgian point of view and play only for their own hand;
the Armenians and the Tartars in the south, and the Terek
and Kuban Cossacks and the Daghestanis in the north, do
the same.[1]

In a place as complicated as this, a little knowledge can be a dangerous
thing. In this conjunction of the deeply local and the global, the small
players can overestimate their importance, and the big players can promise
too much. The history of the Caucasus is littered with mistakes based on
these kinds of assumptions and miscalculations. In August 2008, Georgian
president Mikheil Saakashvili blundered into a war over South Ossetia, almost certainly believing he had more support in the West than he actually
did. The biggest problem in the South Caucasus, the unresolved Armenian-
Azerbaijani Nagorny Karabakh conflict, is an earlier example of how a dispute about local grievances has caused international havoc. When it began,
it was a local dispute in a far-off Soviet province, but it proved to be the first
link in a long chain that eventually tugged down the whole structure of the
Soviet Union. Nowadays, the dispute literally divides the South Caucasus in
two and, by virtue of its proximity to oil and gas pipelines, has a bearing on
European energy security.

For the West, ill-judged intervention can be dangerous for another
reason: the South Caucasus—or Transcaucasus—was for long periods
part of the Russian Empire or the Soviet Union and remains a zone of intense Russian interest. Russian strategists often regard Western interest in
the Caucasus as dilettantism. Although no one believes that the West will
abandon the Caucasus to Russian interests as the Western powers abandoned it to the Bolsheviks in 1920, there is more than a grain of truth in
this. Modern Russia has a more sustained strategic interest in this region
on its borders than any Western powers are ever likely to have. To take
one example, in 1993 it was Russia, not the West, that agreed to set up a
peacekeeping force for the conflict zone of Abkhazia, in which 120 Russian
soldiers subsequently died. Western countries were not interested in a peacekeeping mission for this remote and unstable area. That decision set the stage

for Russia's subsequent outmaneuvering of the West in Abkhazia many years later. Yet Russia also overestimates its understanding of the Caucasus and confuses agreement with subservience in a place like Abkhazia. Power in the Caucasus is generally in inverse proportion to knowledge: the small peoples of the region, speaking multiple languages and keeping a keen eye open, understand their more powerful Great Power neighbors much better than vice versa.

Thus, there is a big gap in understanding about the South Caucasus, which this book hopes partly to fill. It is part portrait and part history, with an emphasis on the events of the last twenty-five years, since the three nation-states of the region achieved independence from the wreckage of the Soviet Union. My aim is to focus firmly on the local dynamics of the region while putting them within a broader context. To get a proper perspective on this region, you need both zoom and wide-angle lenses.

The South Caucasus is in many ways a constructed region. Some will say that it exists only in the mind, in the memory of a Soviet-era generation, and in the vision of policy analysts who devise concepts such as the "Eastern Partnership" project. Actually, the cynics say, the South Caucasus "region" is just a tangle of roadblocks and closed borders that has no common identity beyond a shared past that is being rapidly forgotten. I make no apology for opposing that view. I believe that the South Caucasus does make sense as a region, and that the future of its peoples will be better served by them thinking as one. As I will make clear, there are strong ties of culture between the different nations of the Caucasus and patterns of economic collaboration that persist, even despite closed borders. A common history of Russian rule has shaped everything from railway systems to schooling to table customs. It is also worth considering the South Caucasus as a region in a negative sense, because its different interconnected parts have the capacity to do real harm to one another. Surrounded by bigger neighbors and entangled with each other's problems, the countries of Georgia, Armenia, and Azerbaijan and their breakaway territories cannot escape their Caucasian predicament even if they wanted to.

1

Among the Mountains

Boundaries

First of all there are the mountains. The Greater Caucasus chain is the highest mountain range in Europe—so long as you accept that the region is within Europe. Marking a barrier with the Russian plains to the north, they curve in a magnificent arc for 800 miles from the Black Sea to the Caspian Sea. Among the crowning peaks are the two extinct volcanic cones of Mount Elbrus (18,510 feet, or 5,642 meters) on the Russian side of the mountains and Mount Kazbek (16,558 feet, or 5,033 meters) in the north of Georgia.

For centuries, the name "Caucasus" was synonymous in Europe with wild cold mountains and with the myth of Prometheus, who stole fire from the gods and was punished by being chained to the icy peaks. In two references to the mountains, Shakespeare asked, "Who can hold fire in his hand / By thinking on the frosty Caucasus?" and wrote of a lover as "And faster bound to Aaron's charming eyes / Than is Prometheus tied to Caucasus." But two centuries later, Shelley had only a very vague idea of where the mountains actually were and set his verse drama *Prometheus Unbound* in "A Ravine of Icy Rocks in the Indian Caucasus." It was only in 1874 that a team of English mountaineers climbed the higher peak of Mount Elbrus.

Thus, these mountains are both a colossal landmark and a powerful barrier, and the South Caucasus, the subject of this book, is defined as the region south of this barrier. In Russian, the region is known as the Transcaucasus, or Zakavkaz'ye, because in Russian eyes it is on the far side of the mountains.

The more politically neutral term "South Caucasus" has only gained usage since the three countries of Armenia, Azerbaijan, and Georgia achieved independence in 1991. Mountains define the southern parts of the region as well. A second chain, the Lesser Caucasus, runs to the south of the main range, giving Armenia and western Azerbaijan a mountainous landscape. These mountains turn south through the highlands that have come to be known as Nagorny—Mountainous—Karabakh. To the southwest of the Republic of Armenia loom the two peaks of the sacred Mount Ararat, which is inside the borders of Asian Turkey but dominates the horizon of the Armenian capital Yerevan on a clear day.

Not all of the South Caucasus is mountainous. It also contains the fertile wine-making plains of eastern Georgia, subtropical coastline on the Black Sea coast, and arid desert in central Azerbaijan. But highland geography is the prime cause of several special features of the region. The first is ethnic diversity: a mixture of nationalities lives within a relatively compact area with a population of only about fifteen million people. The Arabs called the Caucasus *djabal al-alsun,* or the "mountain of languages," for its abundances of languages, and the North and South Caucasus together have the greatest density of distinct languages anywhere on earth. The South

Highland landscape in Tusheti, Georgia. Thomas de Waal.

Caucasus contains around ten main nationalities. Alongside the three main ethnic groups—the Azerbaijanis, Georgians, and Armenians—are Ossetians, Abkhaz, both Muslim and Yezidi Kurds, Talysh, and Lezgins. Most of them speak mutually unintelligible languages.

The main nationalities also contain linguistic diversity within themselves. If history had taken a different turn, some provinces might have ended up as their own nation-states. Mingrelians and Svans in Georgia speak their own languages, related to but distinct from Georgian. Karabakh Armenians speak a dialect that is hard to understand in Yerevan. North and South Ossetians speak markedly different dialects of Ossetian and are divided by the mountains. With ethnic diversity come strong traditions of particularism and local autonomy. Abkhazia, Ajaria, South Ossetia, Karabakh, and Nakhichevan were given an autonomous status under the Soviet Union that reflected older traditions of self-rule.

We inevitably end up calling the South Caucasus a "region," but in many ways it isn't one. Centrifugal forces are strong. The South Caucasus—or Transcaucasus—was first put together as a Russian colonial region in the early nineteenth century. The only historical attempt to make a single state, the Transcaucasian Federation, collapsed into three parts after just a month in May 1918. That breakdown created for the first time three entities called Armenia, Azerbaijan, and Georgia, which were then preserved under Soviet rule.

Three of the borders of this region are defined by geography, but the others less so. The first border, the Greater Caucasus chain, was established as a natural boundary thousands of years ago. The Greek geographer Strabo, writing in the first century AD, said it "overhangs both the Euxine and the Caspian Seas forming a kind of rampart to the isthmus which separates one sea from another."[1] The North Caucasus region on the other side of the mountains is mostly a separate world, sitting on the southern fringe of the Russian Federation with few links to the outside world. The North Caucasus is a mosaic of mainly Muslim nationalities inhabiting seven autonomous regions. The largest of them, Dagestan, was so important it was sometimes referred to as the "Eastern Caucasus." The Russian Empire only fully conquered these territories in the 1850s and 1860s, a full fifty years after the takeover of Georgia. Three small ethnic groups have a foot in both the North and South Caucasus and make a narrow bridge between the two regions. In the west, the Abkhaz on the Black Sea coast have been part of Georgia for long periods of their history but also have strong ethnic ties with the Circassian nationalities in the North Caucasus. In the middle of the region, Ossetians live on both the Russian and Georgian sides of the mountains, in both North and South Ossetia. In the east, on the Caspian Sea coast, the Lezgins are divided between Russia and Azerbaijan.

The other two natural boundaries of the South Caucasus, the Black and Caspian seas, have opened up the region to trade and invasion from both Europe and Asia. For centuries, the South Caucasus was located on the major east-west trade routes between Europe and Asia, forming a kind of lesser "Silk Road" passing through the ancient cities of Baku, Derbent, and Tiflis. The only historical exception to this was in Soviet times, when international borders were closed, this route was shut down, and all trade went north.

The fourth boundary to the south is mostly set by the river Araxes, or Aras, which was fixed as the border between the Russian and Persian empires in 1828. The Araxes runs for 660 miles from eastern Turkey between Armenia and Azerbaijan on one side and Iran on the other, until it meets the other main river of the region, the Kura, and flows into the Caspian Sea. Modern Azerbaijan extends south of the Araxes at its eastern stretch, encompassing the mountainous region where the Talysh people live.

Finally, the southwestern border south of the Black Sea, between Turkey on the one hand and Georgia and Armenia on the other, is the one defined most by history and least by natural geography. This area is called both Eastern Anatolia and Western Armenia, which gives some idea of its changing status over the centuries. In 1913, what is now the Turkish city of Kars was a Russian frontier town—a Russian travel guide of that year recommends that visitors take a look at its new granite war memorial. In the years 1915–21, this borderland was the scene of horrific bloodshed, as most of its Armenian population was killed, along with members of many other communities, and Turkish, Russian, and Armenian armies fought over it. The border was eventually drawn between Turkey and the new Bolshevik republics of Armenia and Georgia under the Treaty of Kars in 1921. The treaty established that the port of Batumi would be part of Georgia and conclusively gave Eastern Anatolia, including the Armenians' holy mountain, Mount Ararat, to the new Turkish state. It thereby set the western frontier of the South Caucasus, which was further cemented by Soviet and Turkish border guards and the Cold War.

Belonging

Is the South Caucasus in Europe or Asia? By one definition, proposed by the eighteenth-century German-Swedish geographer Philip Johan von Strahlenberg, the region is in Asia, and the border with Europe runs along the Kuma-Manych Depression, north of the Greater Caucasus range. Other geographers, a bit more tidily, have made the mountains of the Caucasus themselves the border between Europe and Asia. Nowadays, the consensus is to place Georgia, Armenia, and Azerbaijan in Europe and make the Turkish border and the river Araxes the Europe-Asia frontier. The strange result of this is that "Europe" in Armenia and Azerbaijan is directly due east of the "Asian" Turkish towns of Kars and Trabzon.

No definition is satisfactory because the South Caucasus has multiple identities. It is both European and Asian, with strong Middle Eastern influences as well. Politically the three countries, and Georgia in particular, look more towards Europe. They are members of the two European institutions, the Council of Europe and the Organization for Security and Cooperation in Europe (OSCE)—but then so is Turkey. The Georgian politician Zurab Zhvania famously told the Council of Europe in 1999, "I am Georgian and therefore I am European." But Armenians maintain links with their diaspora communities in Iran, Lebanon, and Syria, and Azerbaijanis have affinities with the Turkic nations of Central Asia. In the end, it comes down to a matter of self-identification. At the beginning of Kurban Said's classic 1937 novel of the Caucasus, *Ali and Nino*, set in Baku before and during the First World War, a Russian teacher informs his pupils that the Russian Empire has resolved the ancient geographical dispute over the Caucasus in favor of Europe. The teacher says, "It can therefore be said, my children, that it is partly your responsibility as to whether our town should belong to progressive Europe or to reactionary Asia"—at which point Mehmed Haidar, sitting in the back row, raises his hand and says, "Please, sir, we would rather stay in Asia."[2]

The Caucasus also has its own identity. Anthropologists identify its customs and traditions fairly easily, and they get more marked the closer to the mountains one gets. The Caucasian nationalities share similar wedding and funeral ceremonies, and all mark the fortieth day after the death of a loved one with strikingly similar rituals. The same elaborate rituals of hospitality and toasting are found across the region, even among Muslim Azerbaijanis. Foreign mediators between "warring" Armenians and Azerbaijanis or

Georgians and Abkhaz have frequently seen how once the two sides sit down to dinner together, political differences are forgotten and convivial rituals of eating and drinking precisely observed.

WINE

The Caucasus may be the home of wine. Archaeological finds in southern Georgia, northwestern Azerbaijan, and northern Armenia suggest that Stone Age people took advantage of a temperate climate and the availability of wild fruit species to experiment with cultivating grapes.

In the 1960s, archaeologists in northwestern Azerbaijan found what seemed to be domesticated grape pips in their excavations dating from around 6000 BC. More recently, the American scholar Patrick McGovern found traces of wine in huge narrow-necked, five-liter ceramic vessels from this period excavated from the citadel of Shulaveri in Georgia. The wine had been treated with resin as a preservative. Around 2000 BC, craftsmen of the Trialeti culture in the same area were carving scenes of banquets on gold and silver goblets. And a millennium after that, the Greek historian Herodotus wrote that Armenian boatmen brought wine down the Tigris River to Babylon.[1]

Ceramic wine jars buried in the ground have survived through the centuries under different names. In 1829, Alexander Pushkin wrote, "Kakhetian and Karabakhi are worth several Burgundies. They keep the wine in *maranis*, huge jars, buried in the ground. These are opened with great ceremony. Recently a Russian dragoon secretly unearthed one of these jars, fell inside and drowned in Kakhetian wine, like the unfortunate Clarence in the butt of malmsey."[2]

All three South Caucasian countries make and drink both wine and cognac. Azerbaijan's vineyards were ravaged by Mikhail Gorbachev's antialcohol campaign, and the revival of Islam has restrained drinking habits since then. Armenia is most famous for its cognac. Brands such as Nairi and Dvin are admired all over the world—although the story that Winston Churchill liked to drink Dvin seems to be a legend disseminated by a popular Soviet spy television serial.[3]

Georgia is utterly inseparable from wine. It has more than 400 indigenous varieties, of which forty or so are commercial brands. The most popular brands are semi-sweet reds like Kindzamarauli and Khvanchkara and drier whites such as Tsinandali. The drinking of wine at the table is central to the nation's collective identity. Caucasian banqueting and toasts attain an extra level of intensity in Georgia. A proper Georgian *supra* (banquet) lasts for many hours. A man is designated *tamada* (toastmaster) to lead the toasts and direct and entertain the other guests. The German anthropologist Florian Muehlfried argues that the rituals of the table became a way for Georgians to assert their difference from others and in particular vodka-drinking Russians:

"Since the Russians, unlike former invaders, shared the same religion as the Georgians, religion was no longer a distinguishing factor between 'us' (the Georgians) and 'them'

Farmers in Kakheti, Georgia, bringing in the harvest. Vladimir Valishvili.

(the Russians). The 'self-othering' of the Georgian nation had to be based on something else: folk culture. The *supra* soon became a symbol of that cultural otherness, a manifestation of 'Georgian' hospitality based on a distinct way of eating, drinking and feasting."[4]

Russia's ban on Georgian wine was lifted in 2013. Disastrous in the short term, the embargo had an overwhelmingly positive long-term effect on Georgian winemaking. Production volumes dropped sharply, but quality improved radically. A series of new high-end wineries opened, many using the technique of making wine in a large ceramic jar known as a *qvevri*. In 2016, Russia was again the major export destination of what was now a much more diversified and higher-quality industry.[5]

1. Patrick E. McGovern, *Ancient Wine: The Search for the Origins of Viniculture* (Princeton, N.J.: Princeton University Press, 2003).
2. Alexander Pushkin, *Journey to Erzerum.*
3. See Irina Petrosian and David Underwood, *Armenian Food: Fact, Fiction and Folklore* (Bloomington, Ind.: Yerkir, 2006), 160–61. If the story has any basis in reality, it may be—although this is best not repeated in Yerevan—that Stalin introduced Churchill to Eniseli Georgian cognac when they first met in Moscow in August 1942 and Churchill flew a consignment home. See Cheryl Heckler, *An Accidental Journalist: The Adventures of Edmund Stevens, 1934– 1945* (Columbia: University of Missouri Press, 2007), 205.
4. Florian Muehlfried, "Sharing the Same Blood—Culture and Cuisine in the Republic of Georgia," *Anthropology of Food* (December 2007), http://aof.revues.org/index2342.html.
5. "Official: 50 Million Bottles of Wine Exported to 53 Countries in 2015," *Hvino News*, January 4, 2017.

Ethnic and religious differences have always existed but are much more accentuated by modern politics. A century ago, attitudes toward religion could be deeply pragmatic. In her memoir of early twentieth-century Abkhazia, Adile Abas-oglu writes, "Arriving in Mokva for the Muslim festivals I always laughed when I observed how people drink wine and vodka at them and some families cooked holiday dishes from pork."[3] The émigré historian Aytek Namitok wrote:

Common shrines revered by followers of both religions are by no means rare. The tomb of St. George in the Church of Mokus-Su and the Christian shrine of Dzivar are honored by both Georgians and Armenians on the one hand and by Azerbaidzhan and Moslem Kurds on the other. According to a local tradition the former was built by a Christian and a Moslem shepherd. Similarly the Moslem shrine of Pir-Dovgan (or Saint Dovgan) was revered as earnestly by the Armenians as by the followers of Mahomet.[4]

Before that, in the 1840s the German traveler Baron August von Haxthausen said he saw more hostility between adherents of the same religion than between different faiths:

> The Mohammedan Tatars, Circassians, and Persians, and the Christian Georgians and Armenians, inhabit the same villages, maintain friendly intercourse, and sometimes even eat together on the same carpet; each however strictly complying with the requirements of its own faith, and adhering to their respective national manners, customs and dress. Only between sects of the same religion—as between the Shiite and Sunnite Mohammedans, and those Armenians belonging to the National and to the Romish Church—is there enmity.[5]

The South Caucasus has a long tradition of decentralization, which comes with the landscape. In Georgia, mountain people in Svaneti, Khevsureti, or Tusheti were barely linked to central rule from Tbilisi until the modern era. Azerbaijan, which also did not exist as a single political unit before the modern era, is also characterized by regional divides. Political regionalism, with local politicians having strong local power bases and distributing power and favor to people from the same region, is still alive in Azerbaijan, and even has a name: *yerlizabliq*. Under the last two presidents of Azerbaijan, father and son Heidar and Ilham Aliev, the ruling elite has been dominated by a so-called Nakhichevan clan, made up of people originating from the homeland of the Aliev family. To be a "Nakhichevani" does not mean that one has to live there—President Ilham Aliev has never done so—yet place of origin is still an important marker of identity.

The three main capital cities of the region have their own distinct histories. A century ago, neither Tbilisi (Tiflis), Baku, nor Yerevan had a majority population of Georgians, Azerbaijanis, or Armenians, respectively. Tbilisi can lay claim to being the capital of the Caucasus, but its Georgian character has been much more intermittent. For 500 years it was an Arab town, while the older city of Mtskheta was the old Georgian capital. Then, in the medieval period, the city was taken over by the Armenian merchant class. They were the biggest community in the nineteenth century and finally left en masse only in the 1960s. Famous Tbilisi Armenians have included the world chess champion Tigran Petrosian and the filmmaker Sergei Parajanov. Baku became a cosmopolitan city with many different ethnic groups from the late nineteenth century. Russian became its lingua franca. Garry Kasparov, the Jewish-Armenian world chess champion, who was born in Baku but is unable to return there because of his Armenian roots, describes his nationality as "Bakuvian" (*Bakinets* in Russian). Baku only turned into a strongly Azerbaijani city with the end of the Soviet Union, the Nagorny Karabakh war, and the mass emigration of other national groups.

By contrast, up until the First World War, Yerevan, the capital of Armenia, had a Persian flavor and a Muslim-majority population. Its major landmark was a blue-tiled mosque, and there was no big church. Von Haxthausen wrote, "In Tiflis, Europe and Asia may be said to meet, and the town has a divided aspect; but Erivan is a purely Asiatic city: everything is Oriental, except a few newly-built Russian houses, and occasionally Russian uniforms in the streets."[6] More Armenians lived in Tiflis, Baku, Shusha, and Van. Yerevan became an Armenian city only after the mass flight of Armenians from the Ottoman Empire and of Azerbaijanis from eastern Armenia in 1915–18.

Arguably, strong national identities only began to emerge in the three countries of the South Caucasus in the Soviet era. A consolidation of national identity created a demographic pull such that Armenians moved to Armenia and Azerbaijanis to Azerbaijan, and Tbilisi became a strongly Georgian city for perhaps the first time in its history. The biggest losers were the smaller minority peoples of the Transcaucasus, who feared assimilation, even though their rights were nominally protected by Soviet law.

Half a dozen smaller nationalities form sizable communities in the South Caucasus. Kurds are spread throughout the region. So-called Yezidi Kurds are Armenia's biggest minority, and there are large numbers of Muslim Kurds in Azerbaijan. The Abkhaz and the Ossetians (discussed in chapter 5) are both few in numbers. There are just over 100,000 Abkhaz in Abkhazia

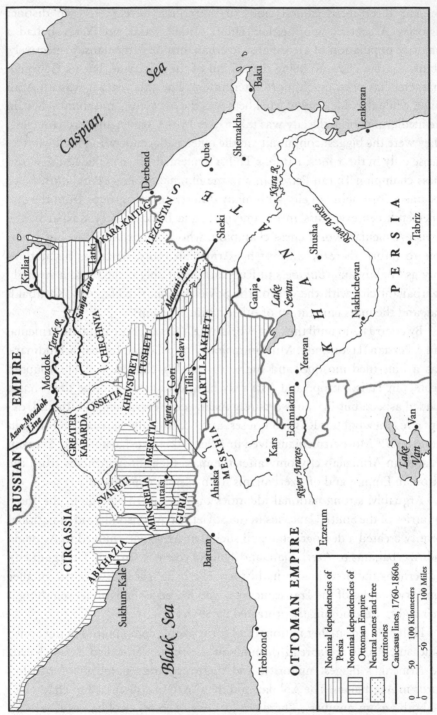

The Caucasus circa 1780

Caspian Sea

Black Sea

RUSSIAN EMPIRE

OTTOMAN EMPIRE

PERSIA

K H A N A T E S

CIRCASSIA

ABKHAZIA

SVANETI

MINGRELIA

GURIA

IMERETIA

MESKHIA

OSSETIA

GREATER KABARDA

KHEVSURETI

TUSHETI

CHECHNYA

KARTLI-KAKHETI

LEZGISTAN

KARA-KAITAG

Azov-Mozdok Line

Mozdok

Terek R.

Sunja Line

Alazani Line

Kura R.

Kura R.

River Araxes

River Araxes

Lake Sevan

Lake Van

Kizliar

Tarki

Derbend

Quba

Shemakha

Baku

Lenkoran

Sheki

Shusha

Nakhichevan

Ganja

Yerevan

Echmiadzin

Tabriz

Van

Kars

Ahiska

Tiflis

Gori

Telavi

Kutaisi

Sukhum-Kale

Batum

Trebizond

Erzerum

Nominal dependencies of Persia

Nominal dependencies of Ottoman Empire

Neutral zones and free territories

Caucasus lines, 1760–1860s

0   50   100 Kilometers
0   50   100 Miles

and even fewer Ossetians in South Ossetia—many more Ossetians live in Russian North Ossetia. Azerbaijan's main two minority ethnic groups are the Lezgins in the north and the Talysh in the south. The 200,000 Lezgins (according to official figures) live in the north of Azerbaijan across the border from around 400,000 of their ethnic kin who live in the Russian republic of Dagestan. They are Sunnis, and they speak a language apparently indigenous to the Caucasus. The Talysh live in southern Azerbaijan near the Iranian border and speak a language related to Farsi. Officially, they number 80,000, but the Talysh themselves give much higher figures. Neither of these ethnic groups plays a political role in the country, although there are occasionally glimmers of discontent about their cultural rights.

KURDS

Kurds have lived for a millennium across the Caucasus as well as in half a dozen countries of the Middle East. The mother of Nizami, the twelfth-century Persian poet from the city of Ganja, was Kurdish. The Kurds of the Caucasus divide into two main groups. The Muslim (mostly Shiite) Kurds are now resident mainly only in Azerbaijan. The so-called Yezidi Kurds, who live in Armenia and Georgia, are not Muslim; some of them do not identify themselves as Kurds, although they speak a language that is identifiably Kurdish.

How many Kurds there actually are is hard to say because they have undergone heavy assimilation and the majority no longer speak Kurdish. According to the all-Russian census of 1897, around 100,000 Kurdish-speakers were living in the South Caucasus.[1] Most were still nomadic herders. In the 1920s, they nominally benefited from the Bolsheviks' "nativization" projects. A region named Red Kurdistan was established in 1923 in six districts of western Azerbaijan between Nagorny Karabakh and Armenia, with its center in the village of Lachin. The 1926 census listed 37,470 Kurds in Red Kurdistan. However, there is no evidence that the Soviet authorities invested any resources in making the experiment work. In the 1926 census, only 17 percent of the Kurds identified Kurdish as their mother tongue.

Red Kurdistan was abolished in 1929. In the 1930s Kurds, were identified as a "backward" and "enemy" group, with ethnic kin on the other side of Soviet frontiers. They were heavily assimilated as Azerbaijanis. In 1937, they were one of the first Soviet nationalities to be deported to Kazakhstan and Siberia. Tens of thousands died. The Kurdish language was banned. Although they were allowed to return home in the 1950s, Kurds virtually disappeared as an ethnic group in Azerbaijan.

No Kurds at all were listed in the 1979 census. The assimilation was part enforced, part willing. Kurds spoke the Azeri language, intermarried with Azerbaijanis, and practiced the same religion as them . Even the leading Kurdish historian of Azerbaijan, Shamil Askerov, listed himself as "Azerbaijani" on his passport. This meant that Muslim Kurds suffered the same fate as Azerbaijanis in the Nagorny Karabakh war. In 1992 and 1993 Armenian forces captured the regions of Lachin, Kelbajar, and Kubatly, which had formerly been "Red Kurdistan," and drove out the entire mixed Azerbaijani-Kurdish population. Shepherds who had summered there were forced to settle permanently on their winter grazing grounds.

Armenia's own Yezidi Kurds stayed in Armenia, thanks to their distinct identity. Neither Christian nor Muslim but with their own ancient religious practices, they had mainly moved to Russian Armenia from the Ottoman Empire in the nineteenth century. By the Yezidis' own estimates there are 30,000 to 40,000 of them still in Armenia, comprising about 3 percent of the population. They are mostly poor farmers or shepherds with limited political influence in Armenia. The Yezidis exist at one remove from other Kurds, and many even deny that they are related. Many have emigrated to Russia, and this unique ethnic group is at risk of disappearing.[2]

1. Julie Flint, *The Kurds of Azerbaijan and Armenia* (London: Kurdish Human Rights Project, December 1998), 4.
2. Zhanna Alexanian and Andrei Liankevich, "Armenia's Yezidi Kurds," Institute for War and Peace Reporting, Caucasus Reporting Service (August 2005), http://www.iwpr.net/galleries/yezidi/yezidi_text.html.

Beginnings

The ancient history of the Caucasus is fairly mysterious. For the purposes of this book, two statements can be made with confidence: the region is a treasure trove for archaeologists, and its ancient past has very little bearing on the present. Some of the earliest-ever skulls, dating back 1.8 million years and named (with more than a hint of patriotism) *Homo georgicus*, were discovered by archaeologists in Dmanisi in southern Georgia. A Neanderthal jawbone found in a cave at Azykh in Karabakh has been dated as over 300,000 years old. There was a flourishing Stone Age culture in the region around 6000 BC that may have invented wine-making. There are rock engravings at Gobustan, south of Baku, that are almost 4,000 years old. All this indicates continuous patterns of settlement since ancient times.

Two ancient Greek and biblical stories are still part of the national narratives of the Caucasus. In Armenia, cafes, shops, and a news agency are named "Noyan Tapan," or "Noah's Ark," in honor of the story that in the biblical flood, the ark came to rest on Mount Ararat. Georgians are still named "Jason" or "Medea" because of the myth of Jason and the Argonauts. The kingdom of Colchis, land of the Golden Fleece and Jason's final destination, can be traced back to a principality that existed on the eastern Black Sea coast in the thirteenth century BC. According to a popular theory, panners for gold used sheep's fleeces to sieve out the precious metals in the streams of Colchis, and that is how the fleeces became "golden."

The first tangible link in the chain of continuity from the past comes with the arrival of Christianity in the region. The tiny stone churches, decorated with carvings, scattered across the landscape are testimony to an ancient Christian civilization that is a defining feature of Armenia and Georgia. The two peoples take pride in having been the first nations to convert to

Christianity in the early fourth century, just before Constantine took up the new faith for the Roman Empire. Today, the national churches have a central role in both Armenia and Georgia, and the Armenian catholicos and Georgian patriarch are national figures, afforded high respect.

Caucasian Christianity still bears strong marks of the pagan and Zoroastrian world that preceded it. The famous Armenian "cross-stones," or *khachkars,* incorporate a fiery Zoroastrian sun-circle beneath the cross. Most Ossetians are nominally Christian, but many still take part in overtly pagan ceremonies. The village of Lykhny in Abkhazia contains a medieval church as well as a pre-Christian shrine where Abkhaz have held mass meetings twice in the twentieth century, in 1931 and 1989, at moments of national crisis.

Both Georgians and Armenians also have long traditions of accommodation with Islam. Historically, Armenians have fared well in the Iranian Empire, and the modern-day legacy of that is a good relationship between overwhelmingly Christian Armenia and the Islamic Republic of Iran. There are also both Armenian and Georgian Muslims. Hemshins, who live in northeastern Turkey, are recognizably both Muslim and of Armenian origin. The Georgians of Ajaria on the Georgian Black Sea coast, which was part of the Ottoman Empire for more than 200 years, are mostly Muslim. For several centuries, Georgian kings and aristocrats converted to Islam and served as courtiers to the Iranian Safavid dynasty, while the feudal lords of the Jakeli family in Meskhia were Muslims who served the Ottoman sultans. These Georgian princes were probably Christian at home and Muslim in public. Deft changes of religious affiliation for political purposes are a recurring theme in the history of the Caucasus—the most recent instance of which occurred in Georgia and Armenia in the 1990s, when the entire Communist Party leadership was suddenly baptized as Christians overnight.

Bearing in mind these caveats, it is still accurate to say that Christianity is central to the identity of both the Armenians and Georgians. The Armenian king Trdat III was supposedly converted by Saint Gregory the Illuminator in either 301 or 314. Georgia became Christian in 327–32, when King Mirian III was converted by Saint Nino. Christianity's grip was strengthened when both nations adopted their own alphabets in the late fourth century, enabling them to write religious texts in their own scripts. For both Armenians and Georgians, the church and the written language provided a source of continuity that kept collective identity alive under foreign rule. As historian Nina Garsoïan wrote of the Armenians, "From the start, the church helped to create a separate Armenian identity and provided a focus for the allegiance of the entire population that was independent of the political framework and consequently from the fate of the realm."[7] The overlap between the Armenian Apostolic Church and the nationality was so strong in the nineteenth century that von Haxthausen commented that Armenians who had rejected the national church ceased to identify themselves as Armenians. He wrote, "Armenians in Tiflis and elsewhere, who have joined the Church of Rome, proudly renounce the name of Armenians, and call themselves Catholics."[8]

To the outsider, one of the mysteries of the Caucasus is why the relationship between the Armenians and the Georgians, two old Christian nations, is frequently fraught and suspicious. The rivalry between the two is a recurring theme in nineteenth-century literature. More recently, it is a comic strand in the popular 1977 Soviet film *Mimino*, in which a Georgian pilot and an Armenian truck driver bicker over the merits of their two nations.

The two nationalities do have a history of collaboration. Armenia has frequently acted as a buffer zone protecting Georgia from invasion from the south, and Georgian rulers often repaid the compliment by inviting Armenians to settle in Georgian towns. The Bagrationis, who were a royal family of Georgia for almost a millennium, were very likely a branch of an Armenian dynasty. But from at least the fifth century AD, the two nations have looked in different directions. Because of a doctrinal quarrel, the Georgian Orthodox Church turned toward Byzantium, and the Armenians stayed separate. The traditional explanation is that the Armenians rejected the formulation on the dual nature of Christ agreed on by theologians at the Council of Chalcedon in 451, arguing instead that Christ was only one person with two natures, divine and human. For this, the Byzantine church labeled the Armenians Monophysite heretics. Whether or not this is the real explanation, within 200 years a schism had opened up between the Georgians and Byzantium on the one hand and the Armenians and the Eastern churches on the other. The Armenian and Georgian churches traded anathemas, and the Armenian catholicos forbade Armenians from communicating with, eating with, praying with, or marrying Georgians.[9]

This split drew the Georgians closer to the Greek world and aligned the Armenians more with the older Christian churches of the Middle East. The Georgians opened a monastery in Mount Athos in Greece named Iveron ("Of the Iberians"), which was home to Georgian monks until the modern era. The Armenians maintained links with the Syrians, Ethiopians, and Copts and kept a foothold in Jerusalem after the Muslims conquered it in the seventh century. The Armenians are still official custodians of one of the four quarters of the Old City of Jerusalem, with a small population of around 2,500 people and their own cathedral. Armenians still keep to some very ancient Christian traditions and celebrate Christmas and Epiphany, which they call *surb tsnund*, on the same day, January 6.

The early medieval period marked a cultural zenith for both Georgian and Armenian Christian culture. Armenian architects were famous church builders. In the tenth century, the Armenian Cathedral of the Holy Cross on Aghtamar Island in Lake Van was built, as well as famous monasteries such as Geghard (in Armenia) and Gandzasar (in Karabakh). Two of the grandest Georgian churches, the cathedral of Svetitskhoveli in the old capital of Mtskheta, outside Tbilisi, and the monastery of Gelati in western Georgia, date back to the eleventh century.

A third Caucasian people also practiced Christianity in what is now Azerbaijan. They are generally called the Caucasian Albanians, after the name the Romans gave them (and have nothing to do with the Balkan people of the same name), and their history is much more shadowy. Most of them lived in lands largely north of the river Kura, known as Aghvank, or Arran. They had their own language and alphabet. According to most historians, traces of the Caucasian Albanians had all but vanished by the tenth century. But their actual history has been overshadowed by a bizarre historical argument about the ancient inhabitants of Nagorny Karabakh (see chapter 4).

Islam

Islam arrived in the Caucasus in the seventh century with Arab invaders who swept in along the Caspian Sea coast from the south. They entered the region north of the river Araxes in 639 and captured Tiflis in 645. The Caucasian Albanian kingdom fell. Jewish Khazars to the north and Christians to the west stopped the Arabs' further advance, leaving the southeastern portion of the region, modern-day Azerbaijan, Islamic. For 500 years, Islam spread throughout Central Asia and along the Volga but not deeper into the South Caucasus. The Mongols of the Golden Horde led another wave of expansion in the thirteenth century, and a vast swathe of territory from western Siberia to Crimea, including much of the North Caucasus, became Islamic in their wake.

Thereafter, two Muslim powers, the Persian and Ottoman empires, dominated the region until the coming of the Russians in the early 1800s. The Christian character of Armenians and Georgians did not change much.

Under the Iranian Safavids, Georgian monarchs and lords converted to Islam, often in rather nominal fashion, while the rest of society remained Christian. Early modern travelers to Tiflis under Iranian rule were surprised to see that there was not a single mosque in the city.

Azerbaijan was different, and Islam gradually became universal there. From 1501, when Shah Ismail I founded the Safavid dynasty of Iran, a kingdom that included Azerbaijan, the Shia faith began to dominate. This gave most Azerbaijani Turks a different religion from the Ottoman Turks and a distinct identity of their own. On the one hand, they had their ethnic and linguistic ties to other Turkic peoples. On the other, they had a religious bond with the Persian-speaking people of Iran, with whom they shared a strong clerical hierarchy and festivals, such as the Day of Ashura, the annual ceremony mourning the martyrdom of the third Shia imam, Ali Hussein.

Not all Azerbaijanis were Shia. Figures compiled by the Russians in the 1830s after they colonized the region show that Sunnis were a majority of the population in what is modern-day Azerbaijan, especially in its northern part. By the 1860s that had changed, as many Sunnis went into exile from tsarist rule. In 1916, of almost two million Muslims registered in Azerbaijan, 62 percent were Shiite and 38 percent were Sunni. Indirectly, Sunni-Shiite strife helped forge a new national identity for Azerbaijan. Frustrated with petty clerical disputes, some Azerbaijanis turned to pan-Islamism, a movement for the unification of Muslim peoples, while others rejected religion altogether and took an interest in secular pan-Turkic ideas.

While Islam was less of a mobilizing force in Azerbaijan than it was in the North Caucasus to the north or Iran to the south, but it still defined a way of life for ordinary people. That way of life was strongly undermined by the Soviet Union. Under Soviet rules, all ties to Iran and the Middle East were cut, and mosques and Islamic schools were shut. What was left of the religious establishment was co-opted by the Communist authorities. Between 1928 and 1980, the number of functioning mosques in Azerbaijan fell from 1,400 to just sixteen. In that context, the Sunni-Shiite schism began to lose any meaning. The Muslims who continued to worship shared use of the tiny handful of mosques that were open, although they still buried their dead in different cemeteries.[10]

The new elite in independent Azerbaijan has allowed Islam to be revived but portrays the country as a secular state on the Turkish model. Fears are expressed about the influence of radical Sunnis from the North Caucasus and the Gulf and of Shiites from Iran. In 2009, the authorities closed down a series of mosques on the grounds that they were harboring extremists. After decades of official atheism, members of the younger generation in Azerbaijan do show signs of being more Muslim than their Soviet-era parents. A survey of young people in 2007 organized by Baku's FAR Center revealed the multiple influences of Europe, Russia, and Turkey as well as the Islamic world. Eighty-eight percent of respondents said they believed in God, with a quarter saying they would be happy to see Azerbaijan ruled by sharia law. Yet only 13 percent said they were actual practicing believers; belief still outstrips worship or the opportunity to worship.

Persians

Until the nineteenth century, Great Power politics in the Caucasus came from the south. There was Iran (Persia) on the one hand and a succession of empires to the southwest on the other, from Rome to Byzantium to the Ottoman Empire. For more than 300 years, the region was shaped by the Persian-Ottoman clash. In the sixteenth century, writes the historian W. E. D. Allen, "the clumsy, lumbering mechanisms of the two Mussulman Empires went slowly grinding on, chipping off and granulating one by one, the little easy-going, anarchical feudalities along the Caucasian borderlands." [11] This imperial push- and- pull made for a shifting west-east line of division across the region, which was formally ratified in two Ottoman-Persian peace treaties in 1555 and 1639. Present-day Georgia was divided into what could be called Ottoman and Persian spheres of influence.

Persian culture can be traced in the South Caucasus from the sixth century BC, and Persians colonized large parts of the region for roughly a thousand years, far longer than the Russians did. The cultural residue of this is surprisingly faint but is there if one looks for it. The Armenian language is so full of Persian loanwords that it was long thought to be an Indo-Iranian language; in fact, it is a distinct branch of the Indo-European language family. The historian Nina Garsoïan argues that the Armenian sociopolitical system, with its tradition of hereditary aristocrats and semidivine monarchy, derived from an Iranian tradition. Medieval Georgia's "Golden Age" was also heavily Persianized. Shota Rustaveli, author of the famous twelfth-century epic *The Knight in the Panther Skin*, called his poem "a Persian work now done into Georgian." [12] Georgian princes served the Safavid dynasty for three centuries.

The Persian-Iranian influence is strongest in Azerbaijan. The river Araxes only became a noticeable border in the nineteenth century. Prior to that, the lands to the north and south were generally part of the same kingdoms. The Azerbaijani city of Ganzak (Ganja) was the location of one of the four great fires of the Zoroastrian religion. The twelfth-century poet Nizami of Ganja is revered as a great Azerbaijani cultural icon, even though he wrote in the Persian language.

In the sixteenth century, the Safavid Empire could lay claim to being a sort of proto-Azerbaijani state. The founder of the empire, Shah Ismail I (ruled 1501–24), came from Ardebil in what is present-day northern Iran, not far from Azerbaijan. Of mixed ethnic descent, he spoke both Persian and Azeri (or at least a form of Turkish that evolved into what is now Azeri) and wrote poems in Azeri under the name Khatai. In Safavid times, an estimated 1,200 Azeri words, mainly dealing with administrative and military issues, entered the Persian language.[13]

The most famous Safavid monarch, Shah Abbas, known as the Great Shah (ruled 1588–1629), has a mixed reputation in the Caucasus, despite having had a Georgian mother. Abbas uprooted the entire Armenian population of Julfa in Nakhichevan and moved its people to his new capital of Isfahan, where they founded a city named New Julfa. Thousands died in the process. His campaigns in Georgia were even more devastating. Suppressing a revolt in Kakheti in eastern Georgia in 1615, he laid waste to the entire territory, killing or deporting tens of thousands of people. The historian Ronald Suny writes, "the population of Kakheti dropped by two-thirds. The former prosperity of the kingdom ended abruptly, and its towns shrank into villages. . . . Shah Abbas, like Timur before him, dealt eastern Georgia a body blow from which the tiny kingdom never fully recovered."[14]

The Persian influence allowed a cross-Caucasian culture of sorts to develop in the eighteenth century. The Georgian king Erekle II, who subsequently made an alliance with Russia, had a strongly Persianized court in which all the Caucasian nationalities were in attendance. One of his courtiers was the Armenian monk Harutiun Sayatian, who became a famous singer and composer under the name Sayat Nova—"King of Songs" in Persian. He composed more than 200 songs in four languages—Armenian, Azeri, Georgian, and Persian—that are still performed to this day. Interestingly, the largest number of them are in the common language of the Caucasus of the day, Azeri.[15]

Iranian political dominance of the Caucasus began to fade with the end of the Safavids in 1722. A succession of military defeats on all fronts led to a slow retreat from the Caucasus that culminated in full capitulation to the Russians in 1828. This marked what some Azerbaijanis call "the parting of the ways" between northern and southern Azerbaijan. The Caucasus lived on in the assumptions of some Iranian statesmen, even as it turned into a Russian zone of influence. At the Versailles peace conference at the end of the First World War, the Iranian delegation caused consternation when it handed the conference a memorandum laying claim to all of present-day Armenia and Azerbaijan and parts of Dagestan. The document explained, "These provinces must be returned to Persia, for they had already formed part of Persia."[16]

Currently, Iran is closer to Armenia than to either Azerbaijan or Georgia. One of Armenia's two open borders is with Iran, and a gas pipeline, opened in 2007, gave the Armenians a new source of natural gas. For Azerbaijan and Iran, the big sleeping issue is Iran's large population of ethnic Azerbaijanis in the north of the country, who may number as many as twenty-five million— or three times the number of Azerbaijanis in the Republic of Azerbaijan. So far, there has been no mass movement there for closer political ties to the north. Fred Halliday writes that after 1979, "in an upheaval in which many dogs barked, Azerbaijani nationalism is the one dog that did not, at least during the first 15 years after the Islamic revolution."[17] Iran would undoubtedly like to play a larger part in the South Caucasus, but it lost two decades of influence after the end of the Soviet Union, due to the international isolation of the modern Iranian regime. If the thaw between Iran and the West persists, then Tehran can be expected to claim a role in the region again, but it has a lot of ground to make up.

Azerbaijanis

The Turkic presence in the Caucasus dates back at least to the seventh century and became stronger with the arrival of Oghuz Turks, who first settled in present-day Azerbaijan in around the ninth century and are probably the ancestors of the modern-day Azerbaijanis. The Turkish-Persian Seljuk Empire overran the Caucasus in the eleventh century, but a major Turkic power only established itself in the region after the Ottoman Empire had captured Constantinople and Trebizond in the mid-fifteenth century. From the end of that century, the Black Sea was known as the "Ottoman Lake," and the eastern Black Sea coast came under Ottoman rule in the early 1800s, with Turkish its lingua franca. The paradox of this historical era is that the main Turkic nation of the region, the Azerbaijanis, were Shiites and separate from the main Turkic power, the Sunni Ottomans, who controlled the western part of the region. The paths of the two only began to converge in the early modern era.

Azerbaijan is the largest country in the South Caucasus, with a population of nine million people, of whom about 90 percent are ethnic Azeris. It is also the least studied country of the region, and its name is much less recognized internationally than those of its two neighbors, Armenia and Georgia, whose historical narratives are more easily told. Many more cultural threads have formed the weave that makes up contemporary Azerbaijan.

The name "Azerbaijan" has been traced back to Atropatenes, a Persian lord in the time of Alexander the Great, or, more poetically, to *azer*, the Persian word for fire, on the grounds that it describes the Zoroastrian fire-temples of the region. Until modern times, the word "Azerbaijan" was more often applied to the northern Turkic-populated part of Iran than to the modern-day state of Azerbaijan. Before the twentieth century, outsiders tended to call Azerbaijanis either "Shirvanis" (from around Baku and Shemakha), "Caucasian Tatars," "Turks," or just "Muslims." Their own self-identification was flexible. In the nineteenth century, Brenda Shaffer writes, "Azerbaijanis could consider themselves as both Turks or Iranians, or Russian subjects, with little conflict. Some were active in political movements in all three of the regions, concurrently or at different times of their careers."[18]

A sense of historical continuity is further fractured by the fact that the Azeri language has been written in three alphabets since the third decade of the twentieth century: the script was changed from Arabic to Roman in the 1920s, to Cyrillic in the 1930s, and back to Roman in the 1990s. That makes it very hard for even an educated Azerbaijani to read his or her recent history. In their identity, Azerbaijanis could be considered the polar opposite of the Armenians, who have maintained a cultural identity through an alphabet and literature that is constant in different lands all over the world. For Azerbaijanis, their land has remained the same, but the culture within it has been buffeted by constant change.

Azerbaijan's strongest neighbor and ally is undoubtedly Turkey, but Azerbaijani-Turkish relations have gone through many difficult patches. Many Russian Azerbaijanis maintained a strongly Shiite and anti-Ottoman identity through much of the nineteenth century. Five Shiite Azerbaijani cavalry regiments fought with the Russian army against the Sunni Turks in the war of 1828–29 and were decorated by the tsar in gratitude. Alexander Pushkin saw the Azerbaijani Shiite "Karabakh regiment" in action fighting outside Kars in 1829 and dedicated a poem to a brave Karabakhi horseman. Later, in the Crimean War, the great-nephew of one of the last khans of Karabakh distinguished himself defending the Russian fortress of Sevastopol against the British, French, and Turks.[19]

In the mid-nineteenth century, a new educated intelligentsia began to exchange ideas with pan-Turkic thinkers in other parts of the Russian Empire. They began articulating a modern Azerbaijani identity. In the 1880s, the magazine *Käshkül* proposed the use of the name "Azerbaijani Turks" instead of "Caucasian Muslims" for the first time.[20] Within fewer than thirty years, the Republic of Azerbaijan had become the world's first parliamentary democracy in an Islamic country. The Soviet Republic of Azerbaijan lost the independence but kept the sense of national identity.

Independence in 1991 again redefined Azerbaijani identity. For the first time, in contrast to the First Republic of 1918, Azerbaijan's borders were internationally recognized. This helps explain why the map of the country has become a national symbol; it is printed on coins, for example. Simultaneously, Azerbaijani statehood has been wounded as a result of the Karabakh conflict with Armenians: one-seventh of its internationally recognized territory is under de facto Armenian control as a result of the conflict. Faced with multiple challenges, Azerbaijani national identity is still evolving. To what degree is it necessary to be Turkic and Muslim to be Azerbaijani? Should the word "Azerbaijani" be redefined as an all-inclusive civic identity that covers all minorities in the country? Can Azerbaijan's lost Armenians ever come to be called Azerbaijani? What links and divides citizens of independent Azerbaijan to and from their ethnic kin across the border in Iran? These questions do not yet have definitive answers.

Armenians

The Republic of Armenia is the smallest of the three South Caucasian states and the official homeland of the world's ten million Armenians. But the fact that an Armenian state is situated in the South Caucasus—or exists at all—is a matter of historical contingency. There was no Armenian political state between the fall of the crusader kingdom of Cilicia in 1375 and the short-lived Armenian Republic of 1918. Instead, the heartland of historic Armenia, known as Western Armenia or Eastern Anatolia, came under the rule of others for centuries.

Living as subjects under various empires, Armenians kept a collective identity through the church, a strong literary tradition written in the thirty-eight-letter Armenian alphabet, and a tradition of yearning for a glorious past. Their golden age could be said to have been all the way back in the first century BC, when King Tigran the Great briefly built the strongest state east of the Roman republic. But the Armenian historical record has more defeats than victories. Just as the Serbs mark the lost battle at Kosovo Field as a key historical moment, Armenians commemorate a defeat at the Battle of Avarayr in 451. At Avarayr, the tale goes, Armenians were defeated by a much larger Persian army and had to submit to foreign rule but were allowed to keep their Christian faith and identity. The Armenian city of Ani, now a deserted ruin on the Armenian-Turkish border, was one of the great cities of the Middle East for several centuries, until it was sacked and destroyed by the Mongols in 1236. Around the same time, with the help of crusaders, the mobile Armenians set up a kingdom on the Turkish southeast Mediterranean coast known as Cilicia, with its capital in Sis (modern-day Kozan). Cilicia was conquered by the Mamluk Turks in 1375.

Without their own rulers, Armenians were scattered from Tiflis to Constantinople to Jerusalem. Later they could be found in Isfahan, Venice, or Calcutta. Then, in 1915 and after, the violent expulsion or death of almost all the Ottoman Armenians, in what is remembered as the Armenian Genocide, created an even greater worldwide diaspora, stretching from Beirut to Los Angeles. Roughly two-thirds of Armenians today live outside Armenia itself, with most of them having roots in Anatolia and speaking a dialect of Western Armenian that is distinct from the language spoken in the Republic of Armenia.

Traditionally, the itinerant Armenians became wealthy merchants, bankers, and craftsmen, rather like the Jews, and the stereotype of the crafty mercantile Armenian has stuck. Armenians' self-conscious pride in their history and resistance to assimilation has made them objects of admiration and resentment, depending on the observer. The Russian Jewish poet Osip Mandelstam was an admirer, writing of "Armenians' fullness with life, their rude tenderness, their noble inclination to work, their inexplicable aversion to anything metaphysical and their splendid intimacy with the world of real things."[21] But many European travelers to the Caucasus preferred the easygoing, aristocratic Georgians and found the Armenians dour and difficult. The stereotype was strongly held by both Azerbaijanis and Georgians, whose national consciousness was to a large degree built in opposition to the supposed economic oppression of Armenians. The Georgian national thinker Ilia Chavchavadze called Armenians parasites who were undermining Georgia from within.

Armenians across the world acquired diverging identities. From 1441, after the fall of Cilicia, they had two catholicoses, one in the ancient cathedral of Echmiadzin near Yerevan and one originally in Cilicia but then based in Lebanon. Both are still functioning today. Although respectful of one another, they represent two different outlooks. From the mid-nineteenth century, other splits opened up between Armenians in the Russian and in the Ottoman empires and between those who wanted national revolt and those who chose accommodation. These divisions were accentuated by the founding in 1890 in Tiflis of the revolutionary nationalist organization the Armenian Revolutionary Federation, or Dashnaktsutiun. Amid worsening persecution of Armenians by the Ottoman authorities, the so-called Dashnaks began targeting fellow Armenians whom they saw as collaborators, even attempting to assassinate the Armenian patriarch of Constantinople.[22]

The tragic years 1915–20 briefly silenced Armenian quarrels, but after the fall of the Dashnak independent republic of Armenia to the Bolsheviks, recriminations began again, this time over attitudes toward the new Soviet regime. The Armenian Apostolic Church of Echmiadzin accepted the Soviet authorities as having saved the nation from the Turks, while the Cilician church rejected them, with the support of the Dashnak Party. The split reached a grisly climax on Christmas Eve 1933, when Archbishop Ghevond Tourian was murdered in the Holy Cross Church of Armenia in New York by Dashnak assassins. Tourian's supposed crime was his supportive attitude toward Soviet Armenia and betrayal of Armenian independence.[23] The critics of the Dashnaktsutiun said the group had made Armenians' tribulations worse. An anti-Dashnak tract of 1934 said, "Its doctrine was, that liberty is won by bloodshed only, and the more the Sultan is goaded into massacring the Armenian people, the stronger will become our claims for autonomy, and the greater will become the hope for European intervention. As we have already stated, this expected intervention never materialized, and the Sultan was left free to deal with the Armenians as he saw fit."[24]

Feuds between pro- and anti-Soviet groups dominated the politics of the Armenian diaspora for much of the twentieth century, displacing even the crimes of Ottoman Turkey as the main political issue for the émigré community. During World War II several prominent Armenian revolutionaries— including General Dro Kanayan, defense minister of the 1918 Dashnak republic—fought with the Nazis with the goal of regaining Armenian independence; at the same time, prominent Soviet Armenian generals took senior positions in the Red Army.[25] During the first decade of the twenty-first century, these intra-Armenian tensions calmed down somewhat. But the polarities between the Dashnak movement and its opponents mean that there are still two Armenian lobbying organizations in Washington and two distinct currents in the Armenian diaspora.

Currently, Armenia is a homogeneous state: 98 percent of the population are ethnic Armenians. The once large Azerbaijani population has gone, and the only noticeable minority, the Yezidi Kurds, have a very low profile in society. The tensions are therefore all intra-Armenian or between the new state and the diaspora—in October 2009, many diaspora Armenians, mostly descendants of Genocide survivors, found themselves in the awkward position of denouncing the Yerevan government for moving to normalize relations with Turkey. Diaspora communities around the world have also unwittingly weakened the Armenian state by acting as a magnet for Armenians dissatisfied with life in the homeland. Since independence, the population of Armenia—3.3 million in 1989—has dropped in real terms, as hundreds of thousands of people have left for Russia or the United States. Many are seasonal workers, but many others—among them the best educated—will never come back.

Georgians

Georgia's landscape, wine, and extravagant people consistently win it friends. In 1947, John Steinbeck heard from Russians about Georgia's charms long before he set foot there. "Wherever we had been in Russia, in Moscow, in the Ukraine, in Stalingrad, the magical name of Georgia came up constantly. . . . [T]hey spoke of the country in the Caucasus and around the Black Sea as a kind of second heaven."[26]

Georgia's distinctive character comes from it being the most "Caucasian" of the three countries of the South Caucasus. Armenians and Azerbaijanis look outward to Iran and the Middle East and beyond and have one foot outside the South Caucasus—their culture and cuisine blends with that of the greater region around them. Georgia has always been a world of its own. Some of its cultural features, such as its beautiful polyphonic singing, have a good claim to being unique. The Georgians have never had a strong diaspora. In Soviet times Georgians were the least likely of the Soviet Union's fifteen main "titular" nationalities—the ethnic groups after whom the USSR's fifteen constituent union republics were named—to live outside their home-land. Very few Georgians live outside Georgia in the South Caucasus, while Georgia itself has large Armenian and Azerbaijani minorities.

With the help of highland geography, Georgians have preserved remnants of an archaic chivalric way of life much longer into the modern era than might have been expected. In the early twentieth century, foreign travelers were amazed to see the Khevsurs, who live high in the mountains of north-eastern Georgia, still wearing chain mail and cloaks adorned with crosses and carrying broadswords, giving rise to speculation that they were in fact "lost crusaders."

Medieval chivalry translated into modern verve. The writer Odette Keun wrote in 1924, "If I were a symbolist, I should portray Georgia as a race-horse—palpitating, furious, rushing forward blindly, it knows not where; rearing at the least check, not having yet learnt what is required of it, or what it can do; falling at the first slackening of the reins into a fantastic, prancing gait; a creature made for parade, and for the pleasure of the eyes rather than utility." But she also noted what she regarded as the reverse side of the charm: "The most deadly weakness of [Georgians'] nature is their faculty of intoxicating themselves with words, their infantile persuasion that in delivering speeches and making gestures they are actively accomplishing something and producing results."[27]

This dashing behavior has more than just touristic value. As the historian Firuz Kazemzadeh writes, independent Georgia was distrusted prior to the Paris Peace Conference of 1919–20 because of its alliance with Germany, but the Georgian delegation managed to charm the Allied diplomats, trumping the Armenians, who had greater claims to sympathy but won fewer friends. Similarly, post-Soviet independent Georgia has punched above its weight in Washington and European capitals in part because of the lobbying talent of a few individuals.

"Georgia" is in fact a place of many regions, and its national iden-tity is both a very ancient and a comparatively recent phenomenon. The name Georgians now use for their country, "sakartvelo " ("a place for the speakers of the language of kartuli"), first began to be used under the eleventh-century reign of David the Builder to describe the central Georgian kingdoms—the region known to the Romans as Iberia. Its strong east-west split, accentuated by a long divide between Persian and Ottoman spheres of influence, only began to end in the 1880s, when Russian engineers first built a railroad across the 3,000-foot Surami highlands in central Georgia, bridging the western and eastern halves of the region with a viable transport route for the first time. Georgia's separate regions and principalities include Kakheti in the east; Kartli, centered around the town of Tiflis; Imereti ("the land on the other side") to the west; Guria and Mingrelia (Samegrelo in Georgian) on the Black Sea coast; Meskhia (Samtskhe) to the south; and Svaneti in the northern mountains. With these regions come strong stereotypes—Kakhetians are said to be direct and honest, Gurians witty, Mingrelians crafty.

Georgia's brief "Golden Age," beginning with David the Builder and ending with the reign of his great-granddaughter, Queen Tamar, provides a touchstone for national identity. The most famous churches were built and a literary language forged during this period. Georgia's national poem, *Vepkhistqaosani* ("The Knight in the Panther Skin"), which contains 1,666 stanzas of four sixteen-syllable rhyming lines, was composed at the end of the twelfth century by Shota Rustaveli. In 1121, King David defeated a Seljuk Turk army at the Battle of Didgori, twenty-five miles southwest of Tiflis, in what is still commemorated as *dzleva sakvirveli*, "the wonderful victory." He then captured Tiflis and made it his capital. David continued to capture territory in Armenian lands and what is present-day Azerbaijan, laying claim briefly to being the ruler of the entire Caucasus.

THE GEORGIAN LANGUAGE

The Georgian language, known to Georgians as *kartuli*, is the chief member of a distinct language family, written in a unique alphabet, and has been the main unifying force in Georgians' expressions of national identity. Georgian is unrelated to any other languages, apart from its close relatives Mingrelian, Svan, and Laz—although some scholars have attempted to make the case that it is a distant cousin of that other lonely European language, Basque. Its exploding "ejective stops" and fearsome consonant clusters—as in *vprtskvni* ("I am peeling it/them") and *gvb(r)dghvnit* ("you [plural] tear us into pieces")—scare away all but the bravest.

The beautiful curly alphabet, originally forty-one letters and now thirty-three, was devised in the fifth century and was the script used for religious texts for several centuries. The poet Shota Rustaveli and others made Georgian a great literary language in the twelfth century. According to the literary historian Donald Rayfield, at that time Georgian probably had the same number of speakers and readers as English did in Shakespearean England.[1]

After Georgia's national church was swallowed up by the Russian Orthodox Church in 1811, the Georgian language became the focus for self-identification among intellectuals. Any attempts to downgrade its status in schools and public life met with passionate resistance. In 1879 the Society for the Spread of the Georgian Language was founded by Iakob Gogebashvili, author of a popular language primer entitled *Deda Ena* (Mother tongue).[2] Language reform and political reform went hand in hand: Gogebashvili held secret discussion meetings for his students at his house, where they also debated subversive political ideas.

Under Georgia's first independent republic of 1918–21, Georgian was entrenched as the national language. It kept its status in the 1920s, and its alphabet was even imposed on Georgia's minorities, the Abkhaz and Ossetians, in the 1930s. Even in the 1960s and 1970s, bilingualism was low in Georgia, with little more than half the population of Tbilisi being fully fluent in Russian.

Despite the persistence of the native language, the threat by Moscow, in the course of imposing a new constitution on Georgia in 1978, to remove the status of Georgian as the official language of the republic hit a raw nerve. Then party boss Eduard Shevardnadze related how he flew to Moscow to discuss the issue with Leonid Brezhnev and the chief Soviet ideologist, Mikhail Suslov. According to Shevardnadze, Suslov regarded the proposal to preserve the status of Georgian as an example of "chauvinism," but Brezhnev's right-hand man, Konstantin

Chernenko, was more sympathetic. Back in Tbilisi, on April 14, 1978, Shevardnadze delivered the speech unveiling the new constitution to a vast demonstration of students and intellectuals who moved along Rustaveli Avenue, shouting "Deda ena!" Some carried placards saying simply "Ai ia" ("Here is a violet"), the first line in Gogebashvili's primer. The demonstrators forced their way past the police to gather noisily in front of the Communist Party headquarters.

There was a real danger of a repetition of the bloody events that had occurred in 1956 during street demonstrations against Moscow's de-Stalinization program, when several dozen people had died virtually on the same spot. It later was revealed that the Moscow leadership had ordered tanks into the courtyard of the party headquarters. As Shevardnadze tells it, "I left the issue of the status of the language to the end of my speech," at which point he announced that Georgian would indeed keep its status under the new constitution. The crowd dispersed, still chanting. In Moscow, Suslov objected to this outcome but was overruled by Brezhnev, who had been briefed about the problem.[3]

With Georgia having achieved this success, Soviet Armenia and Azerbaijan hastily amended their constitutions to give their languages the same status. The issue was in fact a largely symbolic one, but the Russians had placated Georgians on a key issue of national pride, and the decorative "sovereignty" of Soviet Georgia had been reaffirmed. Since 1990, April 14 has been celebrated as the "Day of the Georgian Language."

1. Donald Rayfield, *The Literature of Georgia: A History* (Richmond, England: Curzon, 1994), 9.
2. Ronald Suny, "The Emergence of Political Society in Georgia," in Suny, ed., *Transcaucasia, Nationalism and Social Change: Essays in the History of Armenia, Azerbaijan and Georgia* (Ann Arbor: University of Michigan Press, 1983), 130.
3. Eduard Shevardnadze, interview with author, December 3, 2008, Tbilisi.

It is in the nature of national history to dwell on "golden ages" and say less about what followed. The period from the thirteenth century onward saw repeated Mongol invasions and, as Ronald Suny has put it, "the long twilight of the Georgian kingdoms." They spent most of the succeeding five centuries under either Iranian or Ottoman rule. A series of kings of Kartli and Kakheti went through a less glorious period of negotiated subservience to Persian dynasties that lasted until the late eighteenth century. They were practiced at keeping their options open. Allen says that under the seventeenth-century kings Vakhtang V and his sons, "an apprehending pliable intelligence replaced the erratic heroism of earlier kings in Tiflis. . . . They translated Persian works into Georgian, and carried icons and Psalters with them when they led Persian armies into Afghanistan. They married the Shah's daughters and dabbled in Roman Catholicism."[28]

The different parts of Georgia only came together in the nineteenth century with Russian rule, the coming of the railways, and a generation of patriotic intellectuals keen to foster a new national consciousness. The churches of the Golden Age, the rediscovery of ancient manuscripts, and the poetry of Shota Rustaveli were important cultural treasures in this process of national reinvention and discovery. The dilemma has been that anyone seeking to forge, or reforge, a "Georgian national identity" does so at the risk of suppressing the country's great natural diversity. Georgia's internal differences and regional distinctions, sometimes manifested as centrifugal tendencies, are both a weakness and a strength.

2

Russia's South

The history of Russia in the South Caucasus is more than just that of an outside power. After 1800, the region was absorbed into the Russian state and reshaped with a Russian character. Until recently, most people knew the whole region by its Russocentric name, Transcaucasia, and many outsiders mistook it for part of Russia. Russia unified Transcaucasia (as I will call the region in this chapter) for the first time into a single entity through Russian-built institutions, currency, and railways, as well as making Russian the lingua franca. Europe came to the Caucasus via Russia. The influence also went the other way in a less tangible fashion. Having a presence in the Caucasus moved Russia's foreign policy closer to the Middle East and also created a cultural zone of exoticism. Any educated Russian reader will instantly conjure up a romanticized picture of the wilds of the Caucasus on hearing the lines of Alexander Pushkin's famous love poem: "Dense night has fallen on the hills of Georgia, / I hear the Aragvi's roar in front of me. / I am sad but released, my sadness is bright, / My sadness is full of you."

The tsarist empire differed from the colonial rule of the British or French. As the British historian Geoffrey Hosking has put it, "Britain had an empire, Russia was an empire." The Transcaucasus became the geographic periphery of the expanding Russian state, and over time the tsar's Transcaucasian subjects had as many or as few rights as ethnic Russians. Christian Armenians and Georgians were more favored, but Azerbaijani "Tatars" (Shiite Azeris) could also prosper. The barriers to advancement were more social than ethnic. Caucasians of a certain class could pursue a career in the Russian army, study in Russian universities—and end up in a Siberian prison as well. The problem the Caucasus posed the imperial authorities was mainly one of remoteness and capacity. Even the far more powerful Soviet Union ended up deciding to delegate most of its power to local elites there. The much more limited tsarist administration always had to struggle to keep its grip on the region.

Russia Moves In

For centuries, the Caucasus range was a barrier to the great northern power. The main route across the mountains through the Daryal Pass was simply too dangerous for an army to follow. In 1722–23, Peter the Great bypassed the mountains and moved his southern army along the Caspian coast to Baku, but after his death in 1725 the lands he had captured were handed back to Persian control. Peter's army had been welcomed by Christian Georgian and Armenian princes, but overall strategic considerations prevailed: the Caucasus was only one front among many that Russia faced.

Later in the eighteenth century, Catherine the Great expanded her empire to the northern shores of the Black Sea. She acquired a new ally in King Erekle II, who had united the two old Georgian kingdoms of Kakheti and Kartli in 1762. Portraits of Erekle and his wife show them wearing Persianized dress, but he saw an opportunity to move away from the shadow of the Persian and Ottoman empires, and in 1783 he signed the Treaty of Georgievsk, allowing his kingdoms to become a Russian protectorate. In return for Russian military support, the Georgian monarch and Orthodox Church swore loyalty to the Russian crown but were allowed to keep their former status.

The Georgians soon cried betrayal. The Russian force pulled out of Tiflis, leaving King Erekle to complain bitterly, "Now you are leaving Georgia, to the extreme despair of our subjects."[1] The Iranian shah Mohammad Khan Qajar invaded Georgia in 1795, defeated Erekle II outside Tiflis, and then virtually razed Tiflis to the ground. The English historian Sir John Malcolm wrote, "It is not easy to calculate the number who perished. Bigotry inflamed the brutal rage of the soldier. The churches were leveled to the ground; every priest was put to death. Youth and beauty were alone spared for slavery. Fifteen thousand captives were led into bondage; and the army marched back laden with spoil."[2] Even though the Russians had made the fall of the city possible by leaving it undefended, the 1795 sack of Tbilisiwas cited throughout the nineteenth century by Russians as proof of the Georgians' need for tsarist protection.

The death of Catherine the Great, the assassination of Mohammad Khan Qajar, and the death of Erekle reshuffled the cards. In 1801, the Russian tsar Paul I abrogated the Treaty of Georgievsk, fully annexed Kartli-Kakheti, and deposed the Bagratid dynasty with its millennium-long history. The Georgian royal family was forcibly removed to Russia. Tsar Alexander I, who succeeded Paul, had greater ambitions. In March 1802, he told his ministers that Russia needed to conquer all the territory north of the Kura and Araxes rivers.[3] Alexander appointed Pavel Tsitsianov, a Russian imperial officer with Georgian roots, to lead the new effort. Tsitsianov was successful in Kartli and Kakheti, where he won over the local Georgians by, for example, raising money to restore Tiflis's medieval Sioni Cathedral. But he met resistance in the western principalities of Mingrelia and Imereti, which still harbored pro-Ottoman loyalties. Annexed by force over the next decade, these territories only became fully integrated into the Russian Empire in the second half of the nineteenth century.

Tsitsianov and his officials also behaved like full-fledged colonial invaders in the Muslim regions to the south. He displayed contempt for "Persians" and Muslim "Asiatics" (terms Russians used quite loosely), warning the sultan of the principality of Elisou: "Know until you become a loyal vassal of my Emperor I shall only long to wash my boots in your blood." Tsitsianov rejected peace terms offered him by the khan of the city of Ganja and stormed the city, killing thousands of its inhabitants. Ganja was made into a district of Georgia and renamed Elizavetpol, and its central mosque was converted into a church. In 1806, Tsitsianov was assassinated outside the city walls of Baku as he was negotiating its surrender.

In 1811, Russia's hold on the Transcaucasus was still tenuous. Tsitsianov's immediate successors were less sympathetic to the Georgians: the fourteen-centuries-long autonomy of the Georgian Orthodox Church was abolished, and it was absorbed into the Russian Orthodox Church, recovering its independent status only in 1917. In 1811, the British military historian William Monteith wrote, "The affairs of Russia appeared . . . in a very precarious state, and great disasters would undoubtedly have been the consequence of any vigorous efforts on the side of Persia, but nothing serious was attempted on her part."[4] Despite twice besieging Yerevan, the Russians failed to wrest present-day Armenia from the Persians. Even the two eastern Georgian kingdoms, which were the bulwark of the Russian colonial project, staged a Persian-backed uprising in 1812. Access to the region from the north was limited: the one road across the mountains, the Georgian Military Highway, was still narrow and poorly built. A new 130-mile-long highway, with bridges spanning the multiple gorges, was completed only in 1817.

The Caucasus was called Russia's "southern Siberia," and rough conditions and disease made it an unpopular posting—even later in the century, as conditions improved, large numbers of Russians never settled in the region. The first generation of officials was widely loathed. The tsarist historian Nikolai Dubrovin, quoting a letter of complaint written by Georgians in 1812, wrote: "A former sergeant here . . . while giving out bread or barley compelled one of them to bend into the shape of a chair and another into a table and then he sat down on one and wrote on the other and tormented them inhumanely in this manner."[5]

Russia was still militarily stronger than its main rival, the Persian Empire. Under diplomatic pressure from Britain and France, the shah confirmed Russia's new Caucasian conquests under the Treaty of Gulistan in 1813. In 1826, Persia made one last push and launched a new war in the Caucasus. The fighting lasted only fifteen months. The Persians won initial successes, overrunning most of present-day Azerbaijan, but the Russians rallied, led by a new commander, Ivan Paskevich, who conquered Yerevan and eastern Armenia and forced the Persians to retreat. They were made to sign the humiliating Treaty of Turkmenchai in 1828, accepting Russian control of the whole region, now including Armenia. Paskevich then continued his war against the Ottomans. He captured the cities of Kars and Erzerum in Anatolia and (in modern Georgia) the fortress of Ahiska and the port of Poti, which had been Turkish possessions for two centuries. At the Treaty of Adrianople in 1829, the Turks followed the Persians in formally ceding their claims to the Transcaucasus, and it became an undisputed part of the Russian Empire.

The Tsarist Regime

After the treaties of 1828–29, the Transcaucasus was relatively peaceful, but war intensified north of the mountains. The Dagestani leader Imam Shamil led resistance in Chechnya and Daghestan for almost three decades, finally surrendering only in 1859. The Circassians of the northwestern Caucasus were defeated five years later. Russian policy toward these Muslim rebels was implacable. The decision was taken to rid the Black Sea coast of its native peoples, and up to half a million Circassians, Ubykh, and Abkhaz fled or were deported to the Ottoman Empire, with massive loss of life (see chapter 5). War in the North Caucasus was one reason why in the Transcaucasus the tsarist regime chose more to rule by consent. It opened up its officers's academies to all locals of a certain class and recruited them into its armies to fight both Imam Shamil and the Ottomans. The new soldiers included Shiite Azerbaijani "Tatars"; in 1829 Paskevich praised "the especial bravery of the [Azerbaijani Shiite] Muslim regiments," whose cavalry helped him win victories against the Sunni Turks.[6]

For many Russians, the Caucasus became synonymous with war and heroism. Writing in the 1880s, the Russian Vasily Potto began his history of the wars of conquest with the words: "Caucasus! What Russian heart does not respond to that name, linked by ties of blood and with both the historic and intellectual life of our homeland, speaking at the same time of incalculable sacrifices for it and of poetic inspiration?"[7] In Russian literature, the Caucasus took on the role that the Swiss Alps, the American West, or Pakistan's North-West Frontier had for Europeans or Americans, with an extra oriental and sometimes erotic flavor. The poet Mikhail Lermontov described mysterious captives from the mountains who yearned for freedom and whose beauty destroyed the reason of Russian soldiers.

LERMONTOV

In 1837, the young Russian aristocrat and poet Mikhail Lermontov (1814–41), as punishment for writing an angry poem on the death of Alexander Pushkin, was sent to the Caucasus to serve as a dragoons officer. From exile, he expressed in verse his feelings toward the new southern borderlands and their peoples. Lermontov felt a bond with the freedom of the mountains and their wild inhabitants and reveled in the scenery—but simultaneously he continued to admire the military might of the armies that conquered it.

Lermontov's romantic poems about the Caucasus have helped define how literate Russians feel about the region. The most famous, *Mtsyri*, is the tale of a prisoner from the "highlands" (tellingly, he has no specific nationality) who is interned in a Georgian monastery but who briefly escapes to his homeland before returning to the cloister to die. Taking as his setting is the monastery of Jvari, just north of Tiflis, the poet spins a pro-Russian version of the annexation of Georgia of 1801. A dusty inscription on the floor of the church records "how / discontented with his crown, / a certain tsar in a certain year / entrusted his people to Russia / And divine grace descended / on Georgia! It has flourished / since then in the shade of its gardens, / no longer fearing enemies / because of friendly bayonets across its border." Fleeing the monastery, the highland boy is overwhelmed by the beauty of his native mountains, "fantastic as dreams." He is thrilled by the "wonderful world of alarms and battles / Where cliffs hide in the clouds, / where people are free as eagles." As he dies, the boy asks the monk to have him buried in the mountains.

Lermontov's worldview seems to regard the wild "highlanders" of the Caucasus as a glorious anachronism, not fit for the modern age, while the antiquated Christian Georgians had earned a quiet life contemplating their past, safe behind Russian bayonets. Russian colonial rule is viewed as a necessary but brutal force dragging a backward region into Europe.

Lermontov's brief career in the region—he spent less than a year fighting there before returning to be killed in a duel in the North Caucasian town of Pyatigorsk—points up another aspect of the asymmetrical relationship between Russia and the South Caucasus. The tsar's Caucasian subjects frequently moved to Russia and built careers there—in other words, assimilated into Russian culture— but the movement in the other direction was more limited. Russians served their time and settled in the Caucasus, but very rarely went native or learned the local languages. In the Russian imagination, the Caucasus came closer but still remained elusively "other."

Mikhail Lermontov, Russian tsarist officer and Romantic poet.

The wars in which Lermontov fought faded into myth, but his poetry about the landscape retained its emotional power. From the safe perspective of Soviet times, many Caucasians adopted the verse of the imperial officer as a kind of sacred text. Pushkin had written of the tsarist general Alexei Yermolov, "Bow down your snowy head, submit, O Caucasus, Yermolov is coming." The Soviet Dagestani poet Rasul Gamzatov inverted this in praise of Lermontov, "It was not a general before whom the Caucasus bowed, but the poetry of a young lieutenant."[1]

1. Quoted in Bruce Grant, "Brides, Brigands and Fire-Bringers," in Bruce Grant and Lale Yalcin-Heckmann, eds., *Caucasus Paradigms, Anthropologies, Histories and the Making of a World Area* (Berlin: Lit Verlag, 2008), 6.

European politicians feared that Russia's drive into the Caucasus was the first phase of a bigger expansionist push, perhaps to India. But the historian Muriel Atkin argues that the Caucasus in itself was sufficient for Russia. The conquest, she writes,

> had nothing to do with some legendary Russian drive to obtain warm-water ports or some grand design for the conquest of Asia. . . . Exotic alien lands made attractive targets for colonization because it was believed that they could make their colonial master rich and because the colonial master could in return benefit the subject peoples by introducing them to civilization. Furthermore, all of this would prove that Russia, too, was as great and civilized an empire as those of western Europe.[8]

The civilizing project prescribed different policies for different indigenous peoples. The Christian Georgians with their surviving nobility were the most favored nationality. Armenians did not have an aristocracy like the Georgians but as Christians were also thought to be loyal. In the years 1828–30, up to 60,000 Armenians were encouraged to emigrate from Persia to newly Russian-held Armenia. Although these lands had a strong medieval Armenian heritage and the old ecclesiastical capital of Echmiadzin, prior to the Russian conquest only around a fifth of their inhabitants were estimated to be Armenians. The majority of the population were either "Tatars" or nomadic Muslim Kurds. The Russians reintroduced a strong Armenian demographic presence, which has grown steadily—as noted, ethnic Armenians today constitute around 98 percent of the population of the Republic of Armenia.

Policy in the Caucasus changed with every new regime. In 1845, the tsar appointed Prince Mikhail Vorontsov the first viceroy of the Caucasus, ushering in a period of enlightened autocracy. As governor of the new Russian provinces of Crimea and Odessa, Vorontsov had promoted free trade and ethnic tolerance, and he was given "unlimited powers" by the emperor to work the same magic in the Caucasus. While ferociously pursuing war in the

North Caucasus, Vorontsov tried to rule by consent in the south. He started a new school system with tuition in the native languages and recruited locals into his administration, ridding himself of Russian time-servers in the process. The liberalization had its limits. The lower classes still remained mostly bonded serfs and subject to conscription, but Vorontsov at least allowed them to celebrate their religious ceremonies again.

The Vorontsov reforms gave upper-caste Caucasians access to Russian imperial society. One beneficiary was the composer Alexander Borodin, whose father was a Georgian aristocrat serving in St. Petersburg. Another was the Armenian Mikhail Loris-Melikov, the son of a Tiflis Armenian merchant who studied in St. Petersburg and was appointed to the highest post in the empire, becoming Russia's interior minister in 1880. Azerbaijani "Tatars" also benefited, especially after Vorontsov restored the rights of Muslim landowners in Azerbaijan. Mirza Akhundov, a translator in Vorontsov's chancellery, became a playwright and was called the "Tatar Molière."[9]

Vorontsov especially wooed the Georgian nobility, who comprised around 5 percent of Georgia's population. After the Russian conquest, the nobles continued to inhabit an almost medieval world, living off the land and concentrated on their rural estates. Up until the 1840s, a Georgian nobleman could still give a serf or even a whole family as a gift.[10] The nobles had mostly resented the Russian annexation, and young Georgian aristocrats tried unsuccessfully to stage an uprising in 1832. Vorontsov's reforms led to 30,000 Georgians having their aristocratic status officially recognized in St. Petersburg. They became "service gentry," dependent on the tsarist court, acquiring European culture and habits—and frequently falling into heavy debts that tied them even closer to the Russian administration. The tsarist administration also offered the Georgians a role in its plans to forcibly civilize the smaller peoples of the Caucasus. Russians and Georgians, sharing the same church, proselytized Orthodox Christianity to the remote mountain peoples of the Caucasus, such as the Abkhaz, Ossetians, Lezghins, and Svans. These groups' languages were written down for the first time in the 1860s in scripts based on Cyrillic so their members could read newly translated Christian scripture.

Vorontsov, a classical scholar, argued that the Caucasus was not so much being conquered anew as rediscovered. He encouraged Russian and Georgian archaeologists and ethnographers to uncover the ancient connections of the lands of the Transcaucasus to Rome, Greece, and Byzantium. The new Caucasus Museum in the center of Tiflis that opened in 1867 presented the vision of this new-old Caucasus to the public. The British traveler and diplomat Oliver Wardrop visited the museum twenty years later and wrote that "the student will find geological, zoological, ethnographical, entomological, biological, archeological and numismatic collections of the highest interest." Above the staircase, he saw a painting, "the 'Arrival of the Argonauts in Colchis,' the figures in which are all portraits, the Grand Duke Nicholas Mikhailovich [Romanov] being represented as Jason."[11] The message was that Georgians had received enlightenment from the Russian grand duke, just as Jason, a representative of Greek civilization, had brought enlightenment to the people of Colchis, an ancient but backward kingdom.

Urban Cauldrons

In the nineteenth century, the Transcaucasus was properly urbanized for the first time. The character of the three cities—Tiflis, Baku, and their smaller commercial cousin Batum—began to diverge strongly from that of the rest of the region. In the countryside, villages were neat monoethnic packages, side by side but separate; in these three cities, different nationalities were mixed together in an urban setting that became a cauldron of social and economic change. At the end of the century, all three cities became catalysts for revolution.

RUSTAVELI AVENUE

Rustaveli Avenue is the main thoroughfare in the Georgian capital Tbilisi, but it is much more than that. In 1991 an American journalist wrote of Tbilisi, "This is a city of violent passions, elaborate conspiracy theories and some remarkably good restaurants."[1] All of the above are to be found on Rustaveli.

The avenue was the brainchild of the enlightened tsarist viceroy of the Caucasus, Mikhail Vorontsov. He ordered its construction in the 1840s to change Tiflis from a Persian-style city into a new European metropolis. At the eastern end it flows into the city's main square, which was named successively after Prince Paskevich of Yerevan, Lavrenti

Beria, and Lenin and is now Freedom Square. The avenue itself has had only two names: first, Golovin Prospekt, after an early Russian viceroy; and, since 1918, Rustaveli, after the Georgian national poet. Vorontsov had his own magnificent residence and a new Orthodox cathedral built on the south side of the avenue, but both were destroyed by the Bolsheviks, and the Soviet-era parliament building was put in their place. On the north side were the new opera house and the best hotels in the city. The three-story Hotel Orient, a favorite of European visitors, was the location for at least two major historical episodes. Azerbaijani nationalists hurriedly proclaimed the independence of the Republic of Azerbaijan in the hotel in May 1918, when Baku was under Bolshevik control; and in December 1936, Nestor Lakoba, the party leader of Abkhazia, retired there to die after being poisoned by his Georgian rival, Beria.

Political demonstrators adopt Rustaveli as a place of protest, because if they can occupy the avenue they will bring the city to a halt. The authorities know that too. In 1956 Soviet troops shot down demonstrators who had claimed the streets in anger at Nikita Khrushchev's denunciation of Stalin. In 1978 protestors marched along Rustaveli demanding equal status for the Georgian language. On the tragic night of April 9, 1989, protestors were asphyxiated and trampled to death by Soviet soldiers. Then, in December 1991, the street became the epicenter of the short civil war that culminated in the overthrow of President Zviad Gamsakhurdia. More than a hundred people died and the grand buildings on the eastern half of the avenue were gutted.

It took a decade for Rustaveli to be fully rebuilt. In 2003, on a more euphoric note, crowds gathered there to stage Georgia's bloodless "Rose Revolution." Only four years later, in November 2007, the hero of that revolution, President Mikheil Saakashvili sent in riot police to break up a demonstration against his own rule, and Rustaveli was again filled with teargas and the sound of breaking glass.

> With its tall plane trees and elegant buildings, Rustaveli Avenue is loved by the people of Tbilisi, but most of them would probably rather have it as a street and not a stage for endless political drama. The Georgian author Guram Odisharia writes, "Without the emergence of a new political culture, without a harmonic relationship between the authorities and society, the people's hopes will always be deceived and the main player in our country's political history will be Rustaveli Avenue, and not Georgian politicians."[2]
>
> 1. Michael Dobbs, "Nationalists, Minority Battle in Soviet Georgia; Moscow Accused of Arming Ossetians," *Washington Post*, March 21, 1991.
> 2. Guram Odisharia, "Rustaveli Avenue," in *Histories of Hope in the First Person*, European Bank for Reconstruction and Development, 2008, available online at http://www.ebrd.com/pubs/general/hhe.pdf.

Tiflis (officially called by its Georgian name Tbilisi only in the twentieth century) had long been the largest city in the region. When King David IV reconquered the town from the Arabs in 1122, he invited Armenian traders and artisans to settle there, and they became its largest community. For centuries the Armenians ran the city, as Georgians tended to be either rural nobility or peasantry. After the Russian takeover in 1801, Tiflis became the seat of imperial rule. In the 1840s, Prince Vorontsov finally cleared away the last ruins of the 1795 Iranian assault and transformed the main part of the city into a European-style capital. He laid out a new central boulevard that became the main artery of the city (now Rustaveli Avenue; see box). The first theater and public library were built; newspapers were opened. The viceroy invited an Italian opera company to come and perform Rossini, Bellini, and Donizetti and was pleased to hear them instead of the "semi-barbarous sounds of Persian music" that had filled the town a few years earlier.[12]

In 1899, Tiflis had 172,000 inhabitants. Armenians were just over a third of the population; Georgians and Russians each formed a quarter. The remainder included Ossetians, Azerbaijani "Tatars," Persians, Greeks, Poles, Germans, and Jews. Caucasian towns were not melting pots, and each community had separate places of worship, different holidays, and special trades.

The Armenians dominated business, trade, and municipal government, running the hotels, restaurants, cafes and taverns, wineshops, and caravanserais. Wardrop said the Armenians were called "Shylocks" and like the Jews were disliked by other ethnic groups for their alleged sharp practices: "A local proverb says 'A Greek will cheat three Jews, but an Armenian will cheat three Greeks.'"[13] This kind of racial stereotyping caused tensions between Armenians and Georgians but generally did not spill over into street violence.

The same was not true in the other major city of the Caucasus, Baku. Here, social and political tensions eventually caused mass bloodshed. Situated on a peninsular overlooking the Caspian Sea, Baku was a small ancient desert fortress, home to a powerful dynasty, the Shirvanshahs, in the Middle Ages. The commercial exploitation of its oil wells in the 1870s changed it virtually overnight into the world's foremost oil city. In 1883, the British writer Charles Marvin noted, "What was ten years ago a sleepy Persian town is to-day a thriving city. There is more building activity visible at Baku than in any other place in the Russian Empire." Old houses were being pulled down while the "wretched booths of the Persians were being replaced by spacious Russian shops." As in Tiflis, Armenians had a leading role in both business and municipal government, while tens of thousands of Muslim peasants, many from Iran, immigrated to earn a wage in the oil fields.

The third main urban center of the region, the Black Sea city of Batum (called by its Georgian name Batumi after 1936), became the Caucasus's window on the world after the Russian takeover in 1878. Within a generation, it had a string of foreign consulates and a British yacht club and cricket pitch. Again, this all depended on Baku oil, sent to Batum first by railway and then through the world's first oil pipeline. It was refined in a factory built by the Rothschilds—to which the young Stalin set fire in 1903. Like Baku, although smaller (its population in 1897 was 28,000), it was a place of commerce and intrigue. A 1913 Russian guidebook describes the rich urban mix of the city:

> Georgians predominantly are salesmen, tavern-keepers, cooks, servants, bartenders, carriage drivers; the Armenians are traders and shopkeepers, porters, draymen; the Greeks are bakers, shoemakers, blanket-makers, traders; the Persians are gardeners, vegetable and fruit growers, keepers of eating houses and tea-houses; the Turks are fishermen,

felucca sailors, port workers, keepers of coffee-houses; the Jews are traders; the Ajarians are immigrant peasants, farmers, and wardens. Apart from that, there are a lot of foreigners, thanks to the many different offices and steamship companies.[14]

Reform, Revolution, and Nation-Building

In the second half of the nineteenth century, the Russian Empire oscillated between reform and reaction. In Russia, rebellion was driven by social and political grievances, but in the Transcaucasus national issues came to the fore.

Following Russia's defeat in the Crimean War of 1854–56, the "tsar liberator" Alexander II began an age of liberalization. His major reform, the abolition of serfdom, caused as many problems as it solved in the Transcaucasus. The peasants themselves acquired little land, and thousands were forced to migrate to towns (Stalin's mother, for example, moved to the town of Gori from the village of Gambareuli), while the nobility lost cheap labor and revenue. The main beneficiaries of the era were the Caucasian intellectuals. The tsarist administration still had not opened a university in the Transcaucasus—and never would—so a new generation of Europeanized men from the Caucasus went to study in Russia. There they mingled with the most progressive and radical students of the day and reimported the new liberal ideas to their homelands.

The leading Georgian nationalist thinker was the writer Ilia Chavchavadze (1837–1907), who studied law in St. Petersburg and became the most prominent of the *tergdaleulni*, "those who have tasted the waters of the Terek" (the river on the Russian side of the Caucasus). These were men who had gone to live in Russia and returned to Georgia inspired with ideas of reform. Their Russification equipped them with new ideas but also moved them further away from the people, leaving them in an awkward in-between state. As the historian Zurab Avalov said in 1908, "By skinning himself, a Georgian doesn't become a Russian, but simply a skinned Georgian."[15] Back in Georgia, Chavchavadze wrote popular verse and promoted language reform to make written Georgian more modern and accessible. His generation believed that the Georgian language and the rediscovery of the medieval past were tools that could combine Georgia's diverse regional identities into a new Georgian nation.

In 1881, Tsar Alexander II was assassinated and was succeeded by his more reactionary son, Alexander III. The new tsar abolished the viceroyalty of the Transcaucasus, reducing the region to the same status as other parts of Russia. Russian patriotism was proclaimed in a series of new "military cathedrals" that were built from Baku to Kars and mostly named after the Russian warrior-saint Alexander Nevsky. The most magnificent of these was the forty-meter-high neo-Byzantine cathedral in the center of Tiflis, whose interior was filled with the shields of the regiments that had triumphed in the Caucasian wars and whose exterior was ringed with captured cannons. (The cathedral was demolished by the Communist regime in 1930.)

Armenians were losing their status as some of the most loyal Russian subjects. Russia had three images of Armenians in the nineteenth century, Suny writes: "as Christian, as commercial, and as conspiratorial."[16] The conspiratorial role grew in response to state policy. In 1885, Armenian-language schools were closed, and in 1903, after the death of Alexander III, the state expropriated land and buildings of the Armenian Apostolic Church (a policy that was so unpopular it was reversed two years later). Two Armenian revolutionary movements were founded: Hunchak ("Bell") in 1887 in Geneva and Dashnaktsutiun in Tiflis in 1890. Hunchak was more socialist and was soon eclipsed by the radical nationalist Dashnaks, who espoused revolutionary tactics against the governments of both the tsar and the sultan. The Dashnaks won a similar reputation to the Bolsheviks for terror tactics, and in 1905 both movements all but waged a competition to see who could assassinate more tsarist officials.

In political terms, the Azerbaijanis were the late developers of the three main nationalities in the region. In the 1880s, a European scholar wrote that Transcaucasian Turks "very rarely revolt against the rapaciousness of Russian civil and military officers, and they peacefully submit to all kinds of vexations, as long as their family and religious life is not touched upon."[17] Levels of education were low. According to the all-Russia 1897 census, only 4.7 percent of the "Tatar" population could read or write. Despite this, under the influence of pan-Turkic thinkers, Azerbaijani intellectuals mobilized themselves with amazing speed. According to the historian of Azerbaijan Tadeusz Swietochowski, "In 1905 Azerbaijan was still merely a geographical name for a stretch of land inhabited by a people whose group identity consisted of being Muslims. The period between this date and the fall of the independent Republic in 1920 witnessed the rise of, for the Muslims, a novel type of community, the nation."[18] The new Azerbaijani national identity was a synthesis: Turkic but separate from Turkey, Shiite Islamic but rejecting the clerical establishment. The effort to combine these different aspirations within one movement led leading Azerbaijani editor and intellectual Ali bay Huseynzade to coin the slogan "Turkify, Islamize, Modernize." The main Azerbaijani nationalist party, Musavat, was founded in 1911 and by 1918 had pulled off the feat of founding the first democratic Islamic republic in the world. The three colors of the republic's flag—blue, red, and green— reflected Huseynzade's slogan, symbolizing the Turks, modernity, and Islam, respectively.

In the early part of the new century, the new Armenian and Azerbaijani national movements inevitably collided. For centuries, Armenians and Azerbaijanis had coexisted as neighbors in a patchwork quilt of towns and villages across the Transcaucasus. They spoke each other's languages, traded freely, and had a shared culture with strong Persian influences. Yet mixed marriage was rare, and differences of religion, social status, and now national ideology caused divisions. These tensions were contained by Russian colonial rule, but when that rule weakened in 1905 and 1917 (and again in 1988) the geography of mixed ethnic cohabitation turned peaceful communities into places of violence.

The revolutionary year of 1905 saw the outbreak of what was called the "Armeno-Tatar War." The bloodshed spread the entire length of the South Caucasus, from Baku in the east to Nakhichevan in the west. Up to 10,000 people were killed, and whole urban districts and villages were gutted. The British author James Henry called Baku "the greatest blood-spot in the mysterious, rebellious and blood-stained Caucasus" after it saw two bloody pogroms in one year.[19] The conflict horrified and puzzled both locals and outsiders. One Azerbaijani intellectual in Ganja, Ahmad bay Aghaoghli, "sternly lectured crowds in a Ganja mosque that 'even wild animals do not devour their own kind' reminding them that Muslims and Armenians had for centuries lived in peace before the coming of the Russians."[20] The Russian socialist author Maxim Gorky expressed shock at what had happened, lamenting, "how hard it is to believe that these simple noble people now stupidly and senselessly are killing one another, giving in to provocation by evil and dark forces."[21]

The tsarist empire came to an end in the Caucasus not with mass repression but with a slow surrender of control. The relatively small colonial administration was simply unable to deal with a steady rise in political protest. The biggest challenge came from the previously most loyal nationality, the Georgians, whose social profile had changed strongly. The authority of the nobility had faded, and Georgia now contained all the ingredients for a revolutionary movement, with workers in Tiflis and Batum, a radical peasantry, and what came to be known as the "third generation" of Marxist intellectuals. In 1903, the leading Georgian Marxist, Noe Zhordania, was confident enough to split from Lenin's Bolsheviks and take his followers over to the Menshevik faction of the revolutionary party. In 1905, revolutionaries seized the railway and cut the Georgian provinces in two. In order to keep order in Tiflis, the elderly viceroy, said to be on the verge of a nervous breakdown, tried and failed to impose martial law. Its authority in tatters, the tsarist regime authorized the first ever elections in the Russian Empire. In the voting in Georgia for Russia's new assemblies, the First and Second Dumas of 1905 and 1906 (both of which were dissolved), the Mensheviks strongly outperformed the Bolsheviks and came out on top.

Russia's grip on the Transcaucasus was further loosened when war broke out in Europe in 1914 and the Ottoman Empire allied with Germany against Russia, Britain, and France. The region was mostly unenthusiastic about the war. Georgian socialists debated whether or not to declare support for the Germans. As Muslims, Azerbaijanis were exempt from conscription into the army and mostly reluctant to be at war with Turks. Only Armenians were ready to fight, seeing the war as a chance to liberate their brethren from Ottoman rule.

The Armenian Genocide

The years 1915–21 were the bloodiest in the history of the Caucasus, and the scale of the killing puts into perspective the tragic but far less bloody conflicts of the 1990s. The fact that as many as 45,000 Muslim Laz and Ajarians were allegedly killed in 1915 in the Çoruh River valley south of Batum in the campaign of Russian general Vladimir Lyakhov merits only a line in one history of the Caucasus. The deaths of one million or more Armenians in the same period dwarfs anything the region has experienced since.[22]

The main theater of bloodshed was Eastern Anatolia, in what is now eastern Turkey. This area was the troubled borderland between the Russian and Ottoman empires, with a mixed Christian-Muslim population. It was an Armenian homeland—medieval churches and monuments testified to an ancient Armenian presence, and Armenians were still a large community in the six eastern provinces, although they were not a clear majority in any of them. It was also home to Christian Pontic Greeks and Assyrians, Kurds, Laz, Ajarians, and also as many as 850,000 *muhajirs*—Muslims from the Balkans and North Caucasus who had been deported to the Ottoman Empire over the previous two generations.[23] For the large Turkish population, Anatolia was an ancient Turkish heartland the Ottoman Empire could not afford to lose, especially after it lost its Balkan possessions in the wars of 1912–13. Yet the Armenians and Greeks increasingly looked to neighboring Russia as their Great Power protector. All the ingredients were in place, therefore, for both a struggle between the major powers and for local conflict. The last Ottoman sultan to wield serious power, Abdul Hamid II, said that the loss of these lands would be a deathblow to his empire and explicitly blamed the Armenians for it: "By taking away Greece and Rumania, Europe has cut off the feet of the Turkish state. The loss of Bulgaria, Serbia and Egypt has deprived us of our hands, and now by means of this Armenian agitation they want to get at our most vital places and tear out our very guts."[24]

Armenians had an ambiguous place in the Ottoman Empire. In an empire where collective political identity came through religious affiliation, the Armenian Apostolic Church had its own *millet* (the Ottoman word meant "nation") and was for a long time known as "millet-i sadzka," or "the loyal community," to the sultan. Most Armenians remained peasants, continuing a semifeudal way of life in their old Anatolian homeland. Others, as in Russia, became an urban bourgeoisie in towns like Smyrna, Trabzon, or Van. A small minority in Constantinople were extremely privileged and served the sultan as jewelers or bankers.[25]

In the second half of the nineteenth century, the Ottoman Empire began to disintegrate under the strain of economic failure, stalled reform, and nationalist agitation. Armenian peasants, who had lost their land and complained of oppressive administration, received promises of support from their Armenian brethren in the Russian Empire. Western supporters, such as British prime minister William Gladstone, complained to the sultan about the persecution of his Christian subjects. The Treaty of Berlin of 1878, dictated by the Western powers, all but broke up the empire and committed its government to protecting the Armenians, but on the ground the situation only got worse. Armenian revolutionary bands, known as *fedayi*, were formed. An Armenian rebellion in 1894 was crushed, triggering a series of massacres, ordered by Sultan Abdul Hamid II in 1895–96. According to one German observer, 88,000 Armenians were killed, and 546,000 were left destitute.[26]

As the empire decayed, the so-called Committee of Union and Progress was formed. Initially a multinational reformist group—which even collaborated with the Dasnak Party—it increasingly became a vehicle for pan-Turkic nationalism and the so-called Young Turks. In 1908 the Young Turks deposed Sultan Abdul Hamid and brought in a brief era of constitutional government, with a multinational parliament. Then, after the Ottoman defeat in the Balkan Wars of 1912–13, the three most radical Young Turks, the "three Pashas"—interior minister Talat Pasha, minister of war Enver Pasha, and minister of the navy Cemal Pasha—gained power.

In 1914, these three took the Ottoman Empire into the First World War in alliance with Germany. Enver Pasha, who held extreme pan-Turkic beliefs, launched an invasion of the Caucasus that was designed to avenge past defeats and link up Turkish brethren from Azerbaijan to Central Asia (whether they wanted this or not). Enver met the Russian army, heavily supported by Armenians, in bitter wintry conditions at the railway terminus at Sarikamis, south of Kars, in January 1915, and suffered one of the worst defeats in military history. By one estimate, five-sixths of the Turkish Third Army—around 75,000 men—died. Among the Russians, 16,000 were killed or wounded; a further 12,000 were sickened, mostly from frostbite.

This defeat first inspired the Armenian rebels and then provoked a ferocious Turkish response in the town of Van. At the same time, the Young Turk government had launched what has come to be known as the Armenian Genocide of 1915. On April 24—a date Armenians now commemorate as Genocide Day—Talat Pasha ordered the arrest of several hundred leading Armenians in Constantinople, including many prominent intellectuals, such as Armenia's most famous composer, Komitas. Many were executed.

Talat Pasha then gave orders for the mass deportation of the Armenians of Anatolia on the grounds that they were a threat to the survival of the Ottoman state. Ottoman troops and police gendarmes supervised the rounding up of Armenians and the confiscation of their property. Many men were killed on the spot; many women and children were forcibly converted to Islam; many more were deported on foot in death marches to the deserts of Syria. Anatolian Kurds killed, raped, and ravaged the convoys. In harrowing scenes, mothers gave up their children to Kurds or Bedouin rather than see them perish. At Der Zor in northwestern Syria, tens of thousands perished in open-air concentration camps; human bones and skulls are still reported to come to the surface there to this day. Between 150,000 and 300,000 Assyrian Christians suffered the same fate.

There are inevitably disputes about the numbers of dead. Drawing on church archives, Armenian historian Raymond Kevorkian calculates that there were 1.9 million Armenians living in the Ottoman Empire at the time the Genocide began. Already in 1918 there were estimations that one million of them had died. By 1922, it has been estimated, around 90 percent of the Armenians of the Ottoman Empire, a group that had lived in these lands for many centuries, had been destroyed, deported, or forcibly converted to Islam. [27] Donald Bloxham wrote, "Nowhere else during the First World War was the separatist nationalism of the few answered with the total destruction of the wider ethnic community from which the nationalists hailed."[28]

The deportations and killings of the Ottoman Armenians were the worst atrocity of World War I. The killings were widely reported at the time by journalists, whose reports were corroborated by European and American consuls and thousands of eyewitness testimonies. Some Ottoman officials responsible for particularly hideous massacres were prosecuted by the short-lived Allied administration that ruled Turkey after the end of the war. Why then is there still controversy about the issue? Debate continues in part because Armenians and their Russian backers exacted revenge on Muslims in Anatolia, creating an oral memory of atrocities that, although less extensive than the Genocide, left scars on the region. In 1919, for example, Kars Province was put under the administration of newly independent Armenia, to the despair of its Muslim inhabitants. American envoy General James Harbord, reported scenes of devastation caused by both sides:

> Mutilation, violation, torture, and death have left their haunting memories in a hundred beautiful Armenian valleys, and the traveler in that region is seldom free from the evidence of this most colossal crime of all the ages. Villages are in ruins, some having been destroyed when the Armenians fled or were deported; some during the Russian advance; some on the retreat of the Armenian irregulars and Russians after the fall of the Empire. . . . Where the desperate character of the warfare with its reprisals of burning and destroying as one side and then the other advanced, has not destroyed the buildings, which are generally of abode, the wooden beams have been taken for fuel and the houses are ruined. In the territory untouched by war from which Armenians were deported the ruined villages are undoubtedly due to Turkish devilry, but where Armenians advanced

and retired with the Russians their retaliatory cruelties un-
questionably rivaled the Turks in their inhumanity.[29]

Confusion also clings to the topic because from the 1920s it was half-
forgotten for two generations. Surviving Armenians did not make it an
issue of public politics until the 1960s, while the Republic of Turkey
suppressed its recent history and the inconvenient fact that a new, largely
homogeneous Turkish state had been founded at the expense of non-
Turkish ethnic groups.

When the Armenian issue arose again in international politics in the
1960s and 1970s, it was complicated by two new factors. A campaign
of terrorism conducted by two rival Armenian militant groups based in
Lebanon resulted in the deaths of several dozen Turkish diplomats and
many civilians. [30] This associated Armenians internationally with terrorism, while in Turkey it reconstructed an image of Armenians, who had
disappeared from public consciousness for fifty years, as a hostile security threat. In response to this a "denialist" Turkish historical literature
was written for the first time. Simultaneously, Armenians themselves increasingly directed their efforts towards having the deportations labeled
"genocide," using the a term devised by Raphael Lemkin in the 1940s
(see box). Most scholars do use this term, but it has a heavy baggage and
strong emotional associations with the Holocaust, thereby causing many
Turks not just to reject the "genocide" term but to minimize the story of
the Armenian massacres as a whole.

Since the first AKP government took office in 2002 in Turkey, much of
Turkish society, if not the authorities themselves, has begun to look at the
dark pages of the country's history and acknowledge the crimes committed
against the Armenians. Many progressive Kurdish politicians in particular
have opened up on this issue and overseen the restoration of Armenian
churches. A number of Turkish historians have enriched the scholarship of
the period. A newly sophisticated analysis of what happened has explained—
but not excused—the story of the Armenian Genocide by putting it in the
context of World War I. Recent historians persuasively ascribe the massacres
more to the radicalization of a group of desperate leaders within wartime
than to an atavistic urge by Turks in general to eliminate Armenians. Ronald
Suny has written, "Had there been no World War there would have been no
genocide, not only because there would have been no 'fog of war' to cover
up the events but because the radical sense of endangerment among Turks
would not have been as acute."[31]

GENOCIDE

"Genocide" is not a historical term. It is a legal definition devised in the 1940s by the scholar Raphael Lemkin in response to the Nazis' "Final Solution" program to exterminate Europe's Jews, describing the deliberate attempt to wipe out an ethnic group by mass killing. The word was then enshrined in the 1948 United Nations Convention on the Prevention and Punishment of Genocide.

When he coined the word, Lemkin explicitly used it to refer to the killing of the Armenians in the Ottoman Empire. In their own language, Armenians tended to use the phrase *mets yeghern* (the "great catastrophe" or "great slaughter") to describe the killings of 1915–16. This is the term President Obama used when making a statement on Armenian Genocide Day (April 24) in 2009.[1] After 1948, Armenians began to adopt the term "Armenian Genocide" (*tseghasbanutiun*), and it gained wider currency after the fiftieth anniversary of the massacres in 1965. This was a period when the term "Holocaust" began to be used to describe the Nazi destruction of the Jews and when the civil rights movement made it acceptable to talk about one's own victimhood and suffering.

As the usage grew more common, the Turkish government began to denounce the Armenians' use of the phrase, with the result that, along with the historical and personal investigations into the tragedy of 1915, a parallel debate developed on the question, "Was the killing of the Armenians genocide?" Armenians were aligned on one side and most Turks on the other. Some Armenian lobby groups made achieving international recognition of the killings as genocide their main goal.

After years of nondialogue, some Armenian and Turkish historians began to find common ground in meetings in the late 1990s. Taboos of silence were broken, but some of the Turkish citizens who led the process paid a high price. The Istanbul Armenian editor Hrant Dink, who had built bridges between the two communities and had been attacked by extremists on both sides, was murdered in 2007. Dink's position was very specific. While campaigning passionately for Turks to come to terms with their past and the facts of the Armenian deportations of 1915–16, he was skeptical about the benefits of the genocide recognition campaigns and believed that it was vital to begin work inside Turkey, not outside it. Dink said, "I have a hard time accepting the imprisonment of human experience inside a legal term [genocide] that is itself designed to produce a political outcome."[2]

Dink's funeral was another landmark, as thousands of outraged Turks turned out in solidarity with the dead man. This in turn led to a courageous online signature campaign in which Turks endorsed a statement beginning: "My conscience does not accept the insensitivity showed to and the denial of the Great Catastrophe that the Ottoman Armenians were subjected to in 1915."[3] In 2009, the governments of Armenia and Turkey tried, but ultimately failed, to normalize relations between their two states.

In the Caucasus—and not only there—use of the word "genocide" has become a weapon of identity and almost a badge of national honor. In the wake of the Armenians, other ethnic groups have adopted genocide days and called on the outside world to recognize their collective suffering. For Circassians, the key date is May 21, 1864, when they were deported en masse from the Russian Empire. Azerbaijanis have adopted March 31 as such a commemoration, referring to the day in 1918 when Armenians killed hundreds of Azeris in pogroms in Baku. For Pontic Greeks, Genocide Day is May 19, 1919. If all mass killings of recent times are to be honored, other national groups, such as Kurds, Meskhetian Turks, and Assyrians, also have good claims to make—but in their cases it seems that murderous policies were only too successful, as they lack the numbers and resources to mount campaigns on the issue. In an ideal world, it might be more dignified to call for a truce in the duels of genocide claims and a mass honoring of the dead instead. In the very politicized world of the wider Caucasus region, that idea looks sadly unfeasible.

1. Thomas de Waal, *Great Catastrophe: Armenians and Turks in the Shadow of Genocide* (New York: Oxford University Press, 2015), 132–39.
2. Tuba Çandar, *Hrant Dink, An Armenian Voice of the Voiceless in Turkey* (New Brunswick, N.J.: Transaction, 2016), 281.
3. See http://www.ozurdiliyoruz.com.

The repercussions of the *mets yeghern* ("great catastrophe"), as Armenians call it, are far from over. For those in the Armenian diaspora in the Middle East, the United States, and Europe whose grandparents survived the Anatolian holocaust, this is the issue that above all defines their identity and still demands justice from Turkey. For the eastern Armenians who inhabit what is now the Republic of Armenia, it is a very important issue but not the only one: it is to be set alongside the building of their nation-state and the conflict in Karabakh, and it is Azerbaijan more than Turkey that is seen to constitute the hostile power. This situation created tensions and misunderstandings between the Armenian authorities and much of the diaspora in 2009–10, when President Serzh Sargsyan sought to normalize relations with Turkey and open the closed border between the two states, an act that many diaspora Armenians considered a sellout.

Independence

In the midst of the First World War in 1917, the tsarist regime in St. Petersburg collapsed, leaving the Transcaucasus free of Russian rule but without any effective government. Within a year, the three countries of the region had declared independence in what might be called "separatism by default." But the political chaos both inside and outside the region brought out the worst of the Caucasus and triggered a series of civil wars and foreign invasions that ultimately led to a Russian Bolshevik reconquest in 1920–21.

In 1918, the first issue the would-be national governments faced was that they had no means of defending themselves. In 1919, the British colonel Toby Rawlinson was in Tiflis and wrote that the Georgians "had at this time what they were pleased to call an army," which consisted of "very small and indifferent bodies of cavalry, artillery, and infantry, the officers of which swaggered about the town in magnificent uniforms."[32] This was no match for the 60,000 men of Enver Pasha's Ottoman Third Army in 1918—or the 70,000 men of the Bolshevik Eleventh Army in 1920–21. So the small nations of the region looked for bigger allies and fought their neighbors to try to secure defensible borders.

In February 1917, the last Russian imperial viceroy of the Transcaucasus left quietly, handing over power to a diverse collection of socialist and nationalist parties and workers' soviets. The Tiflis Soviet, dominated by Noe Zhordania's Mensheviks, moved into the viceroy's palace, hoisted the red flag outside, and pledged support to the Provisional Government in Petrograd. In Georgia, the pragmatic policies of this overnight Menshevik government were generally popular, but the economy disintegrated. In the meantime, war with the Ottoman Empire continued, and the Bolsheviks—a minority in the Caucasus—exploited this. After the Bolsheviks took power in Russia in the October Revolution, the Russian army, while in possession of most of eastern Anatolia, simply dissolved on the ground. That left Eastern Anatolia and the Armenian and Georgian borderlands exposed to the Ottoman army as it prepared its next campaign.

It is worth emphasizing that in 1917, most of the Transcaucasian leaders did not want a break with Russia and said they would govern the region only until a new constitutional assembly was convened in Russia. They formed a new interim government, the Transcaucasian Commissariat, consisting of three Armenians, three Azerbaijanis, and three Georgians. In November 1917, Zhordania gave a speech to the First Georgian National Soviet in which he warned about the Turkish threat to the Caucasus and condemned the Bolsheviks' "hasty second revolution" but argued that Georgia's best hopes still lay with a democratic Russia. He said: "This union [with Russia in 1801] was not the result of some kind of personal caprice or a matter of simple chance. It was a historic inevitability. At that time, Georgia stood before a dilemma: the East or the West. And our ancestors decided to turn away from the East and turn to the West. But the road to the West lay through Russia, and consequently to go toward the West meant union with Russia."[33]

The Bolsheviks had one island of support in industrial Baku, where they took power and formed the Baku Commune, but they faced strong adversaries in the Armenian Dashnaktsutiun and the Azerbaijani Musavat Party. In the so-called March Days of 1918, Baku descended into a mini–civil war, after the Bolsheviks declared war on the Musavat Party and then stood by as Dashnak militias rampaged through the city, killing Azerbaijanis indiscriminately.[34] The Baku Soviet used the crisis to disband the Dashnak forces and then assumed full control of the city.

In March 1918, the Russian Bolshevik regime signed the Treaty of Brest-Litovsk with the Germans and Ottomans, promising to cede to them large parts of Eastern Anatolia that had been under tsarist control, but the treaty was signed without consultation with the Caucasian countries themselves. The Transcaucasian parliamentary coalition, now called the Seim, faced the dilemma of how to survive the threat of the Ottoman Third Army, as Enver Pasha at the forefront again marched toward the Caucasus. First Erzerum and Ardahan were captured; then Batum fell on April 14.

On April 22, 1918, the Seim in Tiflis made a historic declaration, announcing the region's separation from Russia and the formation of a new independent state, the Transcaucasian Federation. It was the only instance in history of a shared state for encompassing the entire South Caucasus, and it lasted only a month. The three main nationalities went into the project with completely different aims. The Armenians agreed to the move very reluctantly, afraid of an Ottoman conquest and not wishing formally to sever ties formally with Russia. The Azerbaijanis were enthusiastic about seceding from Russia and recapturing Baku with the help of the Turks. The Georgian leadership saw the declaration as an interim measure, and Zhordania himself abstained from voting on the resolution.

On April 25, 1918, Kars was abandoned, and the Ottoman army recovered it, after thirty years of Russian rule. At talks in Batum, the Ottomans demanded more territorial concessions from both the Georgians and the Armenians. The talks showed that the Transcaucasian Federation was untenable. The Azerbaijanis were happy to accept the Ottoman terms, while the Armenians said they amounted to destruction of their statehood. On May 21, the Ottoman army moved forward again and fought the battles of Sardarapat and Kara Kilise with the Armenians. The Ottoman advance was staved off, and its army stopped twenty-five miles from Yerevan.

From the Georgian point of view, with one section of the new state supporting the Turkish advance and another part opposing it, the federation was now bankrupt. The Georgians had been negotiating secretly with Germany for an alliance that would guarantee their survival, and on May 26 they announced the formation of the new Georgian Democratic Republic. A new crimson, black, and white flag was raised in Tiflis alongside the red flag. The Georgians then signed a treaty of alliance with Germany, which gave the Germans the right to use its railways, occupy the port of Poti, and have a monopoly on mining the country's mineral wealth.

Zhordania said the declaration of independence was an act of tragic historic necessity to defend Georgia from the Turkish threat. On May 28, both Azerbaijanis and Armenians then proclaimed independence, in the harshest possible circumstances. The Azerbaijani nationalists unveiled their new state in Tiflis, as Baku was still under Bolshevik control. They soon moved their new government to Ganja, transferring it to Baku only in September 1918, when the Baku Soviet fell. The declaration of an independent Armenia by Dashnak politicians in Tiflis was even more agonized. Independence effectively meant separation from the Armenian communities of Baku and Tiflis and the loss of Georgian economic and military support. The first Armenian statement on the matter on May 30 did not even mention the word "independence," saying only: "The Armenian National Council declares itself to be the supreme and only administration for the Armenian provinces."[35]

The next issue was making terms with the Turks. Independent Georgia signed an agreement that the southern border of the new state would be established as defined by the Treaty of Brest-Litovsk. The Armenians signed on to a deal that truncated what was left of their lands, giving the new republic a territory of only 4,500 square miles (12,000 square kilometers). That left them a state less than half the size of the present-day Republic of Armenia. (After the Turkish collapse in October 1918, a further 6,000 square miles were added.)

The Azerbaijanis happily signed a "Treaty of Friendship" with the Ottomans, whose primary aim was an alliance to oust the Bolsheviks from Baku—even though the Turks did not actually recognize Azerbaijani independence. The Baku commune crumbled, and its successor regime invited the British to help defend the city against the impending Turkish-Azerbaijani offensive, but the British expedition, the so-called Dunsterforce of General Lionel Dunsterville, had only 1,000 troops. When Dunsterville took over the Russian ship *President Kruger* and replaced the red flag with the Russian imperial flag, local revolutionaries objected, so he turned the flag upside down, thereby making it into a Serbian flag. Dunsterville later described himself as "a British General on the Caspian, the only sea unploughed before by British keels, on board a ship named after a South African president and whilom enemy, sailing from a Persian port, under the Serbian flag, to relieve from the Turks a body of Armenians in a revolutionary Russian town."[36]

Dunsterville pulled his British force out of Baku on September 14 in the face of a big Turkish-Azerbaijani offensive. The next day, the Azerbaijanis were back in the city and engaged in three days of revenge attacks for the March Days, killing up to 9,000 Armenians. The Azerbaijani nationalist government then arrived in the city from Ganja. For a brief period, it operated in Baku under Turkish protection until the next upheaval. With the end of the First World War, the Ottoman Empire capitulated to the Allies under the Treaty of Mudros and agreed to withdraw all its troops from the Caucasus. The British now entered Azerbaijan and became the predominant foreign power in the Transcaucasus, overseeing all three governments and— importantly for them—the Baku-Batum pipeline.

The upshot of the whirlwind events of 1918 was that for a short historical moment, the Transcaucasus had three emergent states independent of both Russia and Turkey. These three states shared features in common. All were parliamentary republics that, by the standards of the age, were fairly democratic. But nationalism was the order of the day. For the first time, Armenians, Azerbaijanis, and Georgians were in control of a territory that explicitly bore their name and claimed ownership of it in ways that alienated minorities and neighbors. They set up separate currencies and customs barriers. All the borders were disputed, which soon led to bloodshed, especially between Armenians and Azerbaijanis.

The Democratic Republic of Azerbaijan was the most remarkable of the three in being the world's first parliamentary democracy in a Muslim nation. Women had the vote there before they did in the United Kingdom. But the Musavat Party and the national leader, Mammed Amin Rasulzade, faced almost insuperable problems. They included the task of building a new state with virtually no experienced personnel; hostility from both the Bolsheviks and Whites in Russia; an ongoing war with Armenians over the territories of Karabakh, Nakhichevan, and Zangezur; a British military guardianship that set its own demands, such as forbidding the export of oil to Bolshevik Russia; and tensions with revolutionary workers and peasants who wanted extensive land reform.

Georgia under its Menshevik government was a little better equipped to deal with equally daunting problems. The independent Georgian state was subsequently mocked by Bolsheviks for being a Western puppet state and dismissed by Europeans as a Marxist anomaly, but there were good reasons that it lasted longest of the three. The government was genuinely popular and earned the support of the peasantry for its land reform program, and in Noe Zhordania the Georgian Mensheviks also had a thoughtful and much-admired leader, who makes for an interesting contrast with his younger Bolshevik contemporary, Iosif Jugashvili, or Stalin. Ten years older than Stalin, Zhordania died in Paris only two months before Stalin did. The two men had worked together, and both had attended Tiflis's Orthodox seminary for priests, the main institute of higher education in tsarist Georgia and a hotbed of revolutionaries. But their characters were very different. Zhordania believed in ruling by consensus. An admiring Polish contemporary described him in 1919 as a national patriarch, despite being only fifty years old, writing, "There seemed to be the halo of the tribal prophet around his majestic head with its thin gray hair and full beard."[37]

Nonetheless, Menshevik Georgia had many faults. Its economy was semiruined. Ethnic Russians were alienated by discriminatory policies. Most important, the Mensheviks antagonized Georgia's smaller nationalities. They waged brutal campaigns to incorporate Abkhazia and South Ossetia into their new state and sowed tensions in Ajaria, where the Muslim population resisted school education being imposed in the Georgian language. In 1920 the Menshevik People's Guard killed thousands of Ossetians in a ferocious response to what they said was a pro-Bolshevik uprising (see chapter 5). The jaundiced British journalist C. E. Bechhofer wrote, "I am sorry to say that the record of the Georgian government, in its two years' existence in the Transcaucasus, has been marred by nearly every fault that a State can commit. Chauvinism has run riot."[38] In December 1918, this nationalism helped turn a Georgian-Armenian border dispute over the regions of Lori and Borchalo into a small war. The British and French imposed a ceasefire and made Borchalo a neutral zone to be guarded by British troops.

Dashnak-ruled Armenia was the most miserable of the three new independent states. Most of its tsarist-era territory had been conquered by the Ottoman army in 1918, and there was perpetual conflict with Azerbaijan. Above all, there was the shadow of the massacres of Anatolia that had made Eastern Armenia home to 300,000 refugees, many of them starving. A *Time* correspondent called Armenia in 1919 "the land of the stalking death." In April 1920, Bechhofer traveled through a ruined country: "At all the stations on the line and in the surrounding villages, not a house remains whole, except, sometimes a solitary building, remarkable by contrast with the rest, where the Turkish commander himself was staying. The villages are masses of rubble; the stations wildernesses. Everywhere there is desolation, except where, among the ruins, new inhabitants are sheltering in misery."[39]

The reverse side of this was Armenia's outburst of revenge toward its Muslim neighbors. General Andranik Toros Ozanian expelled tens of thousands of Azerbaijanis from Zangezur, where they had lived for centuries. Then, following the Ottoman collapse at the end of the First World War in October 1918, the Armenians were given possession of the former province of Kars. Colonel Rawlinson traveled through the region and sent a telegram to his superiors in Tiflis recommending that "in the interests of humanity the Armenians should not be left in independent command of the Moslem population, as, their troops being without discipline and not under effective control, atrocities were constantly being committed, for which we should with justice eventually be held to be morally responsible."[40]

The plight of Armenia attracted particular sympathy in the United States, which basically took over the job of feeding the population. Herbert Hoover, the future president, took charge of food relief operations as head of the American Relief Administration because, in his words, Armenia had "only a shadow of a government." He wrote to President Wilson in June 1919 that 200,000 people had died of starvation, describing reports of the Armenian situation as "the most appalling that have yet developed out of [the] war." Americans ran what was the largest orphanage in the world in the town of Alexandropol (now Gyumri) right up until the end of the 1920s. For a generation afterward, American children were told to remember "the starving Armenians" when they did not finish the food on their plates.[41]

Toward the end of 1919, Harbord, sent by his government to assess the situation in the South Caucasus, painted a picture of utter breakdown:

> The three Governments from an occidental standpoint are now thoroughly inefficient, without credit, and undoubtedly corrupt. . . . [T]wo of them have no outlet to the Black Sea except through Georgia over the railroad. They have no present intermonetary, postal, or customs union, and, as stated, no definite agreement for common control and use of the railroad, and are in continual squabbles over boundaries. Azarbaijan has no educated class capable of well administering a government; Georgia is threatened by bolshevism; Armenia is in ruins, and partial starvation.[42]

The three countries now faced a sterner test, with a resurgent Bolshevik Russia and a resurgent Turkey under Mustafa Kemal (soon to be Ataturk) showing renewed interest in the region. The British had always been unclear about the purpose of their mission in the region and had not recognized the independence of the three states. British policy was made first with reference to

Russia, Persia, or India, ahead of the needs of the region itself. A Foreign Office memorandum of November 1918 said: "If Russia recovers rapidly, they might conceivably rejoin her in some federal relation; if the anarchy in Russia lasts many years, their present separation from her will probably be permanent. Our policy toward the Caucasus should be framed to meet either eventuality."[43]

In the end, differences in outlook fell away as lack of resources and the looming Red Army on the horizon decided Whitehall in favor of withdrawal. Even the arch anti-Bolshevik Winston Churchill said that using the small republics to keep back the Bolsheviks was like "using a piece of putty to stop an earthquake."[44] The British pulled out of most of the region in the late summer of 1919. They made promises that the fate of the disputed territories, primarily Karabakh, would be settled at the forthcoming Paris Peace Conference. In fact, all the disputes were settled by force of arms or Bolshevik politicians. The British left the Transcaucasus in the summer of 1920, just as the Bolsheviks completed their conquest of Azerbaijan.

The Bolshevik Takeover

For the Bolsheviks, there was no question of simply leaving the southern Caucasus alone. There were many Caucasians in the Bolshevik movement, such as Stalin, Anastas Mikoyan, and Sergo Orjonikidze, who dreamed of spreading the revolution to their homelands. There was also Russia's traditional interest in the Transcaucasus as its southern flank and gateway to Asia and the Middle East. Stalin told *Pravda* in November 1920: "The important meaning of the Caucasus for the revolution is determined not only by the fact that it is a source of raw materials, fuel, and food supplies but by its position between Europe and Asia and in particular between Russia and Turkey and the presence [there] of the most important economic and strategic roads."[45]

The immediate priority was to get possession of the Baku oil fields. In January 1920, the White Army was defeated in the Civil War, and the North Caucasus was under Bolshevik control, putting Baku within reach, just across the border. However, the Bolsheviks were split by differences over strategy between the Caucasian comrades, who wanted to conquer the whole of the region immediately, and more cautious Moscow politicians. "Our policy is a world policy and is not restricted by the Caucasus alone," foreign affairs commissar Georgy Chicherin told Orjonikidze in a telegram on May 7, 1920.[46]

The Bolsheviks won useful support from the new nationalist government of Kemal in Turkey. He was more pragmatic than his predecessors and rejected pan-Turkism in favor of a policy of establishing a new Turkey within secure frontiers. He was prepared to abandon the nationalist government in Baku and see Azerbaijan turn Bolshevik if its nominal sovereignty was respected. The Bolsheviks even enlisted some Turkish officers to help with their takeover of Azerbaijan. The plan was for a workers' uprising in Baku to be synchronized with the advance of the Eleventh Army. In the event, Red troops entered Azerbaijani territory on April 27, 1920, the day before the workers' rebellion was due to start. The Musavat government, with much of its army in Karabakh fighting the Armenians, barely resisted. Many workers of Baku, who had been marginalized by the new regime, welcomed the return of the Bolsheviks, but it took them two more months to crush resistance in the rest of the country.

The Bolsheviks initially announced that they were not threatening the independence of the Caucasian republics. When Baku fell, Lenin sent a telegram congratulating "the liberation of the laboring masses of the independent Azerbaijani republic."[47] On May 7, 1920, his government recognized the independence of Menshevik Georgia in what was soon to look like a cynical maneuver. The Georgian Bolshevik Party was legalized, and prisoners were freed from jail. In an independent Georgia, representatives of Bolshevik Russia and the Western powers briefly coexisted.

Armenia's borders continued to expand and contract dramatically. In the summer of 1920, Armenians were driven from the disputed territory of Nakhichevan, but this was also the high point of their ambitions in eastern Anatolia. On August 10, the Treaty of Sèvres was signed between the Allies and the Ottoman Empire in Istanbul, effectively partitioning the empire. Independent Armenia was to be a major beneficiary, thanks to the lobbying of Woodrow Wilson, and with the treaty giving it a vast new state, comprising much of easternAnatolia, including Trabzon on the Black Sea. However, "Wilsonian Armenia" existed only on paper and had little relationship with the situation on the ground. The Ottoman government only had authority in a small area, and Kemal's nationalist administration rejected the treaty and set itself the goal of ousting the Western allies from Turkish soil. In the autumn of 1920, Kemal launched a new offensive in Anatolia, again capturing Kars, and then Alexandropol (Gyumri), and threatening to overrun the whole of Armenia. The Armenians were forced to repudiate the Treaty of Sèvres and accept the loss of territory under the Treaty of Alexandropol on December 2.

At the same moment, the Bolshevik Eleventh Army crossed into Armenia and captured Yerevan on December 4, after only a brief show of resistance from the Dashnak government. Armenian independence was given up as the price of protection from the Turks, and the new Soviet Republic of Armenia was declared. The Dashnaks had one final stand in the spring of 1921; with the Red Army tied down in Georgia, they mounted a rebellion and briefly recaptured Yerevan, until the Bolsheviks again reestablished control. Then the Treaty of Moscow between Bolshevik Russia and Kemalist Turkey on March 21, 1921, finally drew the frontiers of present-day Armenia. The Armenians were forced to renounce claims to the town of Iğdir, the old city of Ani, and Mount Ararat.

By New Year's Day 1921, only independent Georgia remained free of the Bolsheviks. Georgia's Western patrons had pulled out all their troops. They belatedly recognized Georgia's de jure independence on January 27, 1921, but this was an empty gesture. The next day, Stalin wrote to Orjonikidze that an assault on Georgia should begin "after the treaty with England."[48] The British government was negotiating a treaty, eventually signed on March 16, that recognized Russian influence "with regard to countries which formed part of the former Russian Empire and have recently become independent" in return for promises not to incite "any of the peoples of Asia to actions hostile to British interests any more, especially in India and Afghanistan."[49]

By then, the Red Army had already entered Georgia and captured Tiflis, on February 25, after using an uprising in the Armenian-populated district of Borchalo as a pretext to intervene. The Red Army then conquered western Georgia and, with the support of many Abkhaz, Abkhazia. The terms of Menshevik capitulation were relatively mild and took into account the relative weakness of the Georgian Bolsheviks on the ground. Mensheviks were offered an amnesty, and many of them agreed to join the new regime. Menshevik troops continued to be paid and were allowed to keep their uniforms.[50] Another key factor was the fate of Batum, the main port of the Caucasus, which was again threatened by the Turks. Georgian solidarity trumped ideological differences as the ousted Mensheviks helped the Bolsheviks to recover the city from a two-day Turkish occupation. On the same night that Batum was retaken, March 17–18, the Menshevik government, led by Zhordania, sailed into exile on an Italian ship.

With the departure of the Mensheviks, a separate story of a Caucasus in exile began to unfold. From Istanbul, the Menshevik government issued a message, to "all socialist parties and workers' organizations" of the world, protesting the invasion of Georgia, but it went unheeded.[51] In exile, the leaders of the Caucasian independence movement slowly faded into irrelevance. In his memoirs, the British-Soviet double agent Kim Philby gives a disparaging account of Zhordania in postwar Paris as an anachronistic figure out of touch with his homeland. For the first two decades of exile, two émigré journals, *Prométhée* and *Kavkaz*, engaged in hand-wringing and mutual recriminations about how and why the independent republics had been lost to the Bolsheviks. The tone of their polemics suggested why it had all gone wrong. National groups quarreled with one another. *Kavkaz* accused the Georgian Mensheviks of having been too sympathetic to the Bolsheviks, while the "Promethians" despised their rivals for having backed the Russian monarchists and the Turks. The Caucasian émigré movement later fractured again in World War II when some decided to support the Nazis in the war against Stalin and others backed the Western allies.

The mirage of Caucasian independence vanished almost as quickly as it had appeared. In a sense, the three countries had not so much had independence as a forced decoupling from Russia; when the renewed Russian state decided to come back, it eventually got its way. What remained within the region was a vague collective memory of injustice, civil war, and stifled statehood. Even after 1991, the new post-Soviet national leaders—many of them Communist Party officials who had jumped ship at the right moment—mostly only paid lip- service to their forebears of 1918. Redjeb Jordania, the son of the leader of Georgia's first independent state, wrote that he returned to Tbilisi in 1990 to find "ignorance and indifference" about the republic his father had led. The younger Jordania attributed this in part to antagonism towards a state that had been both socialist and secular.[52] In 2004, Georgia's new government further rejected the link by replacing the flag and national anthem of the First Republic that had been adopted at independence. In all three countries, it transpired, the new elites were far more marked by the Soviet experience than by the only dimly remembered experience of the first republics.

3

The Soviet Caucasus

I n the spring of 1921, the Bolsheviks were masters of the Caucasus. Their takeover of the region was different in many ways from the Russian conquest in the nineteenth century. Many of the leading Bolsheviks, beginning with Stalin himself, were also Caucasians. They overcame strong resistance from the defenders of the national governments but also had support from workers, peasants, and small national groups. They themselves called their conquest a liberation from the captivity of oppressive nationalist bourgeois regimes and from "Great Power Russian chauvinism."

It is tempting but misleading to see the seventy-year Soviet experiment as just a second Russian imperial project. Ultimate power resided in Moscow and Russia played the role of big brother, but the Soviet Union was complex and contradictory. The Soviet state modernized, terrorized, and Russified the Caucasus but also gave it new kinds of nationalism. It also went through radically different phases, from the Bolshevik would-be utopia of international class liberation to the Stalinist authoritarian state of the 1930s to the corrupt, Brezhnev-era multinational state. Modernization meant both the destruction of old traditions and emancipation for women and technological progress. Policy toward the nationalities veered from the implementation of a liberal "affirmative action empire," which gave new opportunities to non-Russian nations, to genocide. While some small ethnic groups benefited hugely from "nativization" programs, others were subjected to deportation and mass terror.

One constant feature of Bolshevik-Soviet rule was that the borders of the Transcaucasus were closed and the outside world shut out. This helped form a new kind of Soviet Caucasian identity. As an example, a wide gulf opened up between the ordinary Azerbaijanis who lived in Soviet Azerbaijan on the one hand and those who lived on the far side of the Araxes River in Iran on the other. In 1920, these people led very similar existences in terms of family life, religious practice, and culture. By the time the Soviet Union ended in 1991, Iranian Azerbaijanis had kept most of those cultural practices, while Soviet Azerbaijanis had been entirely altered by the Soviet experiment. Millions of Azerbaijanis had served in the Soviet armed forces, learned to drink vodka, studied in universities or technical colleges, or worked in Russia—and had never set foot inside a working mosque. Standards of health care and literacy were undoubtedly higher in Soviet Azerbaijan, and women had far greater opportunities, but Soviet Azerbaijanis also lacked basic political and cultural freedoms.

Bolshevik Consolidation

In July 1921 the Bolshevik commissar for nationalities, Joseph Stalin, made his first visit to Georgia since the 1917 revolution. He chaired a key meeting of the Caucasus Bureau, which adjudicated outstanding territorial disputes— among many important decisions, the bureau allocated Nagorny Karabakh to Azerbaijan. Stalin and his chief lieutenant, Sergo Orjonikidze, favored a centralizing policy that would break the back of Georgian nationalism. But they were under orders from Lenin to show restraint in their approach to national issues (Lenin told Stalin to "undersalt" his national policies). The eventual compromise was a Transcaucasian Federation that would have a unified economic structure but still maintain within it three distinct republics of Georgia, Armenia, and Azerbaijan.

Stalin was an unpopular figure in Georgia and was given a hostile reception at two Party meetings. He chided his audience for "the absence of the old solidarity among the workers of the various nationalities of the Caucasus," which he said he remembered from the days of the revolutions of 1905 and 1917. But he told his listeners that plans for a federation would not mean an end to their independence: "This does not mean of course that there should no longer be an independent Georgia or an independent Azerbaijan and so on. The draft project circulating among certain comrades of the restoration of the old provinces (Tiflis, Baku, Yerevan) with a single Transcaucasian government is in my view a Utopia, moreover a reactionary Utopia."[1]

The Transcaucasian Federation was set up in March 1922. The Georgian Bolsheviks were resentful, and in an unprecedented show of defiance, they resigned en masse in October 1922. Two months later, the Soviet Union was created, with the new Transcaucasian Federation, or ZSFSR, as one of its constituent parts. The dispute between Lenin and Stalin and their supporters was both political and personal. On the political level it was about the nature of the new Soviet state, about the "national question"—in other words, what distinct rights the different nationalities of the new state should have—and about the best way to reorganize the Transcaucasus. The dying Lenin accused the Georgian Stalin and Orjonikidze of being "Great Russian chauvinists" and ignoring national sentiments in the Caucasus. On the personal level, the clash was the first phase in the so-called Georgian Affair, in which the dying Lenin, worried about what the quarrel told him about Stalin's character, tried to block Stalin's approval as his successor but failed. Lenin's very last letter was written in a sympathetic tone to two of Stalin's Georgian Bolshevik rivals.

Whatever the long-term agenda of the different factions was—and we now know that Stalin's was very sinister indeed—both sides had strong arguments. The majority of the Georgian Bolsheviks, later labeled "deviationists," correctly warned that centralizing measures would alienate the Georgian population and provoke a backlash—an armed rebellion did break out in Georgia in 1924. The Armenians and Azerbaijanis were generally supportive of the Federation on economic grounds. Stalin and Orjonikidze argued that the region was threatened by interethnic violence and economic fragmentation and that a strong federation with centralized powers was needed to drag it into the modern era. Debate between the two camps was unleashed in April 1923 at the Twelfth Congress of the Communist Party. Read on the page, the arguments come across as a little bizarre, given that the Federation, founded in 1922, failed to deliver on its promise of Caucasian integration and was abolished altogether in 1936. But they provide a fascinating snapshot of a dispute on the future of the Caucasus, one that was soon to go underground.

Critics of the Georgian "deviationist" Bolsheviks accused them of being nationalists who wanted to deport Armenians from Tiflis and claim territory from Soviet Armenia. The Georgian Bolshevik Ilia Tsivtsivadze told the Congress that Georgians feared a new Russian chauvinism. He said that they had been impoverished by the devaluation of their currency, which had been forcibly placed in parity with the Russian ruble, and were unhappy about the closure of churches. Tsivtsivadze warned, "In Russian this will sound like merely a bureaucratic absorption of the 'local' by the 'center'; but in Georgian and in the interpretation of the Mensheviks this will sound like national oppression and Russifying policies and much else besides."²

Stalin took on the role of a self-sacrificial Georgian, saying his nation had had a "privileged position" and needed to accept a federation for the sake of its neighbors. Orjonikidze made a strong defense of the new federation on the grounds that the Bolsheviks were determined to build a united, peaceful Caucasus where their bourgeois predecessors had failed. The dangers were still present, he said: the previous decade had seen six civil wars in the Transcaucasus, which the Bolsheviks had ended: "The mutual slaughter, in the literal sense of this word, of Muslims and Armenians filled the atmosphere of the Transcaucasus with the poison of hatred. The republics shut themselves off from one another with a Chinese Wall of customs barriers. Then Soviet power entered this overheated atmosphere of national hatred. The population sighed with relief."

The administrative construction that emerged from these quarrels was a balancing act. The Transcaucasian Federation took on mainly economic functions. Georgia, Armenia, and Azerbaijan survived as separate Soviet republics with their own governments, parliaments, party structures, and universities. The result was that the national elites remained in charge and a residual sense of nationhood was maintained. An Azerbaijani, Nariman Narimanov, was made leader of Bolshevik Azerbaijan in 1921, for example, in contrast to the Baku commune of 1918, which had been multinational and led by an Armenian. At the same time, moves were made to empower the region's small indigenous nationalities, such as the Abkhaz and Ossetians, who had mostly welcomed the Bolsheviks. The Abkhaz were initially given their own Soviet republic, associated with Georgia by treaty, and then had their status downgraded to that of "autonomous republic" in 1931. The Muslim Ajarians had their own autonomous republic, and the South Ossetians their own "autonomous region." Armenia, the most homogeneous of the three republics, did not have any autonomous territories. In Azerbaijan, the borders of the new Nagorny Karabakh Autonomous Region were drawn to give it a 94 percent Armenian majority. The exclave of Nakhichevan, which did not share a border with the rest of Azerbaijan but had a clear Azerbaijani majority, was made into an autonomous republic.

There has been much scholarly debate about the impact of the Bolsheviks' decision to devise an "ethnofederal system" for the Soviet Union, which created autonomous territories on ethnic principles. In the Caucasus, scholars have observed, this preserved national divisions, which eventually fractured the Soviet state and turned into armed conflicts. It could be argued, however, that the Caucasus set the blueprint for the Soviet Union, not the other way around. In other words, the fragile situation in the Caucasus in 1921, still broken by numerous interethnic conflicts, may have caused the Bolsheviks to invent the ethnofederal system under duress.

It was also a Caucasian, Stalin, who presided over this complex construction once it had been created. His approach was both ruthless and pragmatic. The primary aim appears to have been to build a system that would survive the shocks of both internal and external threats. National interests were balanced out and could eventually be eliminated. Small nationalities would be modernized, with Russia the engine pulling them into the future. Lenin, who disapproved of Russian nationalism, might have been content to see Georgia detached from Russia so long as it remained Bolshevik. Stalin believed that Russia, the center, and the Caucasus, the borderlands, needed one another. In 1920, he wrote, "Central Russia, the hearth of world revolution, cannot hold out long without the assistance of the border regions, which abound in raw materials, fuel, and foodstuffs. The border regions of Russia, in their turn, are inevitably doomed to imperialist bondage without the political, military, or organizational support of the more developed Central Russia."[3]

HOW GEORGIAN WAS STALIN?

People who know only a little about Georgia know that Stalin was a Georgian. It is commonplace to see his bloody personality as coming from a Caucasian tradition of violence and blood revenge. Many Georgians still claim Stalin as one of their own; Georgia is almost the only place in the world where you still come across monuments to the great dictator, such as the giant statue of him in the central square in Gori, his hometown, which was taken down only in 2010.

Closer examination of Stalin's biography suggests a different picture, in which he became who he was to a large degree by rejecting Caucasian tradition. To begin with,

Stalin came from a culture where the family is central, but he entirely rejected the family. He was an only son, both of his wives died young, he had no close friends, and he spent all his time in the company of revolutionary comrades or Politburo leaders. He did not move his widowed mother from Tbilisi to Moscow but entrusted her care to Lavrenti Beria, his Georgian alter ego. When she died in 1937, Stalin did not attend the funeral—something unheard of for a Georgian son—and Beria was the chief mourner.

The historian Alfred Rieber calls Stalin a "Man of the Borderlands," with a triple identity that was simultaneously Georgian, proletarian, and Russian. In a speech to railway workers in Tbilisi in 1926, Stalin himself called his revolutionary career a journey in three parts: "From the profession of student (Tiflis) via the profession of apprentice (Baku), to the profession of being one of the masters of our revolution (Leningrad)—that, comrades, was the school of my revolutionary learning."[1]

The man born Iosif Jugashvili kept changing his name and refining his identity. His first pseudonym, Soso, was his childhood nickname. He took the second, Koba (a name Georgian and Bolshevik colleagues called him into old age), from the hero of *The Patricide*, a lurid novel by the nineteenth-century Georgian author Alexander Kazbegi. Kazbegi's Koba is an outlaw with a strong sense of honor who takes revenge for the death of a friend by killing a despotic Russian-appointed governor. It was presumptuous for a small man with a pockmarked face and withered arm to assume the name of a manly Georgian heroic character. Maybe the young Jugashvili was trying to expunge the shame his drunken father's behavior had filled him with. Vissarion Jugashvili, writes the historian Ronald Suny, "was a 'failure' as a Georgian because of weaknesses—his inability to provide the means for display and magnanimity valued by Georgians, his lack of authority within the family (defeated by his strong-willed wife), and his loss of personal control (violence, alcoholism)."[2]

At home, Stalin remained very much a Georgian into old age. He spoke Russian with a strong Georgian accent and drank wine rather than vodka in the Georgian manner (his favorite varieties were the semisweet red Khvanchkara and the white Chkhaveri from the Black Sea coast). He put Georgian folk songs on the gramophone and sang along and spoke Georgian to his old comrades. His conservative attitude toward his teenage daughter's behavior was that of a typical Georgian father. He appears to have harbored some old-fashioned Georgian prejudices, such as a dislike of Turks (though not of Armenians).[3] But all this stayed within his inner circle. His political identity was built on adopting a kind of Russianness.

From 1913, Jugashvili began to use the Russian name Stalin ("Man of Steel"). There was nothing of the Caucasian outlaw in the way Stalin murdered his enemies. He ordered the wholesale arrest and execution of both women and children in complete rejection of Caucasian codes of honor. He even had his own relatives from the Svanidze family executed. He also authorized what was a shockingly blasphemous practice in Georgia—the bodies of victims of the Terror were not returned to their families, as custom required, but were thrown into unmarked graves. The historical figure he now said he most admired was the old Russian tyrant Ivan the Terrible.

By the 1930s, Stalin had shed all Georgian elements from his public persona. He last visited Tbilisi—a city he apparently never liked—in 1935. When he met a group of Georgian historians in 1950, they were struck by how he talked of both Georgians and Russians as "others," saying, "They, the Russians don't appreciate. . . . You, the Georgians, have failed to mention."[4]

Stalin's career can be seen as a progression—Rieber calls it a "pilgrimage"—in pursuit of total power. Everything was a work in progress toward a final goal—only the goal itself was sacred. Stalin, the student of Georgian history, crushed

Stalin and two fellow Caucasian Bolsheviks, Mikoyan
and Sergo Orjonikidze, in 1925.

the Georgian cultural elite. He saw Russia as the Great
Power locomotive that would drag smaller peoples into the
modern industrialized age—something that explains why
this thickly accented Georgian is still fanatically admired by
many Russian nationalists.

The irony is that the longer Stalin stayed away from
Georgia, the more he was revered there. In 1921, Tbilisi
workers heckled him, seeing him as an agent of Russia.
In the 1930s, Beria began the cult of Stalin in Georgia. In
March 1956, Nikita Khrushchev's efforts to undo the cult
of personality led to riots in the streets of Tbilisi. Today
some small-time Georgian nationalists still honor a man
who ravaged their national culture.

1. Alfred J. Rieber, "Stalin: Man of the Borderlands," *American Historical Review* 106, 5 (December 2001): 1651–92.
2. Ronald Suny, "Beyond Psychohistory: The Young Stalin in Georgia," *Slavic Review* 50 (Spring 1991): 53.
3. See Sergo Beria, *Beria, My Father: Inside Stalin's Kremlin* (London: Duckworth, 2001).
4. Donald Rayfield, *Stalin and His Hangmen* (London: Penguin, 2005), 14.

Soviet Nation-Building

Once Soviet power had been consolidated in the Caucasus, Stalin's all-controlling instincts began to emerge. Despite the promises he had made to respect the "independence" of Armenia, Azerbaijan, and Georgia, he abolished their independent institutions and slowly crushed all dissent. Armenia's Dashnak and Azerbaijan's Musavat parties were both dissolved in 1923. Resistance was strongest in Georgia. The new regime abolished the Menshevik Party and redistributed land much more radically. In response came an uprising in western Georgia in August 1924, which the Bolsheviks extinguished and used as an excuse for mass repression: as many as 4,000 people were killed, and thousands more were sent into exile in the far north of Russia. "Only with the language of revolutionary, merciless power can one talk to the pitiful cowardly Mensheviks," declared a leading Georgian Bolshevik in the pitiless language of the new era.[4]

The repression was done in the name of modernization. Despite the brutality of the new regime, the 1920s was an era of nation-building and economic reconstruction in the Caucasus. In Armenia and Azerbaijan in particular, there was a message that new nations were being built out of the chaos of the past. In Azerbaijan, high hopes were invested in the idea of a new, progressive Muslim republic. Mosques were closed and women ordered to tear off their veils. The Tatar Communist Sultan Galiev proclaimed, "Soviet Azerbaijan, with its old and experienced proletariat and its already unified Communist Party, will become the Red beacon for Persia, Arabia and Turkey."[5] Soviet Armenia was seen as the haven of surviving Armenians under Soviet Russian protection. Arthur Koestler visited Yerevan in 1932 and observed:

> The more I saw of Erivan, the more it reminded me of Tel Aviv. The enthusiasm, the muddle, the errors and bad taste which accompanied the fever of construction were all touching and familiar reminders. Here, too, drab, cheap, ugly utilitarian buildings were superseding the charming, colourful and filthy Orient. Erivan, too, was an informal and chaotic pioneer-town, the unfinished streets, between half-finished buildings, a labyrinth of pipes and cables. There were as yet so few telephones that calls were made by asking the exchange for the name, and not the number of the subscriber. Familiar, above all, was the Babel of languages,

for a sizeable part of the population were refugees and immigrants from Turkey, Armenia, Europe and America.[6]

The late 1920s were the heyday of what Terry Martin calls the "affirmative action empire," with the implementation of the new ideology of *korenizatsia* (literally "rooting," or "nativization") and the sponsoring of programs to modernize and assist the non-Russian Soviet nationalities. The Azeri, Abkhaz, Ossetian, and Lezgin written languages were all given a new Roman alphabet. Large numbers of people received an education for the first time in their native languages. The Communists declared that in the first ten years of Soviet rule in Georgia, half a million people had been taught to read and write.[7] In 1940, Armenia claimed that the entire adult population was literate for the first time.

For years, scholars of the Soviet Union concentrated on its centralizing policies, and some called it the "prison-house of nations." Only recently have scholars and commentators begun to analyze how, beginning with the *korenizatsia* program, the Soviet authorities actually defined and strengthened national identities. As Ronald Suny put it in 1993, "rather than a melting pot, the Soviet Union became an incubator of new nations."[8] The tsarist empire had categorized its people by religion, mother tongue, social class, and regional location. The Bolsheviks held that "nationality" was a useful transitional phase between the backward culture of small ethnic groups and an advanced state of socialism. But the national identities persisted, and the transnational socialist future never came. As Martin writes, "in order to implement affirmative action programs, monitor their success, delineate national territories, assign children to programs, the Soviet state constantly asked its citizens for their nationality."[9] So to be "Ossetian" or "Azerbaijani" acquired real meaning for the first time, and this category became a formal badge of identity when it was written into the first Soviet internal passports in 1932.

There was a hierarchy of nations. Two of the three main nationalities of the Transcaucasus, the Armenians and Georgians, were classified as "advanced" Western nationalities, alongside Russians, Ukrainians, Jews, and Germans, while Azerbaijanis fell into the category of nations in formation, requiring developmental aid.[10] In practice this meant that, as in tsarist Russia, Armenians and Georgians could advance more quickly up the Soviet career ladder. Two Karabakh Armenians from village backgrounds were cases in point. One, Levon Mirzoyan, served as head of the Communist Party first in

Azerbaijan and then in Kazakhstan; the other, Suren Sadunts, served as first Party secretary in Tajikistan in 1935–36. Both were shot in Stalin's purges. It would have been impossible for a Kazakh or an Azerbaijani to be given an equivalent post in Armenia or Georgia.

The Age of Terror

The Transcaucasus escaped the worst of Stalin's excesses until the 1930s. Collectivization was imposed from 1929. It was a brutal experiment— peasants resisted by killing their livestock rather than submitting to the new collective farms—but relatively speaking, the region got off lightly, compared to Ukraine and parts of Russia, which were decimated by manmade famine. In Georgia, the redistribution of land proceeded very slowly, while the collectivization in Azerbaijan has been called "socialist in form, traditional in content," because many old social practices survived. The Black Sea region of Abkhazia managed to escape collectivization altogether, thanks to its skilful Bolshevik leader, Nestor Lakoba.

In 1932, Stalin made Georgian secret police chief Lavrenti Beria first Party secretary of the Transcaucasian Federation at the age of thirty-two. The small, bespectacled man had the right qualifications to bring terror to the Caucasus. He was an outsider, being a Mingrelian from a peasant family in Abkhazia; he was formidably efficient and intelligent—after the Second World War he created the Soviet Union's nuclear program from scratch; and he was sadistically cruel, later winning a reputation for kidnapping and raping teenage girls. Beria used Stalin as well and inserted himself into Stalin's family circle. In the words of historian Robert Tucker, he was able to "supply Stalin with ever new objects of distrust and condemnation." In 1935, Beria organized the publication of the book *On the History of Bolshevik Organizations in Transcaucasia,* which retrospectively made Stalin the leader of all tsarist-era revolutionary plots in the Caucasus. Beria took two whole days to read the new work aloud to several thousand party members in Tbilisi.

Beria began to integrate the Transcaucasus into the rest of the Soviet economy with a policy of industrialization, and he promoted its attractions as the "Soviet South," a place of exotic produce and vacation resorts where the Soviet worker could relax. In an era when Soviet leaders were obsessed with America, they promoted the subtropical Transcaucasus as the new "Soviet Florida."

Politically speaking, it was no Florida. Beria exerted total control and from 1936 unleashed the local version of Stalin's Great Terror. Most of the old Georgian Bolsheviks were killed—among the many victims were Budu Mdviani, the recipient of Lenin's last letter, and Abel Enukidze, the godfather of Stalin's first wife. More Georgian Mensheviks probably died in their beds than did Georgian Bolsheviks. Beria either personally killed or forced into suicide the Armenian party chief, Agahasi Khanjian. He poisoned Nestor Lakoba, the party chief of Abkhazia. Fear was spread with the help of secret policemen, who committed hideous tortures in Tbilisi's Ortachala Prison. Whole families were arrested. In her moving memoir of the Stalin era, Adile Abbas-oglu, an Abkhaz woman who married the brother-in-law of Lakoba, tells how Beria systematically arrested all of Lakoba's extended family as "enemies of the people" and had most of them killed. She herself endured ten years of prison and exile but managed to survive. So, for a while, did Lakoba's young son Rauf, but Beria was meticulous. According to one version, Rauf reached the age of eighteen in prison and wrote to Beria on the outbreak of war in 1941, asking to be sent to the front; he was executed instead. Yet Beria had known Rauf as a child, once giving him a book by Jules Verne as a birthday present.[11]

SOVIET FLORIDA

In 1934 the Moscow magazine *Ogonyok* published a 218-page book full of color illustrations entitled *Soviet Sub-Tropics* and devoted to the southern borderlands of the Soviet Union and the Transcaucasus in particular. The famous Soviet journalist Mikhail Koltsov edited the book, and some of the best writers of the day contributed to it. Poems by the Georgian poets Titsian Tabidze and Simon Chikovani were given in Russian translations by Boris Pasternak.

The tone of the book is aggressively celebratory, taking its cue from Stalin, who had recently declared, "Life has got better, life has got more cheerful." Happy workers are shown vacationing in Abkhazia. Newly liberated women in Muslim

Ajaria sort through overflowing boxes of tangerines. The final picture in the book is what must have been the nearest thing to an erotic photograph in the Soviet Union of 1934: on a beach a young woman in a swimming costume with a bare midriff throws out her arms with delight as an adoring man looks up at her. The caption reads, "It's a good life in our country!"

The book displays an obsession with "catching up to America." We are told that the Lenkoran region of Azerbaijan is "finer than the lands of California." Andrei Lezhava, head of the new Soviet "Department of Sub-Tropical Cultures," exhorts, "Let's create a Soviet Florida!" Abkhazia's party boss, Nestor Lakoba, pledges that Abkhazia will supply the Soviet Union with high-quality tobacco. What is more, it is declared that the Soviet South will soon be turning out tea, grapes, olives, figs, geraniums, eucalyptus, and a new discovery, *greipfrut*, or grapefruit. Caucasus party boss Lavrenty Beria promises readers, "If earlier citrus fruits were an object of luxury, available only to the bourgeoisie, then nowadays we have an honorable task ahead of us—to put lemons, tangerines, oranges on the table of the worker of the Soviet country."

Soviet Sub-Tropics was published as Stalin unveiled his doctrine of "socialism in one country," according to which the USSR rejected internationalism and aspired to be a state complete unto itself. Within this self-contained world, republics like Russia and Ukraine could bear the burden of heavy industry and major politics. The more marginal Transcaucasus was assigned another role, that of a place of luxury, health, and sunshine for Soviet workers—in other words, a Soviet Florida. Within a few years, Stalin had killed at least half the writers and heroes of *Soviet Sub-Tropics*, among them Lakoba, Lezhava, Koltsov, and Tabidze. The Transcaucasus never overtook California or supplied Soviet workers with billions of tangerines—let alone grapefruit—as promised. But the role ascribed to the region in the Soviet universe stuck. The Black Sea became the Soviet Riviera—although by the 1970s it was a rather tawdry concrete version of it. Much of Soviet Russian writing about the Caucasus kept the same tone of celebration, verging on the patronizing. Georgia was called "sunny socialist Georgia." Subtropical Abkhazia was a resort zone, longed for by a cast of cold Soviet workers in which the Abkhaz themselves had a barely visible supporting role.

Beria also exterminated the intelligentsia of the Caucasus. The Georgian poet Paolo Iashvili committed suicide in public; his fellow poet Titsian Tabidze was executed, along with the popular novelist Mikheil Javakhishvili and the orchestral conductor Evgeni Mikeladze. The Abkhaz playwright Samson Chanba was killed, as were the Armenian writers Axel Bakunts and Yeghishe Charents. In Azerbaijan, the poet Hussein Javid was exiled to Siberia, where he died in 1941. Bizarrely, amid the killing, cultural celebrations carried on. The 750th anniversary of the Georgian poem "The Knight in the Panther's Skin," by Rustaveli, was celebrated across the Soviet Union in 1937 at the height of the purges. Beria planned to tear down the famous thirteenth-century Metekhi church to clear a space for the festivities but desisted at the last moment.

In 1938, Beria earned the reward of a move to Moscow to head the Soviet secret police. One of his jobs was to enforce a new policy of terror directed against entire national groups. Soviet nationalities policy was changing; some nationalities were singled out for advancement and others for punishment. "Nativization" programs were halted, and the Marxist doctrine that the nation was merely a transitory phenomenon was dropped. The luckiest Soviet nations were now said to be primordial, with ancient roots. This was good news for the three main nationalities of the Transcaucasus. Under the new Soviet Constitution of 1936, the Transcaucasian Federation was abolished and Armenia, Azerbaijan, and Georgia were allowed to become full-fledged "union republics" and key pillars of the Soviet state. From 1937, Azerbaijanis were no longer classified as "Turks" but as "Azerbaijanis," a label that asserted their separate identity. The folklore, literature, and history of the three nationalities, stripped of any overt political and ideological content, were officially promoted, and ancient Armenian history and the poetry of Rustaveli and Nizami were put in the school curriculum, albeit in a form highly colored by Soviet ideology. Georgia was also handed primacy over its minorities in Abkhazia and South Ossetia: the two native languages had a Georgian script imposed on them, and schooling in Abkhaz and Ossetian was shut down.

Stalin's overarching ideology was now "the friendship of peoples," in which Russia was afforded the place of a big brother to the other smaller peoples. Russian patriotism made a comeback. Old heroes, from Alexander Nevsky to Peter the Great, became fashionable again. The Russian language was made compulsory in non-Russian schools, and Russian history and literature were brought back into the curriculum. In the Caucasus, the Azeri, Lezgin, (North) Ossetian, and Talysh languages, after a decade of adapting to new Roman scripts, now suddenly had new Cyrillic alphabets imposed on them. The policy was driven in part by Stalin's desire for his state—and the army in particular—to share a lingua franca and in part by his desire for a more effective unifying idea to defend the Soviet Union against its enemies.

The most sinister side of the change was that some nationalities were deemed to be unworthy of membership in the new Soviet family. As early as 1923, the new regime had built high-security, fourteen-mile-deep "frontier zones" along the new Soviet borders. But certain national groups living near the borders were still suspected of harboring sympathies for foreign powers. This was the official justification for a program of mass deportations between 1938 and 1949. Stalin and Beria organized the deportation of almost all ethnic groups with a Turkic connection, among them Crimean Tatars; North Caucasian Karachais, Balkars, and Kalmyks from the Caspian Sea; and Georgia's Meskhetian Turks. In the Caucasus, they also deported Kurds, Armenian Hemshins, Chechens, Ingush, and Pontic Greeks. The execution of this policy virtually amounted to genocide. Soviet secret police troops closed off an entire region, rounded up hundreds of thousands of people—women and children as well as men, Red Army soldiers included—evicted them from their homes, crammed them into disease-ridden cattle-trucks, and sent them into permanent exile in Kazakhstan or Siberia. Their homelands were abolished, their cemeteries dug up, and their cultures erased from the official record. As many as a quarter of the deportees died en route or never returned.

Most of the deportees were permitted to return home in the 1950s by Nikita Khrushchev. In the Caucasus, the exception was the Meskhetian Turks, who were Muslims, probably of mixed Turkish-Georgian origin from the Meskhia (or Samtskhe) borderland of southern Georgia. In November 1944, all of them—around 100,000 people—were deported to Central Asia;

about a fifth died en route. In the Khrushchev era, restrictions were eased on their everyday lives, but they were not allowed to go home, perhaps because of lobbying by Soviet Georgia and the Armenians in their homeland. The Meskhetian Turks' suffering continued. Dozens of them were killed in interethnic pogroms in Uzbekistan in 1989. Those who resettled in southern Russia suffered racial discrimination, and 9,000 of them were eventually allowed to resettle in the United States. Georgia made a commitment in 1999 to allow the Meskhetian Turks the right of return, but since then Georgian politicians have dragged their feet, and only a few hundred are today living in their old homeland.

In May 1945, the Soviet public learned that two young soldiers, a Russian and a Georgian, Mikhail Yegorov and Meliton Kantaria, had hoisted the red flag over the Reichstag in the ruins of Berlin and that Nazi Germany had been defeated. In actual fact, these two soldiers were probably not the first to capture the building—a Muslim Dagestani almost certainly got there ahead of them—but symbolism was more important than reality. Stalin's two favored nationalities were seen to be at the vanguard of the victory over Hitler.

The South Caucasus escaped the worst of the Great Patriotic War of 1941–45. Hitler's armies only reached as far as North Ossetia in the North Caucasus. Georgia, Armenia, and Azerbaijan escaped physically unscathed, apart from a few bombing raids. Nonetheless, the losses within the Red Army were as appalling as within the rest of the Soviet Union. Figures differ, but perhaps 550,000 Armenian, Azerbaijani, and Georgian soldiers died, out of a total population of around eight million people in 1941. These casualty figures were higher than those for either the United States or Britain in the Second World War. The shared experience of war probably made the Transcaucasian peoples feel a fully Soviet identity for the first time.[12] War also made Georgian patriotism legitimate again. The Georgian Orthodox Church was given back its autonomy in 1943. Stalin himself personally edited the script of a patriotic film about the seventeenth-century Georgian warrior Giorgy Saakadze, who had sacrificed his sons fighting the Persians.

Ironically, Giorgy Saakadze was also the name of the German 797 Battalion, one of fourteen Georgian battalions formed by the Nazis to "liberate" their homeland from Communism. There were also eleven Armenian, fourteen Azerbaijani, and five North Caucasian battalions. It is shocking to a modern eye to see old footage of cheerful Caucasian soldiers wearing Nazi uniforms stitched with epaulettes bearing the flags of independent Armenia, Azerbaijan, and Georgia—but as many as 100,000 men from the

Transcaucasus may have fought on the Nazi side. Many of the Nazi recruits were prisoners of war who joined up under duress, but many were Caucasian émigrés who did so willingly, and they included several prominent officials from the independent republics of 1918. The taint of these associations and the Soviet victory helped consign the Caucasian political émigré movements to irrelevance.

After his victory in 1945, Stalin tried to push the borders of his state farther out at the expense of Iran and Turkey. He was not embarrassed to compare the Soviet Union and the tsarist empire, and in June 1945 Soviet foreign minister Vyacheslav Molotov demanded that Turkey "return" the provinces of Kars and Ardahan, which had been part of the Russian Empire until 1918. The Armenian and Georgian leadership backed the claim, but Turkey stood firm and was supported by Western countries. The row helped trigger Turkey's decision to join NATO in 1952. The Soviet attitude toward Iran was even more aggressive. Soviet troops moved into Iranian Azerbaijan, and a short-lived "Azerbaijan People's Government in Iran," led by the Iranian Azerbaijani Communist Jafar Pishevari, was set up in Tabriz in 1945–46. But the Soviet-backed puppet state collapsed in 1946 after Soviet forces withdrew, again under Western pressure.

The Armenian diaspora supported Stalin's unsuccessful land claims against Turkey. In this atmosphere of goodwill, 90,000 diaspora Armenians, mainly from the Middle East, were given permission to immigrate to Soviet Armenia in the 1940s. Tens of thousands of Azerbaijanis were forced to leave Soviet Armenia for Azerbaijan to make way for the newcomers. Many of the incoming Armenians later became disillusioned and emigrated again, but others stayed, among them the parents of the future president, Levon Ter-Petrosian. The perception was that the Soviet Caucasus was here to stay— even if it soon lost its central role in the larger federation.

After Stalin

When Stalin died in March 1953, the Soviet Union faced an existential crisis. Stalin could have argued that he had achieved the narrow goals he had set himself in the 1920s. He had constructed a powerful modern state that had withstood attacks from enemies within and without. The problem for everyone else was that the human cost had been immeasurably high. Stalin had sacrificed everything and everyone—friends, relatives, revolutionary comrades, whole nationalities and social classes—in a sea of blood for the sake of his state-building project.

The historian Alfred Rieber writes that the Soviet Union "was an extension of [Stalin] based on three interlocking frames: the proletariat as the dominant class, the ethno-cultural region as the territorial unit, and Great Russia as the political center of the state. Once having created it, Stalin set himself the task of maintaining a balance among these elements, each of which contained the potential for conflict and contradiction."[13] For almost thirty years this had been a state built in the image of a man who was now gone.

Beria was also executed at the end of 1953, after an aborted bid to take power. With both Stalin and Beria dead, mass fear was no longer a unifying factor, and arguably the Soviet Union carried on for the next four decades as a state without an idea, propelled by inertia and a few common myths. Not that the Communist Party said this aloud. It was content to relax a little now that the threat of a knock at the door and sudden arrest had passed for all but a very few. Local leaders began to exercise authority without fear of reprisal.

The post-Stalin state was no longer a fully totalitarian system. The Kremlin leadership still had the final authority, but it did meet with many disobediences on many levels. Earlier historians of the Soviet era concentrated on top-down politics; only recently have we had more information about the bottom-up politics of the Soviet Union. We now know that there were frequent serious street protests and riots in the postwar period, many of them in the Caucasus. In 1956, there were mass protests in Tbilisi at Khrushchev's denunciation of Stalin. In 1963, there were violent riots in the Azerbaijani town of Sumgait. Two years later, Yerevan was shut down by demonstrators calling for commemoration of the Armenian genocide. Often the unrest had an ethnic flavor. Soccer matches were a frequent source of trouble—people knew to stay at home when Baku's Neftchi was playing Yerevan's Ararat. In each case, the Soviet authorities still had both the means and the will to suppress the protests as brutally as they thought necessary. In 1956, the army killed dozens of people when it cleared the streets of Tbilisi. This issue helps explain why the Soviet state proved so fragile in the 1980s; Mikhail Gorbachev faced the dilemma of whether or not to suppress political protest, and when he decided not to, the street politics emerged from below the surface of his state with full force.

Despite these occasional flashpoints, the post-Stalin era in the Caucasus is remembered by much of the older generation as a kind of golden age. Although people had to cope with a chronically inefficient political and economic system, their everyday standard of living improved immensely. Russians and Ukrainians gasped at the well-dressed people and full shops they found in the Transcaucasian republics. For providing the sunshine, landscape, and fresh food that the rest of the Soviet Union lacked, the Caucasus—and Georgia in particular—became a favored holiday destination and playground for the Soviet elite. As early as 1947, John Steinbeck visited Georgia and found it an enchanting contrast to Russia, still recovering from the ravages of war. "The people of Tiflis were better dressed, better looking and more full of spirit than any we saw in Russia," he wrote.[14]

After the death of Stalin, the three republics were allowed to undergo a kind of national revival. In Tbilisi and Yerevan, the huge statues of Stalin were replaced by monuments of Mother Georgia and Mother Armenia. In 1966 Armenians were allowed to build a genocide memorial on a hill overlooking Yerevan. Creative artists in all three republics benefited from the cultural thaw of the Khrushchev era. The Azerbaijani poet Sabir Rustamkhanli said,

> That period, the 1960s, 70s and 80s were the period of a small renaissance in the Soviet Union. In different republics a process of self-identification began, national consciousness began to rise. . . . Despite the fact that when we were students, they were always making us study literature connected with Stalinism and so on, our generation completely rejected this. In our verse, in our works there isn't a single word about Soviet ideology, brotherhood with Moscow.[15]

This "renaissance" was manifested in a period of extravagant, state-funded cultural production. Between 1961 and 1991, Soviet Georgia produced 1,200 movies, more than 100 of which won prizes at international festivals. The Tbilisi Armenian director Sergei Parajanov did not bother to make ideologically useful films but produced a series of dreamy, visually stunning works exploring the medieval history of the Caucasus. Baku was a center of cosmopolitan painting, theater, and jazz (see "Baku Jazz" box). The ballet *Spartacus*, written by the Armenian composer Aram Khachaturian, was a hit across the Soviet Union. In 1963, the whole of Yerevan watched, move by move, as another Armenian, Tigran Petrosian, became the world chess champion in Moscow. A giant chessboard was set out in the center of the city so that his games could be played out in public.

The dark reverse side of this coin was that the chauvinism the Bolsheviks had campaigned against in the 1920s showed signs of reemerging. Nominally Marxist historians wrote histories of Armenia, Azerbaijan, and Georgia that stretched back into the distant past and disparaged the claims of their neighbors; in the 1980s some of these Soviet-era works became ideological fuel for conflict. Moreover, much of what was celebrated as "national culture" in Tbilisi, Yerevan, and Baku did not look so attractive to minorities. Abkhazia and South Ossetia benefited from the death of Stalin and Beria in that some of the worst assimilationist Georgian policies were reversed but never recovered the autonomy they had been promised in the 1920s. Some members of minority communities felt nervous, and some voted with their feet. Tens of thousands of Azerbaijanis left Armenia, while large numbers of Armenians moved out of Tbilisi, a city that Armenians had dominated for centuries. In 1989, these trends led the Soviet Union's best-known dissident, Andrei Sakharov, famously to warn that the republics had become "little empires": "We need to begin by fully dismantling the imperial structure," he said. "That's the only way of solving the national problem in the little empires that essentially the union republics are—for example Georgia, which includes Abkhazia, Ossetia, and other national formations."[16]

BAKU JAZZ

Baku and jazz are a natural combination. Baku in the twentieth century was the Soviet Union's most cosmopolitan city. The main nationalities living there were Azerbaijanis, Armenians, Russians, and Jews, but it was considered bad manners to draw attention to someone's ethnicity. Mixed marriages were common and the lingua franca was Russian. It was also a city with a vibrant musical tradition. In 1908 the "first opera of the Muslim east," *Leyli and Majnun* by composer Uzeir Hajibekov, was staged there. The opera combined the Western classical style with the Azerbaijani improvisatory folk tradition known as *mugham*, played on traditional instruments.

Jazz first hit Baku in the 1930s. The Soviet Union had a love-hate relationship with jazz. Its times of favor began in 1932, when American jazz took the country by storm. In 1933 a *New York Times* correspondent reported, "One visitor scoured Tiflis hoping to find an orchestra playing the old Georgian music, noted for its wild harmony. He heard jazz pieces which were popular only a year and more ago in the United States. He finally bribed an orchestra to play some native pieces."[1] Three years later the British traveler Fitzroy Maclean saw the phenomenon in a restaurant in Baku: "Obedient to the Party line, the chief citizens of Baku, Russians, Tartars, Jews, Georgians and Armenians, clasping their peroxide companions to them, shuffled solemnly round to the strains of 'I ain't nobody's baby' rendered with considerable feeling by a Tartar band, which presently broke into a swing version of the 'Internationale.'"[2]

During another time of cultural thaw, the 1960s, the Baku jazz scene summed up the devil-may-care apolitical spirit of the city. Frederick Starr, the historian of Soviet jazz, wrote, "No city in the Soviet Union was more receptive to the fiercely rhythmic cadences of hard bop than the Turkic capital on the Caspian. The Azerbaijani jazz musicians lived a rougher and more bohemian existence than did the Russians, and their playing showed it."[3]

Vagif Mustafazade, Azerbaijan's most talented pianist and jazz composer, was born in Baku but frequently performed in Tbilisi with Armenian musicians and married a Georgian singer.[4] His music, which borrowed from Bill Evans and Azerbaijan *mugham*, was hard to categorize but was wildly successful. Mustafazade died in 1980 at the age of thirty-nine. The Baku jazz tradition lives on in his daughter Aziza, who has become a star pianist and singer in her own right and now lives in Germany. Jazz remains hugely popular in Baku—and also in Tbilisi and Yerevan—and is now celebrated in an annual Baku Jazz Festival.

1. Quoted in Frederick Starr, *Red and Hot* (New York: Oxford University Press, 1983), 111.
2. Fitzroy Maclean, *Eastern Approaches* (London: Jonathan Cape, 1949), 32–33.
3. Starr, *Red and Hot*, 281.
4. See Vagif Samadoglu, "The Emergence of Jazz in Azerbaijan [Vagif Mustafazade: Fusing Jazz with Mugam]," *Azerbaijan International Magazine*, Winter 1997.

Soviet Little Empires

Beginning in the 1960s, the Caucasian republican party bosses came to resemble powerful feudal princes. In the thirty-two years between the death of Stalin in 1953 and the coming to power of Gorbachev in 1985, both Armenia and Azerbaijan had just four leaders, while Georgia had only two, Vasily Mzhavanadze and Eduard Shevardnadze. In the late Soviet era, three men dominated. Shevardnadze was party leader in Georgia from 1972 to 1985 before being appointed Soviet foreign minister by Gorbachev. In Azerbaijan, former Soviet secret police general Heidar Aliev was first party secretary from 1969 to 1982 before being promoted to become a full member of the Soviet Politburo, a position he held for five years before Gorbachev forcibly retired him in 1987. The third powerful national party boss was Karen Demirchian, who was party leader in Armenia from 1974 to 1988.

These three men were rivals and competed for the allocation of resources in Moscow. Aliev and Demirchian were especially bitter opponents. Demirchian, for example, discreetly supported Igor Muradian, a nationalist dissident, in blocking Aliev's plans for a new highway across Armenia to the Azerbaijani territory of Nakhichevan. Asked later why the Communist Party boss should have helped a dissident, Muradian said with a laugh that he had been a useful weapon in an internal power struggle. "My dear, the Soviet Union did not exist from the beginning of the 1970s!" he said. "Different republics existed. One republic fought with another and so on. They were not interested in humanitarian ideals."[17]

Moscow was ultimately in charge, but, paradoxically, real Russian influence in the Caucasus weakened even as the feudal Caucasian leaders made ever more extravagant obeisance to the Kremlin. Aliev flattered Brezhnev and showered him with presents when he visited Baku. Shevardnadze famously declared that for Georgia "the sun rises in the north" but also managed to persuade the Soviet leadership to enshrine the official status of the Georgian language in the Soviet Georgian Constitution of 1978. Five years later, he went along with Russian-led celebrations marking the 200th anniversary of the Treaty of Georgievsk between Georgia and Russia in which statues of nineteenth-century Russian poets were erected along the Georgian Military Highway.

Actual statistics tell a different story of a gradually declining Russian presence. Bilingualism was much lower than might have been expected after fifty years of Soviet rule. In 1970, only 56 percent of people in Tbilisi and 63 percent in Yerevan claimed fluency in Russian as well as their native languages.[18] Nor were ethnic Russians themselves prominent in local society. After 1970, the absolute number of ethnic Russians in the Transcaucasus began to fall, and by 1989 they constituted only 1.5 percent, 5.6 percent, and 7.4 percent of the populations of Armenia, Azerbaijan, and Georgia, respectively. As a result, the rights of ethnic Russians did not become an issue in the post-Soviet South Caucasus as they did in the Baltic states or Kazakhstan.

The overall effect of the diminished Russian presence was that by the 1960s, while the Soviet Union had imposed a façade of uniformity, this masked great regional differences. For many Russians, the image of the Transcaucasus was that of an unthreatening, exotic area of their common Soviet state, a holiday destination or a repository of quaint traditions. A series of comic Russian films, such as *Caucasian Captive Girl*, poked gentle fun at Caucasian accents and customs. Georgians had a reputation for owning large cars and being good boyfriends for daughters. But in the Transcaucasus itself, very different processes were afoot—and generally in local languages that Russians could not understand. The locals were taking control, and their attitudes toward Russians shaded into contempt.

A lot of the Caucasian self-confidence was built on prosperity. The Soviet command economy was notoriously inefficient. The three Transcaucasian republics were linked to a Soviet-wide system, and in 1988 they conducted 93–98 percent of their trade with other republics, mainly Russia. Less than one-tenth of Transcaucasia's trade was conducted within the region itself. This situation later led to a dramatic economic collapse once borders and railways started closing after 1989. Poverty was still widespread, especially in Azerbaijan, which lagged behind the two other republics, but was masked by a sharp rise in living standards that began in the 1960s. In the Transcaucasus, some people began to live very well. The rapidly expanding cities had relatively well-off professional classes. Rates of car ownership were very high.

Rates of private ownership of property were also far higher than elsewhere in the Soviet Union—in 1989 almost half of the urban housing in Georgia was already in private hands.

Real wealth was hard to monitor in the late Soviet era, however, because the three Transcaucasian republics were very successful at exploiting the Soviet Union's informal "shadow" economy, in which actual goods, not cash, were the most valuable commodity. The Transcaucasus was rich in produce—fruits and vegetables, wine and caviar—that was hard to trace and easy to sell through the back door. This trade was assisted by the social traditions of the Caucasus: kinship came before state, and helping members of one's extended family was a matter of honor. Much of the Soviet black economy was run by criminal bosses, known in the Soviet Union as "thieves in law," and the Transcaucasus—Georgia in particular—boasted a large number of them. One of the most famous, the writer Jaba Ioseliani, later reemerged as a Georgian nationalist warlord in 1991. Criminal allegiances crossed national boundaries. In 1993, members of the criminal fraternity flew in to Yerevan from places all across the former Soviet Union to attend the funeral of an Armenian criminal boss known as Svo. Although the city was supposedly under an Azerbaijani blockade because of the Karabakh war, planes also arrived from Baku, and the gangsters arranged for gas and electricity to be switched on for three days.

The Caucasian Soviet shadow economy was almost as large as the legal one. Azerbaijani caviar plants contained entire sections for illegal sales. Two experts on the black economy in Georgia, Gerald Mars and Yochanan Altman, describe a biscuit factory in 1970s Georgia that employed 500 people; for every ten biscuits it produced for official sale, it made four illegal, or "informal," biscuits for sale on the side. The three top managers ran both the legal and illegal side of things, with a sophisticated alternative chain of supply, sales, and bribery.[19]

This organized corruption merged with the political system. Communist Party posts were bought and sold: the job of district party secretary cost 50,000–100,000 rubles. When you bought into the system, you committed yourself to a dense web of local obligations. This system of favors and networks would survive into the postindependence era. Georgi Derluguian describes the rules of the game:

> Officials who denied sinecure appointments to their relatives would lose the support of their family networks, and thus the inadequacy of formal political and bureaucratic institutions ensured that such honest officials would

be eaten alive by rival families. Besides that, the ethnic
cultures of the region, much as in the Mediterranean, laid
special stress on conspicuous consumption as proof of social status. The office-holder who could not provide for
his relatives and guests the 'proper' level of entertainment,
guests, and favors would be judged a scrooge and a miserable failure.[20]

The good old days? Leonid Brezhnev fondly remembered in Sheki,
Azerbaijan, 2000. Thomas de Waal.

All of this hollowed out the Soviet state from within. An increasingly independent political elite operated within an economy that enriched it in the short term but was parasitical and eventually unworkable. Essentially, the Soviet state in the Transcaucasus continued functioning thanks to inertia, subsidies from the center, and a Russian-led security apparatus. But once Armenia, Azerbaijan, and Georgia stopped being the margins and wanted to become centers themselves, they found that many of the essential attributes of statehood were missing. Worse, many of the qualities that made the Soviet Caucasus a relatively dynamic place—entrepreneurialism, tax evasion, creative resistance to authority—would only undermine the efforts of these republics to become new independent states.

The Soviet Legacy

The Soviet legacy is stronger than it seems in the South Caucasus. Many things that people take for granted are a product of the Soviet Union. They include urban lifestyles, mass literacy, and strong secularism. All three countries still live with an authoritarian political culture in which most people expect that the boss or leader will make decisions on their behalf and that civic activism will have no effect. The media is stronger on polemic than fact-based argument. The economies are based on the patron-client networks that formed in Soviet times. Nostalgia for the more innocent times of the 1960s and 1970s still pervades films, books, and Internet debates. An engaging website of the former pupils who attended Class B in School No. 14 in Sukhumi in the early 1980s gathers the reminiscences of people now living in Abkhazia, Tbilisi, Moscow, Siberia, Israel, Ukraine, and Greece. The sepia photos of the children in red cravats suggest a multiethnic past in a closed world that has gone forever.[21]

Different perceptions of the Soviet past also confuse the already complex relationship between the three newly independent countries and Russia. The end of the Soviet Union in 1991 meant the decoupling of Russia and the South Caucasus after an enforced union that had lasted 200 years with one small interruption. The rupture was somewhat better managed than in 1918, but independence was again a traumatic experience. Two vital elements of statehood—economic planning and security—had been steered by Moscow, and it took the three republics at least a decade to reconstruct functioning economies and law enforcement agencies.

In 1991, Armenia, Azerbaijan, and Georgia understandably based their legitimacy on the fact that they had been illegally annexed by the Bolsheviks and had the right to recover their independence. Georgia even readopted its 1921 constitution. But this does not tell the whole story, given the fact that the Soviet Union had been not so much a Russian project as a multinational hybrid state with a strong Russian flavor. Besides, in 1991 Russia itself became a newly independent state, which raised the question of what exactly the three new states in the South Caucasus were becoming independent from. On occasion, the new Russia would provide an answer, especially for Georgians, by behaving in a menacing, neo-imperial fashion, but even Vladimir Putin's Russia is a long way from being the heir to that of Stalin or Alexander I. The Russian Federation is still in the process of constructing a new post-Soviet identity for itself and deciding whether it is the direct heir of the Soviet Union, has been liberated from its captivity, or, in some undefined way, is both.

Where Russia goes in its search for a new identity has a strong bearing on its relationship with its neighbors in the South Caucasus. No models from the past are useful: Russia has never had fully independent neighbors before. In 1992, the Russian government coined the phrase "near abroad" as a catchall term for the newly foreign status of the post-Soviet states. The phrase made sense to Russians, but to the other states it was faintly menacing, implying a less than full endorsement of their independence. Russians across the political spectrum have implied as much. In 1992, Andrei Kozyrev, Boris Yeltsin's supposedly liberal foreign minister, visited Tbilisi; one of his Georgian hosts complained later that Kozyrev had stopped patronizingly outside the front door of the new Foreign Ministry and joked, "So, you've already put a sign up." This kind of attitude exudes an overbearing familiarity that grates on the Georgians. Consider also the fact that the three men who succeeded Kozyrev as Russian foreign minister all had connections with Tbilisi: Yevgeny Primakov grew up in the city, Igor Ivanov had a Georgian mother, and Sergei Lavrov's father was a Tbilisi Armenian.

Current Russian policy is still overreliant on "hard power" in the South Caucasus. In the age of Putin and Medvedev, it employs as instruments its presence in Abkhazia and South Ossetia, its military alliance with Armenia, and its gas pipelines to all three countries. Moscow's use of these tools and aggressive behavior in 2008—and later in Ukraine in 2014—summon up some unwelcome ghosts from the past. But the paradoxical result, as in the Soviet era, is that even as Armenian and Azerbaijani (but no longer Georgian) leaders dutifully visit Moscow to pledge the importance of their alliance, they simultaneously work hard to counterbalance the Russian influence and build up relationships with other international players, such as the European Union, NATO, Iran, and China.

Russia has inherited abundant resources of "soft power" in the Caucasus that Europeans and Americans can only dream of, yet it conspicuously fails to use them. As many as two million Armenians, Azerbaijanis, and Georgians are currently working in Russia and sending remittances home—but they are generally regarded as marginal migrant workers rather than a friendly resource. The Russian language, which is still widely spoken in the Caucasus and was the lingua franca of the region for at least a century, is now in decline, in large part because the Russian government is doing almost nothing to support it. University libraries in Baku, Tbilisi, and Yerevan are full of Russian-language books that a younger generation of students cannot read. In 2002, the director of the cash-strapped public library in Tbilisi said he had received donations of books from all the foreign embassies in the city—except the Russian embassy. As a result of actions like these, the better achievements of the Soviet era are gathering dust, while the Russian imperial legacy continues to loom large in the region.

4

Armenia and Azerbaijan

An Intimate Quarrel

A rmenians say, with a little exaggeration, that the end of the Soviet Union began in a small provincial town in the South Caucasus on February 20, 1988. That was the day the regional soviet in Stepanakert, the capital of the Nagorny Karabakh Autonomous Region, voted to ask for borders to be redrawn and for its territory to be transferred from Soviet Azerbaijan to Armenia. The vote turned out to be the first stone in an avalanche that would sweep away the entire multinational construction of the Soviet Union. In 1992, after the Soviet Union had been dissolved, the Karabakh dispute turned into an interstate conflict between Armenia and Azerbaijan. By the time a ceasefire was declared in 1994, the Armenians had won a victory on the battlefield, 20,000 people had been killed, and more than a million people had lost their homes.

The story of the Karabakh conflict is still largely the story of modern Armenia and Azerbaijan. More than twenty years on, as of this writing, the conflict is still unresolved and the center of a big international security tangle. Nagorny Karabakh itself, the highland region at the center of the quarrel, is under full Armenian control and has declared itself an independent republic, although its independence is recognized by no one, not even Armenia. Armenian forces also wholly or partially control seven districts of Azerbaijan around the enclave full of ruined towns and villages, in what they call a "security zone." Branching out from the official Armenia-Azerbaijan border, a ceasefire line runs like a scar for more than 100 miles across the South Caucasus through

A kind of victory. Armenian war veteran in front of Gazanchetsots Church in the war-ravaged town called Shusha or Shushi, Nagorny Karabakh, 1996. Thomas de Waal.

what is still the internationally recognized territory of Azerbaijan, with heavily equipped armies in trenches on either side. The socioeconomic costs of this conflict have been huge. Armenia's two main borders remain closed. The exclave of Nakhichevan is cut off from the rest of Azerbaijan. Railways go nowhere. The major Caspian Sea pipelines run in a sweeping arc north of Karabakh and Armenia, only eight miles from the ceasefire line.

For all its strategic importance and sensitive location, the unresolved aftermath of the war barely flickers on the international news agenda. In part, that is because serious violence is rare, with the four days of bloodshed in April 2016 being an exception. In part, it is because the negotiations over the future of Karabakh have been extremely narrowly defined and closed to outside actors. Armenian and Azerbaijani leaders prefer to keep strict control over the process and do not engage in public discussion about it.

Nagorny Karabakh was the first of three ethnoterritorial conflicts in the South Caucasus to shatter the peace of Gorbachev's Soviet Union. Soon afterward, it was followed by similar disputes in Abkhazia and South Ossetia. In human terms, perhaps its most traumatic feature was the disproportionately large number of refugees and internally displaced persons (IDPs) it created in such a small region. More than a million Armenians and Azerbaijanis were displaced by the upheavals of 1988–94. Together with the refugees from Georgia's conflicts, this has made for 1.4 million displaced people out of an official population of around sixteen million people in the South Caucasus, or almost 9 percent of the total.

Origins

Armenians and Azerbaijanis have not always been enemies. They lived intermingled in the South Caucasus for centuries, and serious political tensions between them are relatively recent in historical terms, going back, as two scholars put it ironically, "into the mists of the twentieth century." In many ways, the two nations are the "twins" of the South Caucasus. For centuries, they coexisted under Persian rule and shared more elements of a common culture than either did with the Georgians. Russian rule tended to suit Christian Armenians more than Muslim Azerbaijanis, but few instances of violence between them are recorded before the end of the nineteenth century. In 1935, writing in a Paris émigré journal, an Azerbaijani author wrote, "As for the Armenians . . . they are even closer to us than the Georgians, since the Armenians almost to a man used to speak in our language. In everyday habits our lives were closely intertwined. In our villages folksingers [*ashugs*] were almost all Armenians. Our cooking, dress, customs, and behavior were

Nagorny Karabakh

the same. For millennia we lived not only in mutual trust and respect but—it will not be an exaggeration to say—with real love."[1]

For 300 years the most sensitive point in relations between the two national groups has been the mountainous part of the province of Karabakh. This highland region is a beautiful, fertile patch of green between arid plains on either side. It has several names: Armenians call it Artsakh, or Mountainous, Karabakh; Azerbaijanis call it Dağliq Qarabağ, a Turkish-Persian name probably meaning "Black Garden," which describes the region's fertile soil. The Russian name, Nagorny (or Nagorno, "mountainous") Karabakh, has stuck since the dispute first caught the world's attention in 1988. Eighteenth- and nineteenth-century travelers described the region's vines, lush pastures, and ancient churches and the rocky fortress of Shusha. In 1824 an Englishman, George Keppel, wrote of "the black and lofty mountains of the fruitful province of Karabaugh."

For the past few hundred years, Nagorny Karabakh has been a borderland with strong connections to both the Armenian and Turkic worlds.

The demographics of the region have fluctuated sharply over time, but an Armenian presence has been recorded there off and on for centuries, and the hills are dotted with medieval Armenian churches, such as Amaras and Gandzasar. From medieval times, fierce Armenian feudal princes, known as *meliks*, ruled the province, often keeping their autonomy when other Armenian lands were under foreign rule.[2] But there has also been a strong Muslim presence there at least since the Persian Safavid dynasty established itself in the sixteenth century, and probably before. The map shows Karabakh's importance to Azerbaijan. Physically, Nagorny Karabakh is on the eastern side of the mountainous watershed that defines present-day Armenia. It has served as the summer pastures for Muslim shepherds who spend the winters in the plains below. For a long time the territory probably had a Muslim-majority population in the summer, when Muslim shepherds were in the high pastures, and a settled Christian majority in the winter, when the shepherds were in the plains.

Up until the Russian conquest in 1805, Karabakh was one of the most powerful principalities in the Caucasus, either under direct Safavid rule or as a semi-independent khanate. In the mid-eighteenth century, the new fortress-citadel of Shusha became the capital of the khanate. Karabakh came to evolve a distinct identity of its own. Karabakh Armenians have the stereotype among other Armenians of being tough highlanders, and their dialect of Armenian is markedly different from the language spoken in eastern Armenia. They also share many of their practices and traditions with their Muslim neighbors. In the early twentieth century the Armenian scholar Stepan Lisitsian noted that the Karabakh Armenians knew Azerbaijani music and spoke Azeri, often gave their children Muslim names, and sometimes even practiced polygamy.

SHUSHA

The old capital of Nagorny Karabakh, Shusha (known to Armenians as Shushi), once one of the great cities of the Caucasus, is now half-ruined. It is still a key issue in the Armenian-Azerbaijani dispute, making it, in more ways than one, the "Jerusalem" of Karabakh.

The city stands for the best and worst in Armenian-Azerbaijani relations, having had the misfortune of being burned three times as the result of interethnic conflict. It was founded in the years after 1747 by Panakh Khan, the new Muslim feudal lord of Karabakh, who made a dynastic marriage alliance with one of the Armenian *meliks*, Shahnazar. Its position on a cliff made it an almost impregnable fortress, and it held out against two long sieges in 1795 and 1826.

In the nineteenth century, Shusha had a large bourgeois population, mosques, churches, caravanserais, broad cobbled streets, theaters, and a grand school in a neoclassical building. It was subsequently called the "conservatoire of Azerbaijan," being the birthplace of many musicians, including Uzeir Hajibeyov, the most celebrated composer of his era. But the town's importance declined with the building of the railways. In 1905, it was ravaged by intercommunal fighting, which the correspondent of the newspaper the *Morning Leader* compared to a natural disaster: "A light smoke was curling up from the ruins when I arrived. It was indeed a deplorable sight. Street after street was in ruin, absolutely nothing left but the bare walls. Whose fault was it that the best part of this fine town of 30,000 inhabitants has been destroyed it would be hard to say."[1]

In March 1920, the town suffered even more when it was sacked by an Azerbaijani army; its Armenian quarter was gutted, and some 500 Armenians were killed. The Russian Jewish poet Osip Mandelstam, visiting ten years later, found a ghost town with "forty thousand dead windows." When Stepanakert in the plains below became the Soviet capital of Karabakh, Shusha became the center of the Azerbaijani community. When the Karabakh dispute erupted again in 1988, the town became an Azerbaijani fortress in an Armenian province. In May 1992, it was the turn of the Armenians to capture and then burn most of the town to the ground. In the last few years, Shusha has been partially reconstructed and its Armenian church rebuilt, but it is still ghostly; its two mosques stand forlorn and empty.

The loss of Shusha is still keenly felt by Azerbaijanis. For most Armenians, it is almost unthinkable to relinquish a town that could be an Azerbaijani strategic fortress again.

This makes the status of Shusha one of the thorniest issues in the negotiations over Nagorny Karabakh. If Armenians and Azerbaijanis can reach an accommodation to live there again, it will be a sign that real reconciliation is happening between them.

1. J. D. Henry, *Baku: An Eventful History* (London: Archibald Constable, 1905), 172–73.

In the late nineteenth century, the decline of the tsarist empire and the new national movements in Armenia and Azerbaijan inevitably drove the two communities into conflict in Karabakh and elsewhere. In 1905 and again in 1918–20, the province was the arena for a brutal civil war. The British, who made independent Azerbaijan a de facto protectorate, briefly occupied Karabakh but then pulled out, leaving the way clear for the Bolsheviks, who captured the region in the summer of 1920.

As every other foreign power had, the Bolsheviks wavered between the competing claims of the two communities. Meeting in Tbilisi over the course of two days in July 1921, the leading Bolsheviks, headed by Stalin, leaned towards the Armenian claim on one day but the next day ruled in favor of Soviet Azerbaijan. Two years later, the new Nagorny Karabakh Autonomous Region was founded, with its borders drawn so as to give it a population that was 94 percent Armenian. The capital of the new region was made the new town of Stepanakert, named after the Armenian Bolshevik Stepan Shaumian and built around the old village of Khankendi.

The 1921 decision of the Caucasus Bureau is a touchstone in the historical debate over the Karabakh issue. Armenians say that Stalin "gave" Karabakh to the Azerbaijanis, while Azerbaijanis maintain that the decision merely recognized a preexisting reality. From the Bolsheviks' standpoint in 1921, it was a logical decision. Consolidating Soviet Azerbaijan at that time was a much bigger priority than satisfying weak and devastated Armenia, and their new ally Kemalist Turkey also supported the Azerbaijani claims. As good Marxists, the Bolsheviks also saw an economic rationale in placing Nagorny Karabakh within Azerbaijan. The move has been called a case of imperialist divide-and-rule politics, but in making Azerbaijan a single economic unit in which farmers could move their flocks between the plains and highlands of Karabakh without crossing a republican border, the Bolsheviks were actually more interested in what could be called "combine and rule." Moreover, there was no passable road at the time between Armenia and Nagorny Karabakh.

Having placed Nagorny Karabakh within Azerbaijan, the Bolsheviks drew the boundaries of the new autonomous region in 1923 to give it an overwhelmingly Armenian population. Only one pocket of territory with a large Azerbaijani population, the semiruined city of Shusha, remained. In the long term, this was an arrangement with a strong structural flaw, in that it made Nagorny Karabakh a place of uncertain allegiances—an Armenian province within the Soviet Republic of Azerbaijan but not far from the Republic of Armenia. Moreover, the map was drawn such that the borders of the new region came close to but did not touch Armenia. In between lay the Lachin region of Azerbaijan (initially known as Red Kurdistan). This eventually had a crucial bearing on the geography of the conflict, as the Karabakh Armenians did everything they could to build a land bridge with Armenia.

In Soviet times, Nagorny Karabakh turned into a backwater. Rumblings of Armenian discontent were audible only to those listening very carefully. In 1945, 1965, and 1977 there were petitions for the region to be united with Soviet Armenia. The local Armenians complained that they had no Armenian-language television and that their church monuments were being allowed to fall into disrepair. The province was relatively poorer than Soviet Armenia but not much worse off than most of Azerbaijan. Its demographic balance slowly changed in favor of Azerbaijanis: in 1926, there were 117,000 Armenians and 13,000 Azerbaijanis; by 1979, the two groups numbered 123,000 and 37,000, respectively. Azerbaijanis settled in new towns and villages, while many Armenians emigrated in search of a better life. Many Karabakh Armenians, unable to get on the career ladder in Azerbaijan, ended up studying in Moscow or Yerevan. A long-term effect of this was that they came to feel more of an allegiance to the Soviet Union as a whole and less loyalty to Soviet Azerbaijan. (A similar process occurred in Abkhazia with relation to Georgia.) Yet these resentments were more or less managed by the Soviet system. The cultural and historical problems only exercised the intelligentsia. Most ordinary people, while living in distinct communities, got on well on a day-to-day level, worked together, and spoke each other's languages. Former Karabakh Party official Sergei Shugarian said, "At the upper levels [of society] there were never clashes [on ethnic grounds] because people were afraid of confrontation. In the middle there were constant tensions on national grounds. Down below they lived in friendship, there were no problems at all."[3]

HISTORY WARS

All the wars in the South Caucasus are not only about the present but about the past. When ordinary Armenians and Azerbaijanis argue the Nagorny Karabakh question, they tend to talk less about international law and to raise gut issues of history, belonging, and "who was there first."

Soviet Armenian and Azerbaijani historians waged their own battles years before a shooting war broke out, laying the ground for what the Turkish historian Halil Berktay calls "hate narratives." Histories were published about Nagorny Karabakh going back thousands of years that pulled off the feat of not mentioning the presence of the other ethnic group at all.[1] Since fighting ended in 1994, official documents and statements on both sides have deliberately ignored or diminished the historical presence of the other ethnic group in the territory under their control.

Armenians deny the Azerbaijani heritage of the lands they control. For example, they have renamed the Azerbaijani town of Lachin Berdzor and the surrounding region Kashatagh. Shiite Muslims lived in what is now Armenia for centuries; the Azeri dialect of Turkish they spoke was widely used throughout the region, and the eighteenth-century Armenian troubadour Sayat Nova composed many songs in it. However, the word "Azerbaijan" did not enter common usage until the twentieth century, enabling the Armenian nationalist writer Zori Balayan to assert, "We can understand the terms Georgia, Russia, Armenia—but not Azerbaijan. By using such a term we confirm the existence of such a country."[2] This linguistic sleight of hand has enabled the Armenian authorities to label the surviving mosques in Yerevan and the Karabakhi town of Shusha "Persian," denying their historic link with Azerbaijanis.

Azerbaijani historical revisionists face a bigger challenge in that Armenians built dozens of churches and there are thousands of inscriptions in the Armenian alphabet across the South Caucasus. To mitigate this, a curious theory was launched in the 1960s by the Azerbaijani historian Zia Buniatov. It centers on the fate of the ancient Christian people, called Caucasian Albanians by the Romans, who mostly lived in what is now Azerbaijan. Only a few fragments of their writing survive. The historical consensus used to be that the Albanians were almost completely assimilated by other local peoples, including the Armenians, from around the tenth century. A tiny ethnic group, the Udi or Udins, mainly concentrated in two villages in northern Azerbaijan and now numbering fewer than 10,000, appear to be their direct descendants. Many are still Christian. However, the name "Albania" persisted even after little evidence of the actual people was recorded. A branch of the Armenian Apostolic Church in Karabakh was called "Albanian" until the nineteenth century. This and a few other facts led Buniatov and his followers to advance the theory that the history of the Albanians had actually been suppressed, they had retained a distinct identity until much later times, and the monuments of Karabakh were in fact "Albanian" and not Armenian, despite their many Armenian inscriptions. This rather bizarre argument had the strong political subtext that Nagorny Karabakh had in fact been "Caucasian Albanian" and that Armenians therefore had no claim to it.

The "Albanian argument" has entered Azerbaijani public discourse and spelled trouble for cultural monuments. In 2005, an inscription in Armenian script that the local people claimed was not authentic was erased during the restoration of a church in Nij in northern Azerbaijan. Norwegian money had been spent on the restoration of the church, and the Norwegian foreign ministry complained.

In 2006, a much larger act of cultural vandalism was reported near the town of Julfa in the Azerbaijani exclave of Nakhichevan. Film shot from Iran across the border suggested that a famous medieval cemetery that had thousands of cross-stones with Armenian inscriptions on them had been bulldozed. An official Azerbaijan statement declared that

Armenian cemeteries or other Armenian religious and nonreligious monuments never existed on the territory of Julfa region and Nakhichevan AR [Autonomous Republic] of the Azerbaijan Republic.... As to stone crosses existing on the territory of Chuga cemetery of Julfa region, their origin dates back to time of Albanian state, where Christianity was the state religion, and it [the cemetery] belongs to Albans—one of the ancestors of Azerbaijanis. This cemetery is a cultural heritage of Azerbaijan and is under protection of the State.

Unfortunately, the available evidence suggests the graveyard was not protected from an act of destruction in the history wars.[3]

1. The most comprehensive account of the Caucasian historians' war is Viktor Shnirelman, *Voiny Pamyati, Mify, Identichnost' i Politika na Zakavkaze* [*Wars of Memory: Myths, Identity and Politics in the Transcaucasus*] (Moscow: Akademkniga, 2003).
2. Zori Balayan, interview, *Armenian Mirror-Spectator* [Boston], February 20, 1988, reprinted in Gerard Libaridian, ed., *The Karabagh File: Documents and Facts on the Question of Mountainous Karabagh, 1918–1988* (Cambridge, Mass.: Zoryan Institute, 1988), 76.
3. Embassy of the Republic of Azerbaijan in Georgia, press release, http://www.azembassy.ge/press19 1.html, in English in the original.

The Karabakh Revolt

When Nagorny Karabakh became the Soviet Union's first dissident region in February 1988, it took almost everybody by surprise. Within the space of a week, the Karabakh Armenians broke a series of Soviet taboos, staging public rallies, strikes, and effectively a public vote of no confidence in

Moscow. Many Azerbaijanis have seen a high-level conspiracy in this. They argue that a remote province such as Karabakh could only have risen up and challenged the status quo on the critical issue of national borders after receiving strong positive signals from the top. This speaks to Azerbaijani fears about the power of the Armenian lobby—and Gorbachev did indeed have two Armenian advisors. Yet the fact that Gorbachev decisively rejected the Karabakhis' demand suggests that there was no conspiracy, but only a tangle of misunderstandings and mixed messages, with the Karabakh Armenians and their Armenian lobbyists believing they had more support in Moscow than they actually did.

On February 20, 1988, after a series of petitions had been presented in Moscow, Armenian deputies in the local soviet voted to ask the central authorities to facilitate the transfer of the region to Soviet Armenia. Azerbaijani deputies refused to vote. The Politburo immediately rejected the request and said the soviet's actions "contradict the interests of the working people in Soviet Azerbaijan and Armenia and damage interethnic relations."[4] The local soviet's bold resolution had repercussions for the whole Soviet Union. Soviets, the basic building blocks of the USSR's system of government, had nominal power but were in practice supposed to be rubberstamping bodies. Once the Karabakh Soviet challenged that consensus and dusted off Lenin's concept of "all power to the soviets," the system faced paralysis. It was the first shot in a "war of laws" between Soviet institutions—later Azerbaijan's Supreme Soviet would reject the Karabakhi move, and Armenia's Supreme Soviet would support it. The deadlock soon spread to Georgia and later to Russia in what came to be known as a "parade of sovereignties," as autonomous entities across the Soviet Union tried to reinvest power in institutions that had been paper bodies since the 1920s.

Gorbachev faced a dilemma in dealing with the Karabakh revolt. To have agreed to the soviet's demand would have set a risky precedent. To have arrested the demonstrators would also have been perilous and against the spirit of glasnost he was trying otherwise to inculcate in the Soviet Union. In the event, he tried to smother the problem. The official media remained silent about it. A battalion of 160 Soviet Interior Ministry troops was sent to Karabakh, and a Politburo delegation traveled to the region to try to talk sense into the rebels. Appeals were made to the "brotherly solidarity" of the two peoples.

Gorbachev was far more liberal than any other Soviet leader before him, but his response revealed the limitations of the Soviet political system.

Real political dialogue had effectively been banned in the Soviet Union for more than sixty years. "I had hundreds of conversations," said a Moscow official who traveled between Armenia and Azerbaijan seeking compromise on the Karabakh issue in 1988. "I didn't meet a single Armenian or a single Azerbaijani who held a compromise position on this question, from shepherds to academicians."[5] The expectation was that Moscow would rule decisively in favor of one side or the other. The party authorities in Baku never thought of inviting the Karabakh Armenians for talks on their demands—even if they had been allowed to—while the Karabakh Armenians traveled to Moscow, not Baku, to push their claims. Within months, dissatisfied with Moscow's handling of the national issue, Armenians and Azerbaijanis were burning their party cards and openly defying the central authorities. Karabakh also exposed the weakness of the interconnected Soviet command economy. One of the first strikes in the Soviet Union in almost seventy years, at an electronic parts factory in the Karabakhi capital, Stepanakert, slowed or halted production in sixty-five radio and television factories across the Soviet Union.[6] As soon as the rigid, authoritarian Soviet system was challenged in a serious manner, it suddenly looked very brittle.

The dispute unleashed huge pent-up nationalist passions. Two young Azerbaijanis were killed when a protest march toward Nagorny Karabakh was stopped by police. In Yerevan, once the Karabakh issue had broken to the surface, it awakened a sleeping giant of Armenian national sentiment, or *hai dat*. Every day greater and greater crowds attended rallies in Opera Square in which protestors chanted the three syllables "Gha-ra-bagh!" On February 25, more than a million people—more than a quarter of the population of the entire republic—turned out. One of the organizers described Opera Square as a "magnetic field." Ordinary people felt they had a cause they could put their hearts into. Communist Party officials were heckled or listened to in silence, and a new political force, the "Karabakh Committee," gained authority instead. Although their initial demands were rejected, Armenians felt a surge of confidence. Soon, the members of the Karabakh Committee, such as Yerevan intellectual Levon Ter-Petrosian, began to raise other political issues besides Karabakh.

There was far less unanimity in Azerbaijan as to the right way forward. Was it right to reaffirm loyalty to Moscow as the guarantor of Azerbaijan's integrity? Or was it better to fight the Armenians in their own game? Azerbaijan, which was much more ethnically and socially diverse than Armenia, was divided. Azerbaijanis were also resentful that Moscow intellectuals, including

Andrei Sakharov, virtually unanimously backed the Armenians. For years, Azerbaijanis were far less effective in getting their message across on the Karabakh issue than the much better organized Armenians.

Azerbaijan was then hit by a cataclysm when the worst interethnic violence in the peacetime Soviet Union for almost seventy years occurred in the town of Sumgait. In February 1988, as tensions rose over Karabakh, hundreds of ethnic Azerbaijanis left southern Armenia for Azerbaijan, complaining that they had been forced out or beaten up. The party leader in Baku moved them on to Sumgait, an overcrowded workers' town on the Caspian Sea. Rallies were held denouncing Armenians. On the evening of February 28, an angry crowd marched through the center of the town and began attacking ethnic Armenians in their homes. An orgy of mob violence was unleashed: apartments were burned and ransacked, and ordinary Armenians were attacked, raped, and murdered. It was twenty-four hours before Soviet troops retook the center of the town, which had come to resemble a war zone.

In the tense situation in Armenia and Azerbaijan, the Sumgait pogroms caused a sudden and irreparable meltdown in ethnic relations. The region had rediscovered the mob violence of 1905. The death toll in Sumgait was thirty-two, twenty-six Armenians and six Azerbaijanis, the latter probably rioters killed by Soviet troops. Hundreds more, including many soldiers, were injured. Almost all of the 14,000 Armenians of Sumgait chose to flee the city. The temperature in Armenia shot up as Armenians denounced what they called a new genocide. The silence of the Soviet media and the lack of an investigation whipped up more anger and resentment. Several conspiracy theories about Sumgait are prevalent to this day in Azerbaijan, blaming the KGB or Armenians for having planned the violence. Yet the clear outline of events and the culpability of a core group of Azerbaijani workers and refugees cannot be denied.

From Politics to Conflict

After the Sumgait pogroms, Armenia and Azerbaijan were set on a collision course, which the Soviet leadership failed to halt. An officially sanctioned exchange of populations began that altered centuries of coexistence. Tens of thousands of Azerbaijanis left Armenia for Azerbaijan under duress, and tens of thousands of Armenians went the other way. In most cases the deportations were peaceful, but many people were beaten and intimidated, and deaths were reported. Azerbaijan sprang into political life with the holding of mass demonstrations in Baku's vast Lenin Square.

On December 7, 1988, a massive earthquake in northern Armenia virtually destroyed the town of Spitak and caused devastation over a wide area. Around 25,000 people were killed. The disaster drew sympathy from all over the world and changed Armenia overnight, bringing international organizations and diaspora groups into the homeland. Gorbachev broke off a visit to the United Nations in New York to visit the earthquake zone and made what was his only trip to the Transcaucasus during his entire tenure as Soviet leader. On a walkabout in Yerevan, a young man questioned him about the Karabakh issue, and Gorbachev, visibly angry, asked him how he dared to raise this issue at such a tragic time. Gorbachev sanctioned the arrest of the eleven members of the Karabakh Committee, but within months they were free and national heroes.

A recurring issue in the Karabakh dispute is whether economic incentives, such as Azerbaijani oil wealth, can be used to induce the Karabakh Armenians to compromise. Gorbachev's failed attempt to use this kind of incentive suggests that national sentiment and security fears trumped economic factors. In 1988, Gorbachev sent the energetic Russian industrialist Arkady Volsky to the province with instructions to give it an economic "renaissance." Volsky was given a special budget of 400 million rubles, the authority to orient Karabakh's economy toward Russia, and powers that covered—as he himself put it—"everything from inseminating cows to military issues." It did not work. The new envoy and the Soviet police force were outwitted by insurgents. Bridges were blown up, roads blockaded, and hostages taken.[7] In similar fashion, the increasingly radical Azerbaijan Popular Front undermined its own government and relations with Armenia. Its members tore a hole in the economy and railroad system of the South Caucasus by mounting a rail blockade against Armenia—yet by doing so, they also cut off the Azerbaijani exclave of Nakhichevan.

As refugees had moved back and forth and violence had flared, Baku had just about managed to keep its status as a haven of multiethnic tolerance. Tens of thousands of ethnic Armenians were still living there in 1989. They now became the next victims of extreme nationalism, targeted by Popular Front activists and Azerbaijani refugees from Armenia. Events reached a head at the turn of the year in 1990. On January 13, anti-Armenian pogroms broke out in Baku. As in Sumgait, there were appalling scenes of savagery, and many Armenians were rescued by their neighbors. More than ninety people died. Many thousands survived because of an evacuation operation that took frightened, freezing refugees in ferries across the Caspian Sea. Within a couple of days, Baku's long Armenian history had been abruptly ended.

This was only the first chapter of Baku's "Black January." The Popular Front had effectively won control of the streets, and the local Communist Party was powerless. The Politburo decided to send in the army. Shortly after midnight on January 20, tanks rolled into the city, followed by troops. A new tragedy unfolded. Civilians were shot at, and cars crushed. Some militants returned fire, and the city became a battle zone. At least 130 citizens of Baku and 21 soldiers were killed. The army's intervention was a moment of mass trauma for Azerbaijan and the worst single act of bloodshed of Gorbachev's perestroika era. Although the Soviet authorities won back physical control of Baku, they basically lost Azerbaijan in the process. Thousands of people publicly burned their Communist Party cards amid scenes of mass mourning. A new party boss, Ayaz Mutalibov, was installed, but real power lay with his Russian deputy, Viktor Polyanichko, who had powerful backers in the Moscow security establishment, and with the Popular Front, which had won a major moral victory.

Following Black January, the year 1990 saw Moscow cast off its mediating role. The Soviet leadership intervened much more directly to support Azerbaijan, while Armenia was by now a leading rebel in the Soviet system. This rebel status helped Azerbaijan in the short term but worked in Armenia's favor in the long run. Later that year, Armenia became the first republic in the Soviet Union to elect a non-Communist government when it chose Levon Ter-Petrosian as speaker of the Supreme Soviet and de facto leader of the republic. The new authorities began both to build new institutions and to equip Armenian insurgents in Karabakh for an armed struggle. Polyanichko was handed the authority to take charge of Nagorny Karabakh and defeat the Armenian insurgency, with the support of Azerbaijani special police units and Soviet troops. In the summer of 1991, they waged a mini–civil war (it came to be known by its Soviet code name, Operation Ring) against the Armenian guerrillas in which the main victims were ordinary Armenian villagers.

The Soviet Azerbaijani strategy was beginning to squeeze the Armenians, but it was spectacularly derailed by the failed coup d'état in Moscow in August 1991. Polyanichko was discredited by being close to the coup plotters and forced to leave Azerbaijan. The Armenians were better able to exploit the power vacuum than the Azerbaijanis. They had been gearing up for independence for three years, while Azerbaijan had not built any new institutions. Azerbaijan rather mechanically declared independence on August 30, 1991, but the same leadership, led by party boss Mutalibov, stayed in charge. Mutalibov was elected independent Azerbaijan's first president in a ballot in which he was the only candidate on September 8. Armenia was a few days behind, but much better prepared. On September 21, it held a referendum on independence that it had been planning for months; the vote was overwhelmingly in favor. On October 16, Ter-Petrosian was elected Armenia's first president.

The independence of Armenia and Azerbaijan—soon to be recognized internationally—made Nagorny Karabakh the subject of an interstate dispute. It was de jure part of Azerbaijan but mostly under Armenian control. This posed a challenge to the Yerevan government: newly independent Armenia did not want to be accused of wanting to annex part of newly independent Azerbaijan. This was one reason that in September 1991 the Armenians of Nagorny Karabakh—officially numbering just 140,000 people—declared independence as a new state separate from Azerbaijan. Armenia did not recognize the independence of Karabakh but unofficially more or less controlled the region's government and armed forces. To this day, the two territories, one recognized and one unrecognized, continue to operate in a strangely choreographed tandem.

In November 1991, the new Azerbaijani parliament, containing many opposition deputies, voted to abolish the autonomous status of Nagorny Karabakh altogether and make it an ordinary province of Azerbaijan. They also voted to rename Stepanakert Khankendi. The Karabakh Armenians responded by holding a referendum on independence on December 10—boycotted by the Azerbaijani population—with 99 percent of voters casting their ballots in favor. In this black-and-white world of contradictory realities, war was all but inevitable when the Soviet Union was formally dissolved on December 31, 1991.

War over Karabakh

All the wars of the South Caucasus are case studies of the strange phenomenon whereby neighbors who have coexisted peacefully for years end up fighting one another. Karabakh is a striking example. One village named Tug in the south of Karabakh had been home to people of both communities, with only a small stream dividing them. At first, the Armenians and Azerbaijanis of Tug said that the dispute would not affect them; then they retreated to their own half of the village, with some families being broken up; finally, in 1991, the Azerbaijanis were driven out by force.

The problem can be described as "mutual insecurity." In tsarist times, pogroms had broken out when the regime had weakened. In Soviet times, order had been maintained by a central "policeman," but when that law enforcer withdrew, the two national groups turned to their own armed men to protect them. Then in 1991 the Soviet armed forces collapsed into indiscipline, arming both sides and providing hundreds of "guns for hire." This helped elevate a low-intensity conflict into an all-out war fought with tanks and artillery.

Another answer to the puzzle of neighbors fighting one another is that generally it was not they who actually started the conflict. Many Armenians and Azerbaijanis, like the people of Tug, did their best to resist the slide toward war. In the spring of 1991, the revolutionary California-born Armenian warrior Monte Melkonian was sent on a commission down Armenia's border with Azerbaijan to prepare villages for impending conflict. He got frustrated as villagers asked him and other would-be defenders to leave, saying they did not want to fight their Azerbaijani neighbors.[8]

Moreover, although ordinary Armenians and Azerbaijanis lived side by side, the views of their intellectual elites were sharply different. In 1988, nationalist intellectuals played a negative role by disseminating narratives of hate. The Armenian writer Zori Balayan wrote that the Azerbaijanis were "Turks" who had no history of their own. The Azerbaijani historian Ziya Buniatov wrote an inflammatory pamphlet suggesting that the Armenians themselves had been behind the killing of Armenians in Sumgait.

After the intellectuals came the men of violence. As the Soviet security apparatus withered, the initiative was handed to people who have been called "entrepreneurs of violence." They were people who were often marginal figures in society but willing or able to fight. Violence became self-fueling. In the later war in Abkhazia, much of the most brutal fighting would be done by people from outside Abkhazia itself—North Caucasians on the Abkhaz side, incoming Georgian paramilitaries on the Georgian side. These guns-for-hire would exact a tithe for their fighting in looting and plunder. In the early phases of the Karabakh war, the Armenian side called on two paramilitary units, named the Arabo and the Aramo, whom Melkonian accused of atrocities and indiscipline. The Arabo, who were later accused of carrying out massacres, were described as "two huddles of dangerous-looking men in black wool uniforms and with up-curled moustaches." Militias in Georgia cultivated the same image of bravado, courage, and criminality. The display of violent intent was often as important as the will actually to inflict it—as in a cockfight, the other side could be intimidated by a show of strength and made to back down without a fight.

There was often a thin line between courageous patriotism and violent criminality. In the early days of the Karabakh war, the Azerbaijani town of Aghdam, which had been a thriving black market center in Soviet times, relied for its defense on six gangs who fought each other as well as the Armenians. The Azerbaijani volunteer soldier Kemal Ali, who saw them in action, commented, "An educated person never goes to war, criminals go to war. And at that time our army was commanded by criminals."[9] The Armenian side was more organized but contained similar types.[10]

In early 1992, the impromptu armies on both sides in the Karabakh conflict were handed larger and more sophisticated weapons. In February, the Azerbaijani side first used two fearsome "Grad" multiple-rocket launchers—named after the Russian word for "hail" and designed for attacks on soldiers—against the civilians of Stepanakert. Rockets were mounted on the back of a truck and fired to rain down over a wide area, causing indiscriminate damage. The city was terrorized; the Armenians retaliated by bombarding Shusha with their own rockets, but they had fewer of them. The Armenians got hold of the remaining tanks from the Soviet 366th Regiment based in Stepanakert, giving them armor that allowed them to sweep through Azerbaijani villages.

International interest in the conflict was intermittent, and the world media failed to give a coherent picture of it. For the distant observer, it was a war of flickering episodes—the shelling of Stepanakert, the killings at Khojali, the mass flight of Azerbaijani refugees in 1993. The Armenian side, helped by the diaspora, was much more effective in getting its message across but gradually faced more critical questions as it won more victories on the battlefield.

The course of the conflict was dictated by geography and demography. The Armenians' goal was to use their demographic majority inside Nagorny Karabakh itself to drive out the Azerbaijani population, make Karabakh a defensible fortress, and cut a road link to Armenia. The Azerbaijanis sought to squeeze Karabakh in a blockade and force the Armenians to surrender.

There were three main reasons for the eventual Armenian victory: the Armenians were a more effective fighting force, the Azerbaijanis were more disunited and disorganized, and the Armenians benefited more from erratic Russian assistance.

To begin with, the Armenians managed to paper over most of their political differences, although there were constant tensions between the Armenians of Yerevan and those in Karabakh. The Armenians also had more military professionals from the Soviet army and had produced generations of Soviet officers, while Azerbaijanis, like other Soviet Muslims, tended to be given noncombat army jobs. Azerbaijan was also riven by political factionalism. Armed units answered to their own commanders rather than the government and sometimes deserted the front and followed their leaders back to Baku. Azerbaijan lost most of its territory when political power struggles were at their most intense. The third factor, the influence of outside forces, is the hardest to assess. Many incomers, from Armenian diaspora warriors such as Melkonian to Chechen fighter Shamil Basayev, fought in the conflict, but most were individuals who did not have a decisive impact. Russian involvement was much greater, but its overall extent is still not clear. In the early part of the war, many Russians (and Ukrainians and Belorussians) fought, but they were mainly freelance soldiers who had stayed on in the Caucasus after 1991 to earn a living. In the summer of 1992 they drove tanks, manned artillery, and flew airplanes on both sides.

Later on, from the end of 1992, official Russian policy tilted toward the Armenians and against the anti-Russian Popular Front government in Azerbaijan. The leading player in Russian policy in the Caucasus at the time was Russian defense minister Pavel Grachev. His closest relationship was with the Armenians: he made his first foreign trip as defense minister to Yerevan in May 1992 and struck up a close friendship with Armenia's Vazgen Sargsyan. Grachev's overall objective appears to have been to maximize the Russian military presence in the South Caucasus by whatever means possible.

The first phase of the conflict in 1992 was a chaotic scramble to capture pockets of territory inside Nagorny Karabakh, which resulted in its worst massacre. The Azerbaijanis tried to smash Stepanakert into submission with Grad missiles, causing mass casualties as hundreds of civilians sheltered in cold, dark basements. The Armenians bombarded Shusha, but less effectively. For the Armenians, the strategic objective was to break Stepanakert out of isolation and capture the only airfield near the Azerbaijani village of Khojali. On the night of February 25–26, the Armenians began their attack on Khojali,

Azerbaijanis in flight. People from the Azerbaijani region of Kelbajar fleeing an Armenian advance during the Nagorny Karabakh war, April 1993. Halid Askerov.

assisted by the remnants of the Soviet tank regiment. About 3,000 people were living in Khojali. The village's road access had been cut off for four months, and it was only defended by about 160 lightly armed men. Early in the morning, both civilians and fighters fled through the town's one remaining exit down a valley ankle-deep in snow. Outside the village of Nakhichevanik, they were met by a wall of gunfire from Armenian fighters. Wave after wave of fleeing men, women, and children were cut down. The official Azerbaijani parliamentary investigation into the killings later concluded that 485 people had died. Even taking into account that this included Azerbaijani militiamen returning fire and some people who died of cold in the woods, this still made it by far the worst atrocity of the Karabakh war.

For several days, the Khojali killings were barely reported on in Azerbaijan as the Mutalibov government tried to suppress what had happened. Slowly, however, word got out, and when a film of the aftermath, revealing a hillside littered with bodies, was shown in the Azerbaijani parliament, the anger was so intense that President Mutalibov was forced to resign. Thousands of men volunteered to fight. Over the years, Khojali has become a touchstone for Azerbaijanis' record of their suffering. Its anniversary has been marked as a day of mourning, and pictures of the dead bodies of Khojali are posted on websites and even shown in schools.

On the other side, the killings at Khojalu (as they called the village) blotted the Armenians' reputation as the victims in the conflict. Many Armenians still deny that their soldiers killed civilians at Khojali, despite plenty of supporting evidence. Human Rights Watch monitors published eyewitness accounts of survivors, while the Moscow human rights group Memorial concluded, "In carrying out the military operation to seize the town of Khojali mass violence against the population of this town took place. . . . The mass killing of peaceful civilians in the 'free corridor' zone and adjoining territories cannot be justified under any circumstances."[11] Melkonian fumed at the "indiscipline" of the Arabo and Aramo paramilitary units in Khojali.[12] Karabakh Armenian commander Serzh Sargsyan—later president of Armenia—subsequently said that reports of Armenian savagery had been exaggerated but that killings had been carried out by survivors of the pogroms in Baku and Sumgait. He said Khojali also showed the Azerbaijani side that Armenians would not be intimidated. But if intimidation was a motive for Khojali, it only led to more savagery: the Azerbaijani side committed its own smaller massacre at the village of Maragha in April, after which the bodies of at least forty-three Armenian villagers were discovered and buried.

In immediate strategic terms, the capture of Khojali in early 1992 lifted pressure off the Armenians, who now had an airfield they could use to receive supplies by helicopter from Armenia. However, the artillery duel between the towns of Shusha and Stepanakert continued. Stepanakert, lying in an exposed plain, was still battered by artillery and ran short of supplies and medicine. This made Shusha the next Armenian target. Again, the Armenian side benefited from internal political strife in Azerbaijan. Built as a fortress, Shusha should have been relatively easy to hold. But most of the Azerbaijani defenders simply left, and Armenians captured the town on May 8–9 after a battle that cost the lives of 300 people. Shusha was taken virtually intact, but Armenian volunteer fighters set fire to the fine old town, and most of it was reduced to ruins in a few hours. To this day, despite substantial rebuilding in recent years, Shusha (called Shushi by the Armenians) is a ghostly place with only a fraction of its former population (see "Shusha" box).

The fall of Shusha was quickly followed by another Azerbaijani catastrophe, as Lachin, the Azerbaijani town linking Armenia and Karabakh, was abandoned and captured by the Armenians. With the "Lachin corridor" open, volunteers, arms, and supplies flowed into Karabakh. After the war, this road was upgraded with money from the Armenian diaspora to become the best-quality road in the South Caucasus, while Armenian settlers began to move into Lachin. Lachin remains one of the most problematic issues in the Karabakh dispute. For Azerbaijanis, it is a fully Azerbaijani region that cannot be subject to compromise; for Armenians, it is a "road of life" that cannot be relinquished.

A Widening Conflict

The intricate geography of Karabakh, the failure of peace initiatives, and an influx of Soviet weaponry all made the conflict burst the boundaries of Nagorny Karabakh itself and become a wider war. This began in the summer of 1992, when the Azerbaijani side regained the initiative. After the fall of Mutalibov, the Popular Front was in the ascendant, and Abulfaz Elchibey was elected Azerbaijan's second president in June 1992. Elchibey briefly rode a wave of patriotic support and launched a new offensive in Karabakh. The Armenian-populated Shaumian region north of Nagorny Karabakh fell, and then Azerbaijanis, assisted by Russian tanks, rolled onward through the northern districts of Karabakh itself.

The Azerbaijanis also benefited more from a handout of Soviet military equipment that was agreed on in May 1992 at a meeting of post-Soviet states in Tashkent. A limit was set on the amount of weapons to be handed over to newly independent republics from Soviet bases on their territory, but in practice a combination of "money, personal contacts, and lots of vodka," in the words of one Armenian, meant that a lot of arms were transferred through the back door.[13] Azerbaijan had been home to many more military units than Armenia and therefore received more weapons. According to Ter-Petrosian, this imbalance persuaded the Russian government to supply him with sufficient weapons so that "we were completely compensated for the gap between us and Azerbaijan. And in 1994, we were on the same level." He insists: "They never gave more than the balance."[14]

The Azerbaijanis' military gains melted away in early 1993 as internal divisions undermined them. The vast Kelbajar district, north of Lachin and situated between Armenia and Karabakh, was left undefended. In April 1993, the Armenians attacked and captured it within a few days. Hundreds of civilians, many of them Azerbaijani Kurds, perished while fleeing over the mountains.

The occupation of Kelbajar, an entire region of Azerbaijan outside Nagorny Karabakh, drew a stern international response. The Turkish government had been sending cargoes of European wheat to Armenia by rail across their common border in what it was hoped would be a prelude to a normalization of relations between the two states. After the Kelbajar operation, the Turks closed the border in solidarity with Azerbaijan. The United Nations passed Resolution 822, the first of four resolutions on the conflict, calling on both sides to cease hostilities but specifically demanding an "immediate withdrawal of all occupying forces from the Kelbajar district and other recently occupied areas of Azerbaijan."

In Azerbaijan, the defeat triggered a loss of confidence in the already erratic presidency of Elchibey. His government collapsed very quickly. On June 4, the renegade colonel Suret Husseinov raised a rebellion in Ganja, having conveniently taken over almost all the weaponry of the recently departed Russian airborne division in the town. Within two weeks, Elchibey had fled the capital. The parliament invited Heidar Aliev to return to assist Azerbaijan against the rebels. In the event, Aliev, the political veteran and heavyweight, swept all before him. He was first elected speaker of parliament, then engineered a no-confidence vote in Elchibey, and then was himself elected president on October 3, 1993.[15]

During the four months of confusion after one president lost office and before another gained it, Azerbaijan lost a huge swathe of territory to the Armenians east and south of Nagorny Karabakh. This was effectively when the war was lost. The towns of Aghdam, Fizuli, Jebrail, and Kubatly were abandoned along with their surrounding regions. Civilians stayed behind longer than soldiers, who did not know who their leaders were. It was less a case of systematic expulsion of people than of people fleeing ahead of an enemy advance. Casualties were light, and the towns and villages were captured virtually intact—only later would they be looted and stripped by Armenian military entrepreneurs. One jaundiced Armenian observer called the operations "military tourism."

The human effect of this was that around 350,000 Azerbaijani civilians fled the Armenian advance in improvised refugee caravans that ended up in makeshift camps. It was one of the biggest refugee exoduses Europe had seen since the Second World War. Even if the official figure of one million refugees or IDPs was an exaggeration, a more accurate number of about 750,000 displaced (about 190,000 from Soviet Armenia and at least 550,000 from Karabakh and its surrounding territories) was still staggeringly high for such a small country, amounting to about one-tenth of the total population.

The veteran returns. Azerbaijani nationalist president Abulfaz Elchibey (*left*)
together with the man about to replace him, Soviet-era leader Heidar Aliev (*center*),
Baku, 1993. Halid Askerov.

For years, the displaced people lived in awful conditions, in schools,
sanatoria, and tent camps in some of the bleakest and hottest parts of central
Azerbaijan. Some even lived in rusting train carriages. There were accusations
that the Azerbaijani government was deliberately letting them live in these
conditions in order to drum up sympathy from the outside world—and
that corrupt officials were pocketing aid money intended for the refugees.
Gradually they were rehoused, with the last camps being shut down in 2007.
Even so, the IDPs are still a marginal group in Azerbaijani society, facing
problems in finding education and jobs and having almost no political repre-
sentation, despite their large numbers.

Aliev came to office—or back to the office he had left in 1982—in
October 1993 with an unlikely 98.8 percent of the vote. He lambasted his
predecessors, vowing that he would build the Azerbaijani state anew. He
disbanded thirty-three battalions loyal to the Popular Front and had many
commanders arrested. He thereby rid himself of a political threat but faced
the challenge of building a new army. For two months, Aliev negotiated with
the Armenians, holding secret talks with Karabakh Armenian leader Robert
Kocharian, but at the same time he publicly prepared his country for war.

As talks again stalled, he sanctioned a new offensive. In the words of Aliev's Armenian counterpart, Ter-Petrosian, "real war began on 17 December 1993 and lasted until 12 May, 1994. That was a war, when both sides had real armies." In the winter campaign between December and February, casualty figures skyrocketed, with the Azerbaijanis losing perhaps 4,000 men and the Armenians 2,000. In the single bloodiest episode of the war, about 1,500 young Azerbaijani soldiers died after a failed offensive in the Kelbajar region. They were crushed by artillery as they tried to flee to safety through the Omar Pass in the mountains to the north of Kelbajar.

In the spring of 1994, both sides were exhausted, and casualties were mounting. Aliev could see that with the exception of some small gains, his military strategy had failed. The Armenians, having conquered wholly or partly seven Azerbaijani regions, had dramatically shortened the frontline around Nagorny Karabakh and had an incentive to make peace. The two states' leaders used their speakers of parliament and commanders to do the public diplomacy for them—neither president ended up signing the final truce. Russian envoy Vladimir Kazimirov negotiated a ceasefire that came into effect on May 12, 1994. Grachev then invited his military counterparts to Moscow to try to implement what he thought would be the second part of the deal, the deployment of a contingent of 1,800 Russian peacekeepers to the Karabakh frontline. Azerbaijani defense minister Mamedrafi Mamedov refused to agree to the Russian soldiers—a position in which he was tacitly supported by the Armenian side. The truce held, but it turned into a self-regulating ceasefire without any peacekeeping troops in between.

In Search of Peace

In May 1994, war ended in Nagorny Karabakh, but there was no peace. Mediation efforts had been under way for more than two years, since the formation of the so-called Minsk Group in the spring of 1992 by the forty-nine states of the Conference for Security and Cooperation in Europe (CSCE; later the OSCE). The initial idea had been for a peace conference in the newly independent state of Belarus, which had offered its capital, Minsk, as a location. When fighting continued, the Minsk Conference became the Minsk Group of nine countries.

During the war itself, the mediation effort of the Minsk Group was poorly coordinated, and Russian and Western diplomats began to act in rivalry with one another. Russia's envoy, Vladimir Kazimirov, increasingly acted on his own and mediated the ceasefire agreement of May 1994 almost single-handedly. The Minsk Group also suffered from a lack of resources. The Balkans peace processes had benefited from a much stronger mediation effort and the promise of peacekeepers to back them up. By contrast, no full-fledged Western peacekeepers were sent to any of the Caucasian conflict zones. Unlike the United Nations, the CSCE had no experience of peacekeeping and no funds for it. The Budapest summit of December 1994 (at which the CSCE turned into the OSCE) devoted much of its time to fixing this problem. It approved a mandate for the organization's first ever peacekeeping force to be deployed when an overall political agreement was reached.

The black-and-white positions both sides had taken since 1988 persisted in even stronger form into the postwar negotiations. Both of the new states of Armenia and Azerbaijan had been built around the Karabakh issue, so any compromise on it looked like the betrayal of a sacred cause. Unlike any other issue in Armenia or Azerbaijan, Karabakh has what the Armenian scholar Alexander Iskandarian calls "frozen potential," the ability to bring tens or even hundreds of thousands of people out into the streets in support of a sacred cause. Very few people believe in making concessions to the other side. In February 2009, an opinion poll in Azerbaijan found that 70 percent of respondents opposed any kind of compromise. Only 0.1 percent of those questioned supported the option of independence for Nagorny Karabakh, and only 0.9 percent the idea of the highest possible autonomy. On the Armenian side, views are exactly the opposite, with polls suggesting that barely 1 percent of the population favors an option that puts Karabakh under Azerbaijani sovereignty.

These mutually contradictory positions have made for constant wrangling over the format of negotiations. The Azerbaijani side sees the Karabakh dispute as a land grab of Azerbaijani territory by Armenia and therefore insists that the Karabakh Armenians are not genuine actors in themselves— if the Karabakh Armenians are to be represented, they argue, it should be as one of two communities from the province, standing in opposition to Karabakh's Azerbaijanis. Armenians assert that the dispute stems from the Karabakh Armenians' desire to decide their own future and break away from Azerbaijan and that they should therefore take the lead in talks with Baku, with the government in Yerevan playing the role of interested bystander. The Baku-Yerevan approach eventually became the established one, and since 1997, the Karabakh Armenians have not been formally represented at talks, even though their territory is at the heart of the dispute. The Azerbaijanis of

Karabakh are even more forgotten players, having neither their lands or an elected government nor any status in the negotiations. The absence of the Karabakhis has certainly undermined trust in the peace process.

Victory in the conflict was a bittersweet experience for the Armenian side. Armenia emerged from the end of the war formally victorious but in a parlous economic state. A series of winters with closed borders had reduced Armenia to premodern conditions with almost no electricity. The trees of Yerevan were chopped down for firewood, and citizens lived by candlelight and kerosene stoves. The popularity of the government of Ter-Petrosian dived, and he only won reelection in September 1996 after a highly disputed election that saw angry opposition supporters storming the parliament building and tanks on the streets.

The military victory had handed great power to the "Karabakh Party," an alliance of Karabakh politicians and Armenian generals. In Karabakh, a former mechanic turned general named Samvel Babayan ran the territory as a personal fiefdom. In Armenia, a veterans' group led by Defense Minister Vazgen Sargsyan captured large sections of the economy. In 1997, the Karabakh Party began to take over Armenia itself. Karabakh Armenian leader and war hero Kocharian was made prime minister of Armenia by Ter-Petrosian but began to challenge his president. Kocharian and his allies held a much harder line on compromise than Ter-Petrosian, who was prepared to do a deal with Baku to see Armenia break out of its isolation. At the end of 1997, Ter-Petrosian pressed ahead with a peace plan but met resistance from Kocharian and his allies. Support for Ter-Petrosian ebbed away, and in February 1998 he was forced to resign. Kocharian was elected president the following month, and in 1999 the powerful Vazgen Sargsyan become Armenia's new prime minister.

Azerbaijan's veteran leader Aliev preferred not to experiment with democracy and began to build a strong semiauthoritarian state to replace the fragile but pluralistic country he had inherited. Aliev faced down two attempted coup d'états and rid himself of a string of potential rivals. The country's nascent democratic institutions were brought under suffocating control. While slowly and methodically consolidating his power at home, Aliev worked to balance his country's foreign interests as well by signing a contract with international companies to develop Caspian Sea oil fields (see chapter 6). When the first "early oil" began flowing, Azerbaijan began to feel a new confidence that it could use its growing economic power to match Armenia.

A Karabakhi president. Robert Kocharian, elected president of Armenia (*center*), with the man he replaced, Levon Ter-Petrosian (*right*), Yerevan, 1998. Ruben Mangasarian.

In Armenia, once the Karabakh Party gained office through Kocharian in 1998, it showed no signs of relinquishing it. Kocharian, who had personally fought in the conflict, seemed to pin his hopes on a settlement that would straightforwardly confirm an Armenian victory. In April 1999, he and Aliev began to negotiate directly with one another and discussed a new option, a version of a "land swap" that would see Armenia grant a land corridor between Azerbaijan and its exclave of Nakhichevan across Armenian territory in return for Azerbaijani concessions over Karabakh.

The new peace plan was derailed by a savage outbreak of bloodshed in the Armenian parliament. On October 27, a gang of gunmen burst into the parliament building, denouncing the politicians inside as "bloodsuckers," and opened fire. Eight people were killed, including then parliamentary speaker Karen Demirchian and prime minister Vazgen Sargsyan. After a tense night, the gunmen, led by an unstable extremist named Nairi Hunanian, surrendered. Conspiracy theories immediately flourished that the gunmen had been acting on orders to sabotage a Karabakh peace deal, but the available evidence still points to the leading gunman being a loner with a grudge against the Armenian political elite.

In 2000, Aliev and Kocharian pressed ahead with a new plan that involved Azerbaijan basically handing over the sovereignty of Nagorny Karabakh to Armenia in return for big concessions on other issues. Aliev, a lonely autocrat, discussed the plan with no one. The Minsk Group mediators got as far as calling a peace conference in Key West, Florida, in April 2001 to take the plan to a new level. But when Aliev returned to Baku and discussed his ideas with his inner circle, its members strongly opposed him. Kocharian had been more positive but had not signed fully onto the plan, which simply faded away. The deadlock revealed a recurring vicious circle in the peace process: the semiauthoritarian leaders are reluctant to open up the issue of compromise over Karabakh to wider debate inside their societies; the societies remain stuck with black-and-white views on the conflict, hoping for a full victory; without a wider constituency pressing for change, the presidents have no mandate for peace in their negotiations.[16]

The mediators had tried to hurry the presidents at Key West for the simple reason that Aliev was getting older and sicker. In April 1999, he underwent heart surgery at the age of seventy-five, making everyone acutely aware that the whole of the Azerbaijani state depended on a man with uncertain health. In the summer of 2003, a few months before the next scheduled presidential elections, Aliev fell terminally ill. He died in December 2003, having barely managed to hand on power to his inexperienced son Ilham. Ilham Aliev was elected president in a controversial election in October, during which police broke up opposition protests by force.

In 2004, the Armenian and Azerbaijani foreign ministers met in Prague and began to work on a new framework plan that came to be known as the "Prague Principles." They foresaw a phased resolution of the conflict, with the most difficult issue of the status of Nagorny Karabakh being postponed to a later date. The idea was promising, but progress was painfully slow. After a failed round of negotiations in 2006 in the French town of Rambouillet, one negotiator speculated that the two presidents might have agreed to jointly reject the deal on the table. Talking details was one thing; actually committing one's country to a deal was another. In the words of one foreign observer, "Putting a signature on that paper is terra incognita. Both leaders are instinctively cautious. Why make that move?"

So long as Armenia was ruled by Karabakhis, for whom the defense of their homeland was the prime issue, compromise would always be difficult. In 2008, one Karabakh Armenian leader stepped down in favor of another. Robert Kocharian served out his second term as president, and Serzh

Sargsyan, his long-term associate and former defense minister and prime minister, ran to become president in his place. But the transition was not as smooth as they had anticipated. Controversy and bloodshed again marred an election in the Caucasus. Sargsyan faced an unexpectedly strong challenge from former president Levon Ter-Petrosian, who made a political comeback and rallied a large section of public opinion behind him. When Sargsyan was declared the outright winner, the opposition staged ten days of street protests in Yerevan. On the night of March 1, riot police moved in to break up the demonstrators. Many were savagely beaten. The protestors tried to regroup, but the government declared a state of emergency, and leading opposition activists were arrested. At least ten people were killed. The violence hung over Sargsyan's entire ten-year presidency, even after those who had been imprisoned were released. It also marked one of the prisoners, a young journalist named Nikol Pashinian, who a decade later made another—much more successful—effort to defeat Sargsyan and his old guard.

Closer to War than Peace

On April 2, 2016, fighting broke out on the Line of Contact dividing Armenian and Azerbaijani forces east of Nagorny Karabakh. Over four days of warfare worse than anything the region had seen since the 1994 ceasefire agreement, up to 200 people died, including several civilians. The Azerbaijani army recaptured two small pockets of territory, but the psychological boost for Baku was more important than the physical one: Azerbaijan was able to proclaim a military success for the first time in more than two decades, reversing long-held feelings of humiliation. Russia negotiated a ceasefire, although nothing was signed on paper.[17]

The fighting reflected many realities, first of all the disturbing fact that the longest-running dispute in the former Soviet Union was nearer to war than to peace. In the more than twenty years following the ceasefire, the conflict zone had become heavily militarized and extremely dangerous, while the only thing keeping the peace remained the modest mechanisms devised in the 1990s to halt the low-tech fighting of that era. There were no peacekeepers, and the truce on the 160-mile-long "Line of Contact" was monitored by just six observers from the OSCE. The Azerbaijani government in particular had used oil revenues for several years to spend up to $4 billion annually on its military budget and acquire modern equipment. In the mid-1990s the ceasefire line had been a quiet network of trenches across which conscript soldiers would occasionally take potshots at one another and sometimes meet to exchange cigarettes in no-man's-land. By 2016 it had become the most militarized zone in Europe. The two sides used battle tanks, helicopters, and heavy artillery. Azerbaijan used an Israeli-built "kamikaze drone" to attack an Armenian bus. Moreover, this short outbreak of fighting demonstrated that the dispute was now a full interstate conflict between Armenia and Azerbaijan, and that any future war would fully involve both countries. The delivery to Armenia of Russian-made long-range Iskander missiles in late 2016 was another episode in an escalating game of bluff.

Another unfortunate—and inevitable—reality was that the Nagorny Karabakh conflict had slipped down the international agenda since the 1990s, crowded out by other fresher and more urgent global issues, such as the conflicts in Iraq, Afghanistan, Sudan, and Syria. The protracted Karabakh conflict could at best command the attention of the leaders of the three Minsk Group "co-chair" countries—France, Russia, and the United States—once or twice a year. That left the diplomatic work to middle-level officials and the burden of resolving the conflict to the presidents of Armenia and Azerbaijan—a burden they were increasingly reluctant to take on.

Russia remains the most important foreign actor in the region. But it is a mistake to conclude that, as in other post-Soviet disputes in Georgia and Ukraine, Moscow is instigating or controlling the conflict. While it has a military alliance with Armenia—a commitment that only serves to fuel suspicions on both sides about Moscow's intentions—Russia also has strong interests in Azerbaijan and sells weapons to both sides (with the Armenians receiving them at discounted prices). It is wary of taking on the burden of "owning" a conflict that could spoil its relations with either one side or the other. At the same time, Russia remains the most active mediator of the conflict. The most serious attempt at peacemaking in the last few years was carried out by Russian president Dmitry Medvedev, who brought his two fellow presidents to an unsuccessful peace summit in the town of Kazan on the Volga in 2011. Since then, Russian foreign minister Sergei Lavrov has led negotiations.

Medvedev and Lavrov both worked on the basis of a sophisticated framework peace proposal known as the Basic Principles or Madrid Principles that dated back to the 2007 OSCE summit in Madrid, when the mediators filed a short document of fourteen or fifteen points. The document demanded compromises from both sides and tried to thread the needle of resolving the issue at the heart of the dispute, the sovereign status of the disputed territory of Nagorny Karabakh. The framework agreement foresaw a phased Armenian withdrawal from the Azerbaijani territories around Karabakh. In the meantime, the Karabakh Armenians would be offered the carrot of "interim status," which would fall short of independence but give them some kind of international legitimacy. Eventually, the Armenians were promised a popular vote on the status of the territory. But here lay the rub. The vote was projected to take part on an unspecified date so far in the future that it was unofficially dubbed a "neverendum." That was politically difficult for both the Armenian and Azerbaijani presidents to sell to their peoples. On the Armenian side, the promise of independence was too remote, while for the Azerbaijani leader, even agreeing to a vote on secession long hence would be condemned by many as a betrayal. Both countries also drew encouragement from events in modern Europe, which superficially seemed to support contrary principles. Kosovo's declaration of independence in 2008, recognized by dozens of countries, heartened Armenian secessionists. The widespread condemnation of Russia's annexation of Crimea in 2014 and support for Ukraine's territorial integrity reinforced Azerbaijani determination.

The four-day war also demonstrated apparently high levels of support in each society for the fighting. There had been hope that mutual aggression would diminish over time, but in April 2016, some of the most bellicose voices were those of younger people. This should perhaps not be surprising considering that, unlike their Soviet-era parents, most members of the younger generation had never met an Armenian or an Azerbaijani in the flesh and derived their views of the other side in the conflict from patriotic media. In Azerbaijan there were spontaneous demonstrations in support of the fighting. On both sides there were reports of young people volunteering to go to the front.

Any visitor to the Armenian and Azerbaijani sides of the Karabakh conflict will confirm that the two peoples live in parallel worlds and that ordinary people, from senior ministers to impoverished villagers, share the same national narrative that justice is on "our" side and that Nagorny Karabakh "belongs to us." Some three decades after the dispute broke out in 1988, Azerbaijan still lives with a national grievance that its lands are occupied (the repeated figure is 20 percent, although the actual amount of territory under Armenian control is around 13.6 percent, if one includes Karabakh itself).

Azerbaijani frustration is understandable, but it does not point any way out of the impasse, and anti-Armenian aggression in Azerbaijan manifests itself in ugly ways that reduce the chance for peace and the return of territories. Anti-Armenian rhetoric has intensified in recent years. Defense minister Zakir Hasanov has claimed that the Republic of Armenia is Azerbaijani land and in 2015 warned that "the Karabakh land will burn under the feet of the Armenian invaders."[18]

Veteran Azerbaijani author Akram Aylisli was vilified after he published a novel in 2012 entitled *Stone Dreams*, which touched on the theme of Armenian-Azerbaijani friendship in the twentieth century and portrayed Armenians in a positive light. Aylisli was stripped of literary awards; his wife and son lost their jobs. Protestors demonstrated outside his house with placards reading "Shame!," "Armenian," and "Why did you sell your soul to the enemy?"[19] The episode came at the start of a broader crackdown on Azerbaijani civil society that targeted several individuals who had been involved in peaceful dialogue initiatives with Armenians. Perhaps even more disturbing was the way the Azerbaijani government welcomed home one of its officers, Ramil Safarov, who had served six years in a Hungarian jail for murdering a fellow Armenian officer, Gurgen Margarian, on a NATO training course in Budapest. Safarov was released from prison in 2012 and sent to Baku, supposedly to serve more time in an Azerbaijani jail. Instead he was greeted with a presidential pardon, flowers, a promotion, and a free apartment. The Azerbaijani authorities later hid Safarov from view, perhaps having belatedly understood how the accolade they had given to a convicted murderer had hurt their own image and the Karabakh peace process. But the damage had already been done.

Public Armenian rhetoric is less aggressive on the Karabakh question, but it does not have to be, given that the Armenians were the victors on the ground in the war of the 1990s. In their own way, however, the Armenians hold just as tough a line, especially on the issue of the seven Azerbaijani territories around Karabakh that they control, either wholly or partially. The captured territories were ordinary regions of Azerbaijan before the war began and home to more than half a million people, almost none of them Armenian. When the Armenians captured these lands, they initially called them a "security zone" or "buffer zone"—lands to be handed back to Azerbaijani control in return for a good deal on the sovereignty of Nagorny Karabakh itself. That is still the official Armenian position. However, in recent years, public Armenian discourse has termed these lands "occupied territories," and in news broadcasts, weather forecasts, and maps, the distinction between Armenia, Karabakh, and the occupied territories has become increasingly blurred. Although few people live there, new roads have been built across them. In 2010, the Karabakh Armenian authorities announced they were giving the Azerbaijani towns new names, with Aghdam, for instance, being called Akna. This altering of the facts on the ground is less noisy than the aggressive Azerbaijani rhetoric but just as dangerous. It could be called "passive aggressive."

Decreasing international attention has left the leaders of Armenia and Azerbaijan as the chief conductors of the negotiating process. The leaders know the problem intimately and know how the nonresolution of the conflict holds back their two countries from development and prosperity. They occasionally make public remarks that hint at the serious discussions they have had with one another behind closed doors. Yet almost all their public rhetoric both reflects and shapes the public narrative of "no surrender" to the other side.

In that sense the leaders are trapped in a vicious circle, created in part by their own stance. The first political priority for them is staying in power. The ongoing Karabakh conflict is a useful short-term instrument in sticking to that goal: opposition forces can be kept off balance by appeals to patriotism, and democratization is held in check by nationalist rhetoric.

Yet even if the short-term political goal is achieved, this hardline stance limits the leaders' ability to make compromises with the other side and build a constituency for peace. It thus perpetuates the risk of war and precludes the chance of either side building a better future for its nation-state. The leaders are trapped in a situation they have helped create.

It is worth taking a step back to consider that there is nothing primordial about the Armenian-Azerbaijani conflict. There is no "ancient hatred" between the two national groups, as evidenced by the continued existence of mixed Armenian-Azerbaijani villages in Georgia just outside the conflict zone where the two communities live together peacefully. People of the two nationalities still do business together in Georgia, Iran, and Russia and sometimes joke that they prefer dealing with one another than with the Georgians. Nor is the dispute over the territorial status of Nagorny Karabakh the most insoluble one in the world; compromises have been struck over even thornier problems.

In that sense, the conflict is "all in the mind," about narratives of national identity and political allegiance that are in flux and could change one day in a different political and global environment. But, as with all conflicts in the Caucasus, identity is also bound up with fears about survival and security in their most intimate senses: both Armenians and Azerbaijanis are apprehensive that their lives will be put at risk if any missteps are made in meeting the other side halfway. That is a problem that only the big powers, with their ability to deploy peacekeepers and to guarantee an internationally binding agreement, are able to enforce, if they can muster the interest to care again about this half-forgotten conflict in the hills of the Caucasus.

5

Georgia's Conflicts:

Abkhazia and South Ossetia

Gamsakhurdia's Revolution

In 1989, Georgia rejected Soviet rule and embraced revolutionary nationalism. Previously, there had been reason to believe that Soviet Georgia might be at the forefront of Gorbachev's perestroika reforms. In 1987, Gorbachev and his Georgian foreign minister, Eduard Shevardnadze, had jointly authorized the release of the film *Repentance* by Georgian director Tengiz Abuladze, which had lifted a twenty-five-year taboo on discussion of the killings of the Stalin era. In fact, nationalist fervor had not been far below the surface. As with Nagorny Karabakh, a reemerging majority-minority dispute lit the fuse. The issue was the autonomous Black Sea region of Abkhazia. On March 18, 1989, the Abkhaz convened a "People's Forum" in the village of Lykhny at which about 30,000 people called for Abkhazia to be separated from Soviet Georgia, given the status of a full Soviet republic, and placed under special rule from Moscow.

The meeting unleashed a wave of counterprotests by Georgians led by two former dissidents, Merab Kostava and Zviad Gamsakhurdia. They denounced not only the Abkhaz for wanting to break up Georgia but also "colonialist" Moscow for being behind the Abkhaz initiative. While in Armenia and Azerbaijan many activists blamed the other side rather than Moscow, the Georgian movement took an openly anti-Russian and anti-Soviet line from the beginning—for Georgians, the "other" was Moscow itself. Some

Georgian intellectuals tried to form a reformist Popular Front organization in support of Gorbachev's perestroika reforms but never gained popular support, having the ground cut from under them by the rush of events.

The radicals set the agenda. Merab Kostava, a music teacher, who had been Georgia's most admired dissident in the 1970s, led a campaign denouncing the Abkhaz, the Ossetians, and Gorbachev. But his death in a car accident in October 1989 handed the mantle of leadership to an even stronger nationalist, his protégé Zviad Gamsakhurdia. Gamsakhurdia was an extraordinary individual who inspired both loathing from his critics and devotion from his followers, who came to be known as "Zviadists." He had an aura and somewhat unworldly presence about him, leading one observer to write, "His sad eyes and deathbed pallor were alarming, as though the man hadn't seen sunlight in years."[1] In part, Gamsakhurdia derived his success from being both inside and outside the Tbilisi elite. His father Konstantin was a famous novelist, and the young Gamsakhurdia also became a talented writer and translator before joining the dissident movement. Yet his family homeland and base of support was in Mingrelia, the western province of Georgia, with a distinct identity of its own. Gamsakhurdia believed he had been entrusted with a special role within the Georgian nation, talking about Georgia's "spiritual mission" and the "ethnogeny of Georgians."

Gamsakhurdia and Kostava held rallies in Abkhazia in the spring of 1989 and then moved their protests to Tbilisi, where a crowd of several thousand camped out on Rustaveli Avenue for several days. By the second day, there were more shouts of "Down with Russian imperialism!" than anti-Abkhaz slogans. On the night of April 8–9, the Soviet army garrison in Tbilisi intervened and broke up the rally with spades and teargas. One teenage girl was beaten to death, and eighteen others died, almost all women, trampled in a stampede and unable to breathe because of the gas. The killings shocked the whole of the Soviet Union. The Politburo dispatched Shevardnadze to Tbilisi to try to calm passions and ensured that the party leaders were sacked, but a flame of anger had been lit.[2] The moral credit was now all on the side of the nationalist opposition, and Georgians saw loyalty to Moscow as complicity in murder. Five months later, an opinion poll recorded that 89 percent of Georgians wanted independence, an even higher level of support than among Estonians.[3]

Georgia began to hurtle toward secession from the Soviet Union. The Communist Party leadership, which had lost credibility after the killings, vied with the opposition to assert its patriotic credentials. In November, Georgia's

Supreme Soviet voted to condemn the Bolshevik takeover of Georgia in 1921 as an illegal act of annexation. New elections were called. Ahead of time, Gamsakhurdia campaigned for a new electoral law that banned parties that were not represented throughout Georgia from standing in the polls. It was a transparent device to exclude minorities such as Abkhaz, Ossetians, Armenians, and Azerbaijanis from gaining seats in the new parliament.

An American reporter described the national mood as "Democracy with a Vengeance The nationalist movement was deeply divided. Political groups now carried small arms they had acquired at cut-rate prices from Soviet soldiers. A Georgian academic said, "We have passed through the romantic stage and now we are in what I call the 'Afghanistan period' of Georgia."[4] The most prominent armed group was the so-called Mkhedrioni (translated as "knights" or "horsemen"), founded by former playwright, bank robber, and mafia boss Jaba Ioseliani. The Mkhedrioni warriors sported a macho look that was almost a parody of Georgian male swagger; combining sunglasses and leather jackets with large amulets bearing a portrait of Saint George that they wore on their chests. One of Ioseliani's fighters memorably told a foreign reporter that

Savior or destroyer? Georgia's first nationalist leader, Zviad Gamsakhurdia, leading a demonstration, Tbilisi, 1989. Vladimir Valishvili.

Mkhedrioni was a "paramilitary charity organization."[5] Along with patriotism and machismo, the third defining element of the group was its roots in the criminal underworld. Former gangster Ioseliani used his warriors to take control of large sections of Georgia's economy, such as the tobacco and gasoline trades.

In October 1990, Gamsakhurdia's Round Table bloc won a resounding victory in elections to Georgia's reconstituted legislature, the Supreme Soviet, and he was elected speaker of the new parliament. He then rolled out a stream of resolutions and legislation aimed at dismantling Soviet power and building a new Georgian national state. The Supreme Soviet unilaterally abolished South Ossetia's autonomous status. It recalled Georgian young men from serving in the Soviet army and established a National Guard— effectively a new Georgian army. Then, on the second anniversary of the bloodshed on Rustaveli Avenue, April 9, 1991, Gamsakhurdia declared full independence from the Soviet Union. The text of the declaration made no mention of Abkhaz or Ossetians, saying: "The territory of the sovereign Republic of Georgia is united and indivisible."[6]

In May, Gamsakhurdia was elected president of Georgia with 86.5 percent of the vote, but the country was already in a state of collapse. Despite predicting that Georgia would become "a second Switzerland" within years, he did nothing to reform the economy. Georgia descended from being one of the Soviet Union's most prosperous republics into dire poverty; its gross domestic product (GDP) dropped by 73 percent between 1991 and 1994. Gamsakhurdia showed no interest in democratic institutions and appointed "prefects" to run Georgia's regions. A new opposition quickly mobilized. The language of political debate was abusive and threatening—a problem that persists, in a milder form, in Georgian political life today. Gamsakhurdia denounced his opponents as "enemies of Georgia" and "agents of the Kremlin." Opposition leader Gia Chanturia called Gamsakhurdia a "fascist" "KGB agent." Chanturia was arrested and jailed along with several dozen other political prisoners.

In August 1991, Gamsakhurdia provoked more controversy by failing to condemn the coup plot in Moscow against Gorbachev, describing it as the internal affair of another country. Shortly afterward, he declared a state of emergency, but he quickly faced armed rebellion from the leader of the National Guard he had created, the former sculptor Tengiz Kitovani, allied with his disaffected prime minister, Tengiz Sigua. The third leader, Ioseliani, joined them after being sprung from jail. This triumvirate moved to overthrow Gamsakhurdia in December 1991, probably with the aid of Soviet troops. Gamsakhurdia retreated to a bunker in the parliament building as heavy fighting raged through central Tbilisi. When Gamsakhurdia finally fled the country on January 6, 1992, at least 113 people had been killed, and the center of the city had been gutted. The ousted president fled and eventually settled in exile in Chechnya in the North Caucasus. His supporters, the Zviadists, fought a low-level war of resistance in western Georgia in which the Mkhedrioni ravaged the region. Gamsakhurdia himself died in 1993 on an ill-fated return mission to his home region of Georgia.

The outbreak of ethnic nationalism Georgia suffered in 1989–91 was so extreme it resembled a collective national fever. In Europe around this time, probably only Serbia experienced something similar. All Georgia's minorities, not just Abkhaz and Ossetians but also Armenians and Azeris, complained of discrimination. It is important to stress that Gamsakhurdia did not seize power but was elected president in May 1991 with a strong public endorsement. Very few people were able to stand against the current. One of those who did, the philosopher Merab Mamardashvili, was vilified by Gamsakhurdia and died an early death in 1990. He famously objected, "If this is the choice of my people, then I am against my people," arguing that Georgia had only replaced one authoritarian system with another.

Georgia has come a long way since 1991, but the appeal of Gamsakhurdia has not entirely faded. He is still revered by diehard nationalists and in Mingrelia, where his supporters were subjected to persecution after his fall. An official figure of hate under Shevardnadze, he was partially rehabilitated by Georgia's third president, Mikheil Saakashvili. In April 2007, Saakashvili had his predecessor's body returned from Chechnya and reburied in a grand ceremony in the national pantheon overlooking Tbilisi. Saakashvili told mourners that Gamsakhurdia was a "great statesman and patriot" and that his reburial was designed to "put an end to disunity in our society."

South Ossetia: Origins

The darkest legacy of Zviad Gamsakhurdia was a conflict in South Ossetia, that could have been avoided.

The Ossetians are a people related to Iranians and probably descended from the Scythian and Sarmatian peoples who inhabited what is now the southern steppes of Russia in the early medieval period. They have three subgroups: the most numerous Irons in the north, the Kudars in the south, and small numbers of Digors in the northwest, many of whom are Muslim. Most Ossetians are Orthodox Christian, but they still make pilgrimages to the shrines of pre-Christian pagan "saints" such as Wasilla, the patron of thunderstorms, and Uastyrji, who shares many traits with the Christian Saint George. The vast majority of Ossetians—currently around 450,000— have always lived in North Ossetia on the north side of the Caucasus. But the historical record also shows that Ossetians have lived south of the mountains for centuries and developed a distinct identity there. The Ossetian language, from the Iranian family, was barely written down until the early twentieth century. Since then, in one of the crazier examples of world language policy, it has had to change its script several times; a Cyrillic alphabet was adopted for the entire language in both North and South Ossetia only in 1954.

Ossetians were poor mountain people who came to the notice of the Russians mostly because their lands adjoined the main southerly route across the Caucasus. In the early nineteenth century, the military historian Vasily Potto wrote: "The subjugation of Ossetia ... was closely connected to the question of the safety of the Georgian Military Highway, which served as the only road linking Russia and Georgia."[7] Since then, geography and religion have given Ossetians a pro-Russian orientation. The Russian fortress of Vladikavkaz ("Rule over the Caucasus"), founded in 1784, eventually became the North Ossetian capital. Ossetians joined both the tsarist and Soviet army in large numbers, and they take pride in having produced more men decorated as "Heroes of the Soviet Union" per head of population than any other Soviet ethnic group. The North Ossetians benefited from this reputation in 1944 when their Muslim neighbors, the Ingush, were deported en masse by Stalin and North Ossetia was awarded Ingushetia's small and fertile Prigorodny region. The territorial dispute over this region was the cause of a small but brutal war between Ossetians and Ingush at the end of 1992.

South of the Caucasus, the Ossetian Kudars were concentrated in a region that came to be known as South Ossetia, north of the town of Gori and west of the Georgian Military Highway. The Tiflis province briefly contained an "Ossetian district" in the 1840s and 1850s, but many Georgians have long resisted the very concept of "South Ossetia," with its implied link to North Ossetia, as constituting a threat to the integrity of Georgia. In recent years, even Georgians who conceded that Abkhazia and Ajaria had the right to be autonomous regions denied the existence of South Ossetia. Instead, Georgians called the region Shida [Inner] Kartli, "Samachablo" (a reference to the estates of the nineteenth-century prince Machabeli), or "Tskhinvali region" after the region's main town, which used to have a larger population of Jews and Armenians than of Ossetians.[8]

On the ground, Ossetians and Georgians generally lived together harmoniously, and there were higher rates of intermarriage between Georgians and Ossetians than between Georgians and other ethnic groups. But South Ossetia's location and links to Russia made it a zone of conflict during periods of Georgian-Russian tension. The worst instance was in 1918–20, when the South Ossetians refused to be part of Menshevik Georgia and staged three uprisings with Bolshevik support.

In May 1920, South Ossetian Bolsheviks declared allegiance to Russia. Bolshevik foreign affairs commissar Giorgy Chicherin complained to the Georgian Menshevik government about an attack on the "Soviet Republic" of South Ossetia; the Georgian foreign ministry responded, "As you know well, the process of the re-creation of Georgia in its inalienable borders has not yet been completed," and, more starkly, "there is no South Ossetia within Georgia."[9] The Ossetian forces pushed south and captured Tskhinvali. In a situation that prefigured the war of August 2008, the Ossetian commander wanted to advance further south and capture the city of Gori, but on this occasion the Ossetians halted. The Georgian Menshevik People's Guard, commanded by Valiko Jugeli, then counterattacked and ravaged South Ossetia. Jugeli described the Ossetians as "our worst and most relentless enemies" and said, "These traitors should be cruelly punished. There is no other way." According to Soviet Ossetian sources, Menshevik guardsmen killed 4,800 people, burned fifty villages, and caused 25,000 refugees to flee over the mountains, many of whom died of hunger and disease. Two generations later, many South Ossetians were still retelling their grandparents' tragic stories from 1920.[10]

When the Bolsheviks overthrew the Menshevik government in Georgia in 1921, they promised to respect the rights of Georgia's minorities, and in 1922 the South Ossetian Autonomous Region was created. Ossetians moved in large numbers to the town they called Tskhinval and Georgians called Tskhinvali. In Soviet times, the region was a relatively poor province of Georgia but blessed with rich farmland. Tbilisi was much closer than Vladikavkaz, and South and North Ossetia were linked by road for the first time only in 1985, when the two-mile-long Roki Tunnel was built through the mountains.

Ossetians were a relatively small minority in Soviet Georgia. Around 65,000 lived in South Ossetia, about two-thirds of the total population. A further 100,000 Ossetians who lived in other parts of Georgia were especially well integrated; according to census data, they spoke the Georgian language more fluently than any other minority. In South Ossetia itself, Georgian and Ossetian villages were mixed up, and many people were trilingual in Ossetian, Georgian, and Russian. According to one estimate, about half the families in the region were of mixed nationality. The war of 1991–92 painfully divided many families.[11]

All this suggests that the South Ossetians could have reached a compromise with any reasonable government in Tbilisi. Small in number, strongly intermixed with the Georgians, and linked to their North Ossetian kin by only one road through the Roki Tunnel, they had no incentive for conflict. Even after the 1991–92 war, intercommunal relations were not irreparably damaged. Many Georgians fled the town of Tskhinvali, but—unlike in Abkhazia—most Georgian villages in South Ossetia stayed untouched, and their inhabitants carried on living there.

However, Gamsakhurdia's rhetoric appeared to threaten the Ossetians' very existence in Georgia. He described them (and other minorities) as *stumrebi*, or "guests," suggesting they were living in Georgia on the sufferance of their Georgian hosts. He said that mixed marriages threatened the survival of the Georgian nation.[12] Gamsakhurdia's prejudices were widely supported, and—as in the Armenian-Azerbaijani dispute— members of the intelligentsia often displayed more ethnic prejudice than easygoing villagers in South Ossetia itself. For example, the 1924 novel by the Georgian writer Mikheil Javakhishvili, *Hisan Jako,* with a crude and deceitful Ossetian protagonist at its center, was revived and made into a film.

Ordinary South Ossetians had a tradition of keeping their distance from political leaders of all types. However, in May 1988 they carried out a spectacular act of politics from below. A typhoid epidemic broke out in South Ossetia because of a contaminated water supply—an extraordinary blunder in an area blessed by abundant fresh mountain water—and a crowd of angry women physically ejected party leader Felix Sanakoyev from his office.

In 1989, the South Ossetians began to mobilize along national lines. A college lecturer named Alan Chochiev founded a movement called Adamon Nykhas ("People's Assembly" or "People's Word") and began to campaign for greater Ossetian national rights. He sent Gamsakhurdia a defiant letter. Chochiev was inspired by the Abkhaz nationalist movement, but in less sophisticated and smaller South Ossetia he failed to emerge as a strong leader, unlike Abkhazia's Vladislav Ardzinba. South Ossetia's numerous Georgians also began to complain of discrimination. A letter published in a Tbilisi newspaper in June 1989 from a local Georgian, Diana Machabeli, almost certainly had provocative intent but probably contained a kernel of truth as well. She wrote, "We should ask A. Chochiev if he was ever concerned about persecution of his Georgian 'brothers.' If you go into a shop [in South Ossetia] and ask a question in Georgian, you don't get an answer. Georgians do not get appointed to important jobs." In other words, the Georgians of South Ossetia faced the insecurity of being a "double minority," caught between Tskhinvali and Tbilisi.

The first confrontation flared over competing claims for Georgian and Ossetian to be the language of public life in Georgia and South Ossetia. The issue of status then raised its head, and a "war of laws" began like the one over Nagorny Karabakh began. On November 16, 1989, the South Ossetians proclaimed their region an autonomous republic (in other words, one step higher than their current status, on a level with Abkhazia), but the Tbilisi authorities rejected the declaration. One week later, on November 23—Giorgoba, or Saint George's Day, and a useful day to mobilize Georgians into action—more than 20,000 Georgians descended on Tskhinvali in a convoy of cars and buses. They were halted by an improvised group of South Ossetians who formed a human chain and put up barricades. Three days of violence followed in which at least six people were killed and dozens wounded.

In 1990, some younger Georgian nationalist leaders argued that confrontation with South Ossetia was a distraction from efforts to achieve the main goal of independence from Moscow. But Gamsakhurdia continued to inflame the situation, saying, "If [Ossetians] do not wish to live peacefully with us, then let them leave Georgia."[13] On September 20, the South Ossetians declared the creation of a new South Ossetian Soviet Democratic Republic separate from Georgia. On December 11, Georgia's new parliament, led by Gamsakhurdia, voted to abolish South Ossetia's autonomous status altogether, "taking into account the fact the South Ossetian Autonomous Region was formed in 1922 against the will of the native Georgian population living in this region and damaging the interests of the whole of Georgia."[14] The next day, the parliament declared a state of emergency in the newly renamed "Tskhinvali and Java Regions." Fighting immediately broke out. There was no mechanism for political negotiation: the South Ossetian local leader, Torez Kulumbegov, went for talks in Tbilisi but was arrested and imprisoned.

The South Ossetian War

In terms of lives lost, the 1991–92 war in South Ossetia was one of the less bloody post-Soviet conflicts.[15] Perhaps 1,000 people died. It was barely noticed by the international media. But at the time it was the worst internal conflict in the Soviet Union since the 1920s and devastating for a region with a population of fewer than 100,000 people. For years afterward, the physical scars of the fighting were visible in South Ossetia, and the playground of School No. 5 in Tskhinvali, where many of the Ossetians killed in the fighting were hastily buried, became an informal shrine to the dead. The repercussions of war were also felt by 100,000 Ossetians in other parts of Georgia who were sacked from their jobs or forced to sell their houses for token prices if they chose to flee to North Ossetia.[16]

South Ossetia

For twenty days in January 1991, there was street fighting in Tskhinvali, and the town was split in two before the Georgian militias withdrew into the hills. Loss of life was not greater mainly because of the primitive weapons being used. South Ossetian fighters converted unguided air-to-surface missiles taken from the helicopter regiment stationed near Tskhinvali into improvised shoulder-launched bazookas that they used in street fighting.[17] In March 1991, the American journalist Michael Dobbs found a place devastated by vindictive acts of violence:

> During a three-week occupation of Tskhinvali in January, Georgian militia units ransacked the Ossetian national theater. The plaster statue of Ossetia's national poet, Kosta Khetagurov, was decapitated. Monuments to Ossetians who fought with Soviet troops in World War II were smashed to pieces and thrown into the river. The Ossetians have repaid the Georgians in kind. About 10,000 Georgian residents of Tskhinvali have fled their homes in fear for their lives. Armed Ossetian bands have fired on Georgian villages. The news that six Georgians, including several policemen, had been killed during a recent shootout was received with grim satisfaction by some Ossetians.[18]

In early 1991, the first contours had were drawn of a geography of conflict that would recur in 2004 and 2008. South Ossetia is a mixed patchwork of Georgian and Ossetian settlements. Tskhinvali was under Ossetian control but under siege from Georgians on high ground around the town. Three of the four roads leading into Tskhinvali were under Georgian control. The fourth road out of the town passed north through a group of four Georgian villages in the Liakhvi River valley, which in their turn were surrounded by Ossetians. In this tangle of conflict, roadblocks were set up and hostages taken.

On April 29, the appetite for violence was dulled by a powerful earthquake that shook the northwestern Java region of South Ossetia and the Georgian region of Racha. It killed 200 people and destroyed nine-tenths of the houses in Java. Fighting resumed again in the autumn of 1991. The Georgians cut off gas and electricity from Tskhinvali, leaving its citizens in desperate conditions in the middle of winter. The Ossetians cut the Georgian villages off from the rest of Georgia. In December 1991 Medea, a Georgian woman from the village of Kemerti, told Human Rights Watch, "We have no groceries, no food, and no way to bring goods in. There is only one road to Tskhinvali, and soldiers shoot along it. To get food we have to go fifteen kilometers through thick woods, and it's dangerous."[19] Soviet interior ministry troops played an ambiguous role, their allegiance uncertain.

The change of regime in Tbilisi in the New Year of 1992 did not bring any new prospect of compromise. The Military Council, which had overthrown Gamsakhurdia, rejected the idea of restoring South Ossetia's autonomy, while the South Ossetians themselves voted massively in favor of full independence in a referendum.

In March 1992, the three men who had deposed Gamsakhurdia invited former party boss and Soviet foreign minister Shevardnadze back to Georgia to lead their administration and lend their putsch some badly needed legitimacy. Shevardnadze returned to a country that was de facto independent but had not been internationally recognized as such; its economy had collapsed, and it was effectively being run by armed militias. He could not even take up residence in government buildings, as they had been shattered by the street fighting of the previous winter.

Shevardnadze's first priority was the conflict in South Ossetia. On April 11, he publicly repented for what had occurred on Georgian television, saying, "It seems to me that the Georgian people cannot wipe away from itself this stain of bloodshed for many centuries."[20] However, he lacked the authority to change the situation on the ground. Heavier arms taken from abandoned military bases were pouring into the country for both sides. Different factions in the newly independent Russia became involved. Shevardnadze traveled to Tskhinvali on May 13 for talks. According to one report, he was in the town when it came under fire from Georgian militias.[21] Ceasefires broke down. The conflict then suddenly went into overdrive. On May 20, a column of Ossetian refugees traveling toward North Ossetia near the village of Zar was attacked by Georgian irregulars. Thirty-six civilians, mostly women, children, and old people, were killed. Although Shevardnadze strongly condemned the massacre, it ignited passions in North Ossetia like a firework. There were mass demonstrations in Vladikavkaz, demanding armed intervention. The road and the gas pipeline to Georgia were cut. On May 29, South Ossetia's Supreme Soviet formally declared independence. In North Ossetia on June 8, crowds consisting mainly of Ossetian refugees from Georgia encircled the army garrison outside Vladikavkaz and were rewarded with gifts of trucks, ammunition, firearms, and howitzers, which were immediately sent to South Ossetia.

The sudden escalation frightened the Georgian and Russian leadership into action. If South Ossetia itself was not a big priority for them, the wider crisis it could create was. On June 10, Shevardnadze met the North Ossetian leader, Akhsarbek Galazov, and the two men agreed to a joint statement. Galazov later said that Shevardnadze had overruled his Georgian colleagues and agreed on the need for a ceasefire and a long-term approach: "What is very important is that in this document, for the first time we moved away from the term Tskhinval region and called South Ossetia by its real name. In a conversation one on one, [Shevardnadze] told me, 'There's no need to hurry. The time will come and we will restore everything: there will be autonomy, there will be friendship, there will be normal economic and cultural relations between our peoples.'"[22]

However, the fighting continued and threatened to turn into a Russian-Georgian war. The political opponents of Yeltsin threatened the Georgians with war, and there were reports of Russian helicopters and Russian tanks attacking Georgian positions. This was the cue for direct contact between Yeltsin and Shevardnadze.[23] On June 24, 1992, the Georgian and Russian leaders met in the Black Sea resort of Dagomys and signed a peace agreement. Two incidents that happened on the same day showed how little Shevardnadze controlled Georgia at this point: in Tbilisi, Gamsakhurdia supporters briefly seized the television station before being driven out; in Sukhumi, the Georgian interior minister of Abkhazia was evicted from his offices and replaced by his Abkhaz counterpart.

The Dagomys agreement on South Ossetia was a short-term fix that turned into a long-term arrangement. It did not touch on any political issues and concentrated entirely on halting the fighting. It stipulated withdrawal of forces, demilitarization of the region, the withdrawal of the remaining ex-Soviet forces from South Ossetia, and the formation of a four-sided "Joint Control Commission" to oversee the conflict zone. The peacekeeping force, with 2,000 Russian, Ossetian, and Georgian soldiers, was deployed in South Ossetia in mid-July. Later, Georgians began to voice unhappiness with this arrangement, which gave them only one-third of the peacekeeping contingent. At the time, peace was the priority. By ending the war, Shevardnadze won political capital internationally, and Georgia was formally admitted to the United Nations on July 31, 1992. The war in Abkhazia began two weeks later.

Three years after the fighting ended, Shevardnadze described the 1989–92 conflict in South Ossetia as the "most senseless and pointless war in the history of Georgia."[24] The South Ossetian leaders, a divided group of men who had no experience of politics beyond their remote small Caucasian province, began with fairly limited goals, wanting merely to forge stronger links with North Ossetia and loosen, but not break, bonds with Tbilisi. In an ideal world, as far as most South Ossetians were concerned, they would not have to choose between Georgia and Russia but would have close connections with both. But, faced with aggression by Georgian militias, they waged a war of self-defense and looked to Russian and North Ossetian allies for support. They then militated for independence, probably more in imitation of other Soviet separatist movements than with a real hope of achieving it.

Motivation on the Georgian side is harder to fathom. Economic and criminal gain cannot be ascribed as major factors in the behavior of Georgian armed men: there was not much besides agricultural produce to loot in South Ossetia. Sufficient numbers of young men seem to have been gripped by a genuine conviction that they were defending the "Georgian nation" against Russian-Ossetian threats. Gamsakhurdia's extremist leadership was a major factor but not the defining one. One paramilitary leader, Vazha Adamia, boasted that Gamsakhurdia repeatedly ordered him to withdraw his men but he disobeyed.[25]

The Dagomys agreement established the conditions for the first of what became known, misleadingly, as the "frozen conflicts" of the South Caucasus. The emphasis was more on maintaining a ceasefire than on establishing a forum for serious negotiations. The Russian military successfully negotiated a role as peacekeepers, as they later did in Abkhazia, which became increasingly problematic for the Georgians. The involvement from the end of 1992 of the CSCE added a welcome international element, but the Conference's mandate for South Ossetia was weak.

After the war Ludvig Chibirov, the former dean of the region's pedagogical institute, emerged as South Ossetia's nominal leader and was later elected its first "president." He held talks with Shevardnadze in 1997 and 1998. At the later meeting in the Georgian town of Borjomi, the two men provisionally agreed on most parts of a deal that gave South Ossetia high autonomous status within a Georgian state. Neither man was in a hurry to complete the deal, and there was a strong economic disincentive to change the status quo, as many senior officials on both sides were using South Ossetia's twilight status to make money. However, Chibirov lost the election in 2001, and by then President Vladimir Putin was in the Kremlin and Russian policy was changing.

After 1992, South Ossetia almost vanished as a political issue for most Georgians. Although the territory remained as a de facto separate political entity, its border with the rest of Georgia was open, and ordinary people traveled freely across it. Underresourced and badly damaged, South Ossetia became the major channel for untaxed and smuggled goods flowing in and out of the South Caucasus. These goods ranged from fruits and vegetables to tobacco and vodka to weapons, and, in one recorded instance, to plutonium. The trade was a key factor in bringing the two communities together after the conflict, and no "confidence-building measures" were required for them to interact with one another. But the black economy was also an incentive for powerful players to see ensure that the conflict remained unresolved and for millions of dollars of untaxed revenue to be earned.

AJARIA: THE CONFLICT THAT DID NOT HAPPEN

In the early 1990s, when conflict erupted in Georgia's autonomous provinces of Abkhazia and South Ossetia, a historians could see that conflict was being resumed after a long interval. After all, both Abkhaz and Ossetians had fought the Georgian Menshevik government in 1918–20. It was as though their unsolved and suppressed problems were now coming to the surface again. But that raises an interesting question: Why was a third conflict from 1918–20, a dispute between the Georgian government and the Muslim people of Ajaria, not revived as well? Why was it Georgia's "conflict that did not happen" in the modern era?

Ajaria, a lush subtropical region on Georgia's Black Sea coast next to Turkey, spent many centuries under Ottoman Turkish rule. From the 1820s, it was an arena of frequent Russo-Turkish warfare. In 1878, the Russian Empire finally took possession of Ajaria and made its city of Batum the main port of the South Caucasus. Its main inhabitants, Ajars or Ajarians, are Muslims who speak a dialect of Georgian and, apparently, converted to Islam mainly in the eighteenth and nineteenth centuries. Despite their ethnic and linguistic ties to other Georgians, they kept strong pro-Turkish affiliations. During World War I, Ajarians fought with Turks against Georgians. In June 1918, they voted in favor of rejoining Ottoman Turkey in a plebiscite, but Menshevik Georgia rejected it as invalid.

When the Bolsheviks took over Georgia in 1921, they spoke of the sufferings of the Ajaria Muslims in the same breath as those of Abkhaz and Ossetians. Ajaria was given the status of an autonomous republic, with Turkey as its guarantor. In the late 1980s, this was grounds for worry that, as in Abkhazia and South Ossetia, an old conflict could restart. Georgian nationalist leader Zviad Gamsakhurdia did his best to inflame the situation, telling Ajarians provocatively that as Muslims they were not proper Georgians.

But no conflict happened. It seems that in Soviet times, Ajarians had come to feel like Georgians. In the 1930s, the Soviet authorities abolished the ethnic category of "Ajarians" and reclassified them as Georgians. Their religious affiliation also meant less in a strongly secular state, and in 1929 the last uprising by Muslim clerics had been brutally suppressed. What is more, in the 1990s, the Ajarian leader Aslan Abashidze secured enough political power for his autonomous republic and secured enough revenues from trade with neighboring Turkey to forestall any ideas of separation from Georgia. Autonomy worked here.

Another reason for the lack of conflict is that Turkey, Ajaria's old Great Power patron, did not want to play the Ajaria card against Georgia, while Abkhaz and South Ossetians could count on Russia for support. This reminds us that the idea of so-called ancient hatreds in the Caucasus must be taken with a pinch of salt. Over the broad sweep of history, Georgian-Turkish relations were much worse than Georgian-Russian ones. A Turkish army invaded Ajaria as recently in 1921. In May 1918, the Menshevik leader Noe Zhordania said he was declaring Georgian independence only because Georgia's traditional protector, Russia, could not defend it from the Turks: "At the present moment the Georgian people says it is ready to accept the dominion of anyone rather than fall under the dominion of Turkey."[1]

If the cliché of "ancient hatreds" were true, then the old legacy of conflict between Georgia and Turkey should have been revived in Ajaria. But it seems that in Soviet times, the image of the "enemy Turk" had receded from the Georgian popular memory. Turkey may have been a member of NATO, but on the other side of a closed border it ceased to be a real presence. When the border reopened, Georgian-Turkish relations actually got off to a very good start. In the cases of Abkhazia, South Ossetia, and Russia there were much more real and recent grievances. Soviet intimacy, not ancient hatreds, led to conflict, not ancient hatreds.

1. Noe Zhordania, *Za dva goda, Doklady i rechi* [Over two *Two* years *Years*, lectures *Lectures* and speeches *Speeches*] (Tiflis, 1919), 94.

Abkhazia: Origins

Georgia's other conflict territory, Abkhazia, was more complex than South Ossetia. The historical and strategic reasons for the conflict were stronger, and Russia had much more at stake in Abkhazia, than in South Ossetia, but in its own way the conflict was also entirely avoidable, and chaos and bad luck helped turn a political crisis into a shooting war in August 1992.

The homeland of the Abkhaz consists of a much-coveted subtropical stretch of Black Sea coastline and valleys rising to the mountains behind it. Abkhazia differs from the other two conflict zones of the Caucasus, Nagorny Karabakh and South Ossetia, in being much larger—its prewar population was half a million—and wealthier. The prime cause of all the conflicts in the Caucasus has been the insecurity of small ethnic groups vis-à-vis one another. Here another key element was a scramble for the resources of a small Black Sea paradise—in which, it should be said, top Soviet leaders took the most valuable prizes while ordinary people picked up the scraps. Abkhazia was extremely mixed ethnically. At least five ethnic groups intermingled there, and many of them spoke each other's languages. More than a quarter of the marriages in urban Abkhazia in the 1970s were of mixed ethnicity, one of the highest rates within the Soviet Union.[26] This was an inbuilt deterrent against conflict. In 1989, the Abkhaz themselves were only 18 percent of the population. The Georgians—most of them Mingrelians—were the other prominent ethnic group, comprising around 45 percent of the population.

The Abkhaz have shared their history with Georgians for at least a thousand years but are a distinct ethnic group, related to the Circassian nationalities from the North Caucasus such as the Cherkess, the Kabardins, the Shapsug, and the Ubykh. The name "Abkhaz" most likely derives from the ancient Greek Abasgoi. They call themselves Apsua and their country Apsny. Their religious affiliation has changed over the centuries. Once Christian, as a number of Byzantine churches in Abkhazia prove, most converted to Islam in the nineteenth century, but many became Orthodox Christian again later in the same century. But pre-Christian religious practices have persisted, leading the Abkhaz historian and politician Stanislav Lakoba, only half in jest, to describe his people as "80 percent Christian, 20 percent (Sunni) Muslim and 100 percent Pagan."[27]

Early medieval Abkhazia was a Black Sea principality linked to the Byzantine world. From the eighth to the eleventh century, it was home to a flourishing Christian kingdom. Its political relationship to the western Georgian kingdoms is much disputed by historians, but there is consensus that they had strong religious and cultural links. Lakoba points out that a chronicler of the great Georgian monarch Queen Tamar gave her son Georgi the second name Lasha, which "is translated from the language of the Apsars as enlightener of the universe." In Abkhaz, the word *a-lasha-ra* means "brightness" or "enlightenment," suggesting that the Abkhaz language was known at her court. From the fifteenth century, Abkhazia came under Ottoman rule and later became an autonomous principality ruled by the Chachba family (known in Georgia as the Shervashidzes). They maneuvered between Russia and the Ottoman Empire, while keeping up close links with their western Georgian neighbors. At the end of the eighteenth century, one of the sons of the Abkhaz prince Keleshbey Chachba allied himself with the Ottomans, while the other married into the Dadiani family, who were the rulers of Mingrelia.

Nowadays, especially following Russia's recognition of the independence of Abkhazia in 2008, there is a widespread assumption that the Abkhaz are strongly pro-Russian or even Russian puppets, while Georgians are the enemies of Russia. In the nineteenth century the stereotype worked the other way around. Abkhazia was made a principality inside the Russian Empire in 1810, but resistance to Russian rule, aided by the Ottomans, continued for much of the nineteenth century, while many Georgians adapted well to Russian rule. The Abkhaz supported their ethnic cousins, the Circassian tribes to the north and east, in their war against tsarist armies. As late as 1852, the Russian general Grigory Filipson complained, "In a word, we occupy Abkhazia but we do not rule it."[28]

In May 1864, the tsarist empire's conquest of the Circassians finally ended, and a victory parade was held on the Black Sea coast just north of Abkhazia, called Krasnaya Polyana ("Red Glade") by the Russians. The principality of Abkhazia was abolished and the area renamed the Sukhum Military District. The Russians systematically punished all the defeated peoples by deporting hundreds of thousands of Circassians, including the Abkhaz and Ubykh, to the Ottoman Empire. This horrific act of ethnic punishment predated the Armenian genocide by fifty years but is far less known. Tens of thousands died of hunger and disease as they were transported in rickety ships across the sea. The Black Sea coast, once densely inhabited by different Circassian tribes, was left depopulated. These so-called *muhajirs* became a large diaspora across the Ottoman Empire, in Turkey, Jordan, and Syria in particular. Ahead of the Sochi Winter Olympics of 2014, Circassians complained that it was insensitive to their ancestors to hold the games at Krasnaya Polyana on the 150th anniversary of the deportations.

In August 1866, the Abkhaz again rebelled and were subjected to deportation. The British diplomat William Palgrave visited the territory in 1867 and wrote, "After entire submission and granted pardon, the remnants of the old Abkhasian nation—first their chiefs and then the people—have at last, in time of full peace and quiet, been driven from the mountains and coast where Greek, Roman, Persian and Turkish domination had left them unmolested for more than two thousand years."[29] After another rebellion during the Russo-Turkish war of 1877, the Russian authorities pronounced the Abkhaz "guilty people" and prohibited them from living in the main towns of Abkhazia or along the coast. This second-class status was lifted only in 1907. Russian, Armenian, and Greek colonists immigrated to Sukhum and Mingrelians, and Svans moved into depopulated Abkhaz villages. By the turn of the twentieth century, the Abkhaz constituted only half the population of Abkhazia amid a host of other nationalities. The town of Sukhum became a cosmopolitan port, with whitewashed villas owned by wealthy merchants, and a *lingua franca* of Turkish. The coastline became a holiday destination for the Russian upper classes.

After the revolution of 1917, Abkhazia navigated between Bolsheviks and Mensheviks and spent the period of 1918–21 under several different rulers. A short-lived pro-Bolshevik administration was defeated in May 1918 by troops from Menshevik Georgia, who took control not just of Abkhazia but of the Black Sea port of Sochi as well.

Abkhazia's status in the early Soviet era was ambiguous and was interpreted differently by different players. With the conquest of Menshevik Georgia by the Red Army in 1921, it existed for ten months as a de facto independent Bolshevik republic. In 1922, the Abkhaz Bolsheviks then agreed to make Abkhazia a "treaty republic" within the Transcaucasus Federation, with substantial powers of autonomy. From 1921 to 1936, Abkhazia was led by the popular Bolshevik leader Nestor Lakoba, who preserved for it a large degree of self-rule. He exploited Abkhazia's status as a holiday destination for the Russian elite and did his old comrade Stalin a favor by providing a home for the sick Leon Trotsky in the crucial early months of 1924 when Stalin made his bid in Moscow to succeed Lenin.

In 1931, Abkhazia had its status downgraded to that of an autonomous republic within Georgia but enjoyed five more years of relative calm. Then Stalin and Beria acted to crush both Lakoba and what remained of Abkhazia's autonomy. In December 1936, Beria invited Lakoba to dinner with his family in Tbilisi and then to a premiere at the opera. Poisoned at one of these locations, Lakoba died the same night. He was given a massive funeral in Sukhum, but Stalin, ominously, did not send condolences. Shortly afterward, Lakoba's body was exhumed, he was denounced posthumously as an enemy of the people, and most of his family were arrested and executed.

Beria then imposed a policy of enforced Georgianization on Abkhazia. Abkhaz officials were replaced or shot. Most of the top party posts were given to Georgians, and a new wave of immigration began, with thousands of ethnic Mingrelians and Svans being given new houses in Abkhazia. By 1939, the portion of ethnic Abkhaz in Abkhazia had dropped to 18 percent. Place-names were given Georgian endings, with Sukhum henceforth being called Sukhumi. The Abkhaz language was transcribed into a new Georgian alphabet, and teaching in Abkhaz was suppressed. This assimilation policy was given intellectual support in the 1940s when the Georgian academic Pavle Ingorokva asserted that the Abkhaz/Abasgoi of ancient sources were in fact ethnic Georgian tribes and that the present-day Abkhaz had only arrived in Abkhazia in the seventeenth century.

Evidently the policy was authorized by Stalin himself. Stalin loved Abkhazia and spent around half of the last eight years of his life there, living in four vacation dachas—and never traveling onward to the Georgian capital, Tbilisi. But he apparently shared Ingorokva's ethnic prejudices about the historical origins of the Abkhaz. The loyal Stalinist Georgian Akaki Mgeladze, who was Abkhazia's party boss and Stalin's host from 1944 to 1952, writes in his memoirs of a lunch the two men shared in 1948, during which Stalin mused on the history of the Abkhaz and said, "They [the Abkhaz] are closer to Georgians than Svans, but it doesn't occur to anyone that Svans are not Georgians. Everyone who knows their history well ought to understand that Abkhazia was always part of Georgia. The customs and beliefs of the Abkhaz basically don't differ from the customs of western Georgians."[30]

Abkhazia the place benefited from Stalin's rule, even if the ethnic Abkhaz did not. Mgeladze's memoir relates how he used Stalin's visits to lobby successfully for infrastructure projects such as new bridges or roads. He also writes that Russian party leaders regarded Abkhazia as an extension of the Russian Black Sea coast and talked aloud about merging it with Russia.[31]

After Stalin's death and Beria's arrest and execution at the end of 1953, the strong assimilation of Abkhazia into Georgia halted, and the territory, while remaining firmly inside Soviet Georgia, again looked toward both Georgia and Russia. In 1954, the Abkhaz language was again given a Cyrillic alphabet—its sixth different script in less than a century. Ingorokva's theories were condemned. Large numbers of Armenians and Russians settled in Abkhazia. With some tacit support in Russia, Abkhaz intellectuals and party bosses campaigned for more rights. In 1977, a group of prominent Abkhaz intellectuals wrote a letter asking for Abkhazia to join the Russian Federation. They were punished, but there were more protests the following year. Georgian party boss Shevardnadze agreed to concessions. A new Abkhaz state university was founded, Abkhaz television broadcasting was inaugurated, and quotas were introduced for ethnic Abkhaz in the bureaucracy. In June 1978, Shevardnadze publicly admitted, "The policy towards the Abkhazian nation in this period was . . . chauvinistic. It was against the interests of both Georgian and Abkhazian nations."[32]

What have been called the "ethnic battles" between Abkhaz and Georgians of the 1970s and 1980s had a strong economic dimension. Shevardnadze's concessions to the Abkhaz dissatisfied ethnic Georgians, who complained that they were being denied privileges. There was permanent low-level instability as different ethnic groups, backed by patrons in the party bureaucracy, vied for control of Abkhazia's wealth and the lucrative tourist industry. In the words of Georgi Derluguian, "for generation after generation the structural tension engendered by the patterns of land tenure, shadow markets, and Soviet nationality policy in the distribution of state offices have reproduced the Abkhaz-Georgian clashes at every historical juncture."[33]

With the start of the Gorbachev reform era in 1985, the future of Abkhazia and its riches was again seen as being up for grabs. In essence, each side accused the other of being a splitter, with the Abkhaz seeing the Georgians as splitting from the Soviet Union, and the Georgians accusing the Abkhaz of breaking away from Georgia. The republic's other main ethnic groups did not intervene openly in politics but, if pressed, tended to support the Abkhaz because they preferred the status quo within the Soviet Union to the idea of Georgia's independence. It was a time of great illusions on both sides. The Sukhumi-born Georgian writer Guram Odisharia recalls, "We Georgians thought we'd become independent, sell our wine and mineral water and live like millionaires. The Abkhaz, with their sea and countryside, thought they would break from Georgia and become a second Switzerland. We were all going to live so well."[34]

As we have seen, a mass Abkhaz rally in March 1989 led to Georgian counterdemonstrations and in turn to the April 9 tragedy in Tbilisi. Abkhazia began to splinter along ethnic lines. Its soccer team and theater split in two. The first casualties came in July, when Abkhaz and Georgian students clashed over proposals to divide the Abkhaz state university into two parts. At least sixteen people died, hundreds were injured, and buildings were ransacked in Sukhumi. A wave of violence broke out in Sukhumi and other towns before Soviet troops reimposed order. In 1990, the dispute duly became a "war of laws." On August 25, the Abkhazian Supreme Soviet, dominated by ethnic Abkhaz, proclaimed Abkhazia a union republic within the Soviet Union, a move rejected in Tbilisi. Gamsakhurdia in his turn proclaimed Georgia independent.

By this time, the Abkhaz had their national leader, Vladislav Ardzinba, an ancient historian and specialist in Hittite. Ardzinba had been head of Abkhazia's Institute of Language, Literature and History before being elected to the new Soviet parliament in Moscow in 1989. In December 1990, he was elected head of the Abkhaz Supreme Soviet. Unlike most of the Caucasian intellectuals who entered politics during this period, Ardzinba proved a skillful political operator, albeit one known for a volatile temper.

In 1991, there was a brief truce in the conflict as the extreme nationalist Gamsakhurdia moderated his position on Abkhazia. Whether for pragmatic reasons or from a genuine shift in ideology, Gamsakhurdia, who had written scathingly only two years earlier of Abkhazia as "Northwestern Georgia," now respectfully referred to the Abkhaz as an aboriginal nation and urged them in a public letter to unite with the Georgians as two "captive nations" against Russia. The Abkhaz leadership replied that Abkhazia was still part of the Soviet Union. There was enough common ground for the two sides to do a power-sharing deal for the formation of a new parliament for Abkhazia in August 1991 along ethnic lines—in strong contrast to the total assimilationist policies the new Georgian government was pursuing at the same time in South Ossetia. Despite their minority status, the Abkhaz were promised twenty-eight seats in the sixty-five-seat assembly.

In the New Year of 1992, the end of the Soviet Union and the fall of Gamsakhurdia left both sides doubly insecure: neither side now knew for sure where its sovereignty resided. The power-sharing deal broke down, and conflict loomed. In May, a direct fight broke out between supporters of alternative Georgian and Abkhaz interior ministers. The Abkhaz faction prevailed. The declaration of peace in South Ossetia ironically diverted war-hungry Georgian militias to the mini–civil war being waged against Gamsakhurdia loyalists in western Georgia on the borders of Abkhazia. In July 1992, the Georgian government inherited the tanks and artillery of the Tbilisi-based Transcaucasian Military District and was equipped to fight a war for the first time.

THE GREEKS OF ABKHAZIA

On August 15, 1993, in the middle of a fragile truce in the fighting in Abkhazia, more than a thousand Greeks were shepherded onto a cruise- liner in Sukhumi Harbor to be ferried out to Greece. As the evacuees stepped on board, they were handed passports of the republic of Greece. Many of them stuck photos they had cut from family albums into their new identity documents.[1]

The evacuation, meticulously planned by the Greek government, was called Operation Golden Fleece. It was called a "repatriation" and a "homecoming"—yet almost none of the passengers on the ship had ever been to Greece. It was an astonishing case of how the power of an idea can change people's lives.

Greek-speakers have lived on the shores of the Black Sea since ancient times. The town of Sukhumi once bore the Greek names Dioskurias and Sevastopolis. But Abkhazia's Greek population mainly dates back to the Russian-Ottoman wars of the nineteenth century. To call them "Greek" implies a connection with the country of Greece most of them did not have. They were are almost all "Pontic Greeks" from the region known as the Pontus in the southeast corner of the Black Sea around the ancient city of Trebizond. The Soviet authorities decided to call them by the Russian word *greki*. In their own archaic dialect of Greek, they generally called themselves *Romaioi*, "Romans," meaning they were descendants of the Roman empire of Byzantium.

These Roman-Christian-Pontic-Byzantine-Orthodox-Greeks lived in large numbers in Ottoman times in and around Trebizond. In a series of Russo-Turkish wars, Russia's Muslims were deported one way across the Black Sea and the Pontic Greeks headed in the other. Religion, not language, was the main criterion of identity: the Pontic deportees who settled in Tsalka in southern Georgia, for example, were Christians with Greek names, but they spoke—and still speak—Turkish as their mother tongue.

The cataclysms of the First World War triggered the final expulsion of the Pontic Greeks from their homeland. Under the 1923 Treaty of Lausanne, Greece and Turkey agreed to exchange almost their entire Christian and Muslim populations. More than a million Orthodox Christians left former Ottoman Turkey. The old Christian civilization of the Pontus was extinguished. Thousands of Pontic Greeks also fled to the Soviet Union.[2]

Abkhazia was a natural refuge for them. Many were merchants or tobacco-growers, skills they could easily transfer to their new location. In Sukhum at the turn of the twentieth century, around a third of the population was already Greek, and eight of the twelve churches were Greek Orthodox. In 1912 the businessman Ioachim Aloizi built Sukhum's theater and adjoining Grand Hotel, complete with garage, casino, and cinema. The Villa Aloizi, an Arabian- Nights--style fantasy of towers and turrets, is still standing. In the early 1930s, the USSR was home to around a quarter of a million "Greeks" along the Black Sea coast and in Georgia. In Abkhazia they were briefly allowed to teach in their own language and publish their own newspaper, *Kokkinos Kapnas* (The Red Tobacco-Planter). But later in the decade, Stalin labeled them enemy "stateless cosmopolitans," linked to Greece, a hostile power.

During World War II, first the Greek schools and newspapers were closed, and then tens of thousands of Greeks were deported to Kazakhstan. In June 1949 Stalin and Beria had most of the remaining Pontic Greeks of the Caucasus deported. In five days, more than 27,000 Pontic Greeks, including 10,000 children, were dispatched from Abkhazia to the steppes of Kazakhstan. In multiethnic Abkhazia, some non-Greek spouses pleaded to go into to exile with their husbands or wives; others escaped deportation because they came from mixed families. "The town felt completely empty," said Nikolai Ioannidi, who managed to stay behind with his German mother. Later, as Abkhazia's chief archivist and historian of its Greeks, Ioannidi studied the files. "I tried to find a single traitor or spy, but there was nothing!" he said. In 1956 the Pontic Greeks were rehabilitated by Khrushchev, but only around a quarter of the deportees came home to Abkhazia. The community went into decline, and in the 1980s many emigrated to Greece. Operation Golden Fleece took away most of the rest.

Black Sea Greeks. A group of Pontic Greeks in Abkhazia before the deportations of 1949. Note the traditional three-stringed instrument, the *lyra* or *kemenje.*

In the early modern era, the Greeks were one of the four main communities of Abkhazia. They were well-off, spoke the two main languages of the region, Turkish and Russian, and they got along well with both Abkhaz and Georgians. "In my childhood, we were not aware of nationality, we were just one thing, a Sukhumian," said Ioannidi. Ioannidi's own life ended in sadness. His archive, including its unique Greek newspaper collection, was burned by the Georgians in 1992. When he died in 2007, his community had all but disappeared. The year before he died Ioannidi spoke wistfully of how the Stalinist deportations had left a hole in Abkhazia's multiethnic identity and how keenly the Greeks had been missed. "If there had not been 1949, the whole situation in Abkhazia would have been different," he said. "If there had been a neutral force in the middle, war would not have been so possible."[3]

1. On Operation Golden Fleece, see an article by Yevgeny Krutikov in *Izvestia*, republished at http://www.greek.ru/forum/forum11/topic1813/messages/.

2. The best survey in English on the Pontic Greeks is "The Odyssey of the Pontic Greeks, Special Issue," *Journal of Refugee Studies* 4, 1 (1991).
3. Author's interviews with Ioannidi. His book *The Greeks in Abkhazia* was republished in Greek and Russian in Greece in 2012.

War in Abkhazia

War began in Abkhazia on August 14, 1992, when the head of the Georgian National Guard, Tengiz Kitovani, marched on Sukhumi. Kitovani justified his intervention as a mission to rescue Georgian officials supposedly being held by Zviadist rebels in Gali, the southernmost district of Abkhazia, and to re-open the railway line. Early on that day, a several-thousand-strong battalion of the Georgian National Guard headed by Kitovani moved into Abkhazia but then marched straight to Sukhumi. Georgian soldiers seized government buildings and began looting the city and burning public buildings. Kitovani announced on television that he had dissolved the Abkhaz parliament and dismissed Ardzinba. The Abkhaz leadership hastily withdrew to the town of Gudauta ten miles north. A day later—confirming that this was a planned operation—another Georgian force landed in the seaside town of Gagra in the north of Abkhazia, hemming in the Abkhaz leadership on two sides.

The operation may well have been a personal initiative by Kitovani to claim glory and loot Abkhazia. The key question at the start of the war was whether the head of the State Council, Shevardnadze, had authorized it. Objectively speaking, the last thing the Georgian leader needed shortly after the war in South Ossetia ended was a new war in Abkhazia. Some of Shevardnadze's critics, however, see the fact that Georgia had been admitted to the United Nations on July 31, just two weeks earlier, as proof that he was waiting for international recognition in order to move to suppress the Abkhaz. Once war started, Shevardnadze was at best equivocal about the attack and was very soon justifying it in public. A few days later he told the *New York Times*, "If we didn't do this, the outcome would have been worse." Pressed about whether Kitovani had exceeded orders, he finally conceded, "I think there was no necessity to seize the Parliament building and the Council of Ministers."[35]

In another interview two years later, Shevardnadze was more outspoken about Kitovani—who was now in jail—and condemned his "irresponsibility." He said that the plan had been to secure the railway line through Abkhazia

Abkhazia and Western Georgia

to Russia and that Kitovani had strict instructions not to enter Sukhumi. Shevardnadze also said that he had spoken to Russian president Yeltsin, who was vacationing in Sochi not far from Abkhazia when the fighting broke out, and that Yeltsin had warned him, "It seems to me that you are being dragged into a serious escapade. What are you planning to do with Sukhumi?"[36]

From the Georgian government's perspective, there was a great fear of "losing" Abkhazia, and far more was at stake there than in South Ossetia: a quarter of a million ethnic Georgians, a large slice of territory, and most of Georgia's Black Sea coastline, not to mention a great deal of pride and emotional and historical attachment. Yet Kitovani's brutal intervention achieved the exact opposite of what had been intended. His ragtag force of national guardsmen was too wild and disorganized either to win a military victory or to gain the sympathy of the non-Georgian population of Abkhazia. Their rampage made young Abkhaz men go north to the other side of the Gumista River to join the makeshift resistance.

The war lasted fifteen months, with several lulls and ceasefires. It loomed large in Russia but was poorly covered by the Western media. Many Western editors picked up a simplistic narrative that barely told the stories of the people involved but focused instead on the tribulations of Shevardnadze, "the man who ended the Cold War." British television cameraman Jon Steele tells how he and his crew were pulled out of besieged Sukhumi in September 1993, as soon as they had secured an interview with Shevardnadze: "'Remember, we are only interested in Shevardnadze. It's a war nobody cares about,' said a voice from London."[37]

Neither side had an armed force capable of "winning" such a messy internal conflict on its own. The Georgian fighters were a disorganized force resented by much of the local population. Many of them were "weekend fighters" who came and went from the frontline. Much of the local Georgian population—including most of the inhabitants of the Gali region—did not fight at all. Halfway through the war, President Shevardnadze himself admitted to a foreign reporter, "It is too early to talk about an army. We've just got armed units. Mostly they are patriots and volunteers. The level of training is none or very low. It is difficult to talk about discipline, it is so very weak."[38] The Abkhaz, their backs against the wall, had more reason to fight but lacked numbers and basic weaponry. They were only able to prevail with the support of North Caucasian volunteers and parts of the Russian military.

The issue of Russian involvement dominates all discussions about the war. Georgians say that they fought a war not with Abkhaz but with Russians; the Abkhaz maintain that there was a Georgian-Abkhaz conflict independent of Russia and that Russians helped both sides in the war. The truth lies somewhere in between. The Abkhaz leader Ardzinba rallied sufficient Abkhaz, aided by local Armenians and Russians, to stop the Georgian advance, but he also received active support and sympathy from inside the Russian military and political establishment, many of whose members regarded Gorbachev's former foreign minister Shevardnadze as a traitor for his role in bringing the Soviet Union to an end. The Abkhaz were able to take weapons from the Soviet military base in Gudauta. In March 1993, *Izvestia* reported that Abkhazian forces had received a mass of weapons, including seventy-two tanks and artillery manned by Russian crews. In the same month, an Su-27 fighter jet flown by a Russian pilot was shot down by the Georgians.[39]

As with the wars in Karabakh and South Ossetia, the Abkhaz conflict has to be put within the context of the disintegration of the Soviet armed forces in 1991–92. Much of the military support the Abkhaz received was probably freelance, coming from unemployed Russian officers. It may be no coincidence that the Abkhaz launched their final and successful assault on Sukhumi, with the help of Russian heavy weaponry, at the end of September 1993, when President Yeltsin had his hands tied by a domestic crisis, which ended with fighting in central Moscow.

Just as important a factor in the Abkhaz victory was the help provided by several hundred volunteer warriors from the North Caucasus, mainly Chechens and Circassians, who crossed the mountains to help them in August 1992. They were inspired by the new idea of a "confederation of mountain peoples," who would bring independence to the small peoples of the Caucasus; the fact that this would be done in Abkhazia with Russian military help was for them an unfortunate accident of history. Chechnya's most notorious warrior, Shamil Basayev, went to fight in Abkhazia because he said "the idea of uniting all the small nations of the Caucasus into one confederate state was dear to me."[40] For his part in the campaign, Basayev was later named deputy defense minister of Abkhazia and made a national hero. All this was later glossed over when Abkhazia got close to Russia and Basayev was identified as Russia's number-one terrorist. Yet his actions early in the war may have saved the Abkhaz side. On October 2–3, 1992, Basayev led a swift operation to capture the resort of Gagra for the Abkhaz, marching straight into the center of the town and taking the Georgians by surprise. Vitally for the Abkhaz, the operation broke them out of their isolation and linked them to Russian once again.

Until the end of the war, the Georgians were in possession of the Abkhaz capital Sukhumi. This occupation in the name of "Georgian territorial integrity" quickly took on an aggressive nationalist character. On the evening of October 22, Georgian forces made a menacing statement of their contempt for Abkhaz identity. A group of soldiers in black uniform surrounded Abkhazia's national archive and set fire to it. When neighbors, including Georgians, put out the fire, the armed men returned, drove away the local people by shooting, doused the archive with kerosene, and this time made sure the building was comprehensively burned. Almost 95 percent of the archival record of Abkhazia's cosmopolitan history was destroyed. The Greek archivist Nikolai Ioannidi kept the remainder in his apartment for the rest of the war.[41]

On August 25, the new twenty-six-year-old Georgian military commander of the city, Giorgy Karkarashvili, appeared on local television to make what has become a notorious statement in which he more or less threatened the Abkhaz with annihilation. He began by warning "the supporters of Mr. Ardzinba" that "we are not the cowardly sort" and that those who resist "will find a brotherly grave here." He then threatenedthose who chose to continue resisting that they would be killed, not taken prisoner. Finally and most chillingly, he said, "I can assure those separatists that if in round numbers a hundred thousand Georgians die, then all ninety-seven thousand of yours, who support the decisions of Ardzinba, will also die."[42] Not surprisingly, this interview is cited by Abkhaz as proof of Georgian willingness to slaughter them all.

The war was characterized by a series of sieges and countersieges. The Georgians besieged the southern Abkhaz-held town of Tkvarcheli, causing misery for Abkhaz and Russian civilians who were trapped there. On December 14, 1992, a Russian army helicopter evacuating civilians from Tkvarcheli was shot down, and at least fifty-two people, including twenty-five children, died. In 1993, Georgian-held Sukhumi came under sustained attack four times. In the first half of the year, the Abkhaz side launched three unsuccessful assaults, bombarding the city with heavy artillery and causing many casualties each time.

An elderly Abkhaz librarian, Lyudmila Tarnava, captured what it was like to live through the war in Sukhumi in a candid, fearful diary. She describes a lawless situation in which basic services have broken down, trees are chopped down for firewood, and Kitovani's "guardsmen" are the masters of the town. This creates a hierarchy of nationalities, with Georgians at the top, Abkhaz at the bottom, and Sukhumi's many ethnic Russians following the prevailing political wind. Tarnava's record is full of bitterness against almost everyone—the Georgians who loot apartments, the Russian neighbors who avoid her, the Abkhaz armed forces who fire rockets at her city from the other side of the Gumista River. Mostly, she fears the indiscriminate violence of the Georgian "guardsmen," especially when they have been drinking. In March 1993 she writes:

> Towards evening my "guardsmen," that is, the people living in my doorway ... decided to have a binge. I can understand that, their work is dangerous. But they'll get drunk and then what can I expect from them? I'm not afraid of them sober. They don't touch people, they're not abusive,

they're calm. But I am afraid of them drunk. . . . I can't see enemies in them. I'm only offended at them. And I feel ha-tred for their politicians. But these young people? They are just young and don't know all the truth about history. Someone is inciting them and they believe in it. They've been inspired with a hatred of the Abkhaz and the belief that they are enemies.[43]

There are more accounts of atrocities, including hideous stories of muti-lation, torture, and rape, from the war in Abkhazia than from the conflicts in South Ossetia or Karabakh. This may be because of the large numbers of outside fighters, in particular Georgian militiamen and North Caucasian volunteers, who lacked the restraints that natives of multiethnic Abkhazia had. In a de-tailed report on the war published in 1995, Human Rights Watch concluded,

"Troops on the ground terrorized the local population through house-to-house searches, and engaged in widespread looting and pillage, stripping civilians of property and food. We have received countless reports on both sides that combatants captured during combat were killed and abused, pri-marily by the Georgians, and that combatants raped and otherwise used sexual terror as an instrument of warfare. Human Rights Watch believes these allegations to be credible."[44]

On July 27, 1993, Moscow negotiated a ceasefire. The two armies withdrew most of their heavy weaponry from in and around Sukhumi. The key player was Russian defense minister Pavel Grachev. Grachev must have given his blessing to Russian military support for the Abkhaz, but he was also a friend of Kitovani. He overtly used the conflict to seek to insert a Russian military presence in both Abkhazia and Georgia as a whole. He pressed to have two Russian military divisions accepted as a peacekeeping force, but the Georgians resisted, in a move that may have sealed their fate. Shevardnadze's position was further weakened by a new rebellion in western Georgia by supporters of ousted president Gamsakhurdia. The rebels took three towns in Mingrelia and the city of Poti.

On September 16, the Abkhaz broke the ceasefire, alleging that the Georgians had not been complying with it. They launched an all-out at-tack, after apparently being given their artillery back by the Russians. Shevardnadze, who had lost most of his heavy weapons to the ceasefire agreement, personally commanded the defense of Sukhumi from a deadly bombardment. The Abkhaz landed a small force south of Sukhumi and held the coastal road. Three Georgian planes flying in to bolster the defense of the city were shot down by missiles fired from gunboats in the Black Sea, with the deaths of more than 100 people on board.[45]

Georgian defenses were overwhelmed, and Sukhumi fell on September 27.[46] Incoming fighters killed most of the members of the Georgian government who had stayed on in the parliament building. Three days later, Abkhaz forces had reached the river Inguri and the boundary with western Georgia, taking control of the whole republic, except for the mountainous Upper Kodori Gorge. Writing on October 6 from a city now controlled by Abkhaz forces, Lyudmila Tarnava observed a situation turned on its head:

> Times and roles have changed around. I got the name-plate that I took down in 1989, with my surname, and put it up, and Darejan [a Georgian neighbor] has already taken hers down. So that's how it is! "'Celebration has begun in our street too!'" [adapted version of a famous quotation by Stalin from 1942]. An unceasing stream of cars is moving toward Gudauta with property stolen off the Georgians. Georgians have taken the things of the Abkhaz to the east, and the Abkhaz have taken theirs west, in the opposite direction.[47]

In Sukhumi, the victorious side carried out an orgy of looting, with the North Caucasian volunteers being especially feared as they claimed their rewards in the captured city. The Abkhaz commanders tried to impose a curfew and sacked their own interior minister to spare their own republic the worst of the ravages. "We do not want to stay here, but we have a right to our trophies," a North Caucasian warrior named Zhena told Reuters reporter Lawrence Sheets. A Georgian told Sheets, "Every day soldiers come to the apartment saying that they are looking for weapons and snipers. They threaten to rape my daughter."[48]

Not just ethnic Georgians but others, such as ethnic Greeks, said they feared for their lives in a territory overwhelmed by lawless violence. This was the situation in which almost the entire Georgian population of Abkhazia fled. With the road south blocked to them, thousands fled over the mountains into western Georgia in desperate conditions of hunger and cold. In late October, one journalist described harrowing scenes of "refugees who had been stranded for weeks, lashed by rain and snow, sleeping fifty to a house or camping out in rickety Soviet-era cars."[49] There are accounts that the misery of the refugees was compounded by their own side, with many refugees in the lowlands turned back by Georgian troops and others in the mountains robbed by local Svans.[50] Of a prewar population of around 240,000 in Abkhazia, only a few thousand Georgians remained.

After the War

The Abkhaz won a victory at a heavy price. The war claimed around 8,000 lives. The city of Sukhumi was devastated by the final round of fighting, and its old center, around the massive Soviet-era parliament building, which went up in flames only when the Abkhaz captured the city, was still a maze of ruins two decades later.

The Russian government was more interested in exerting pressure on Georgia than in lending support to the Abkhaz. Moscow gave support to Shevardnadze in defeating the Zviadist rebels, and Gamsakhurdia himself died in December 1993, apparently having committed suicide on a failed mission to fight in western Georgia. But Shevardnadze was forced to accept humiliating terms: he was made to join the Commonwealth of Independent States on October 9, 1993, ; to agree to the renewal of leases on Russian military bases,; and to accept Moscow's nominee as defense minister.

A ceasefire agreement was eventually signed only the following May. A Commonwealth of Independent States peacekeeping force, which was in fact basically a Russian contingent, was sent to the ceasefire zone area on either side of the river Inguri. A UN mission (the United Nations Observer Mission in Georgia) was established, providing just over 100 unarmed monitors. The weak international commitment to the peace process—in marked comparison to the response in the Balkans—basically made the ceasefire settlement a Pax Russica designed and implemented in Moscow. At first, the Yeltsin government seemed committed to forging a new partnership with Georgia that might involve a deal over the two breakaway provinces. Yeltsin went to Tbilisi in February 1994 to sign a treaty of friendship, accompanied by agreements on military cooperation. However, the treaty was opposed by Yeltsin's new parliament, the State Duma.

After 1993, the Russian government applied as much pressure on breakaway Abkhazia as it did on Georgia. The border across the river Psou was closed to all males between the ages of ten and fifty-five, and Russia applied trade sanctions against Abkhazia. Russian foreign minister Yevgeny Primakov, who knew both Shevardnadze and Ardzinba, tried to press both sides into making a deal. In August 1997, on the fifth anniversary of the outbreak of war, Primakov arranged for Ardzinba to fly to Tbilisi for talks with Shevardnadze. The two men signed a declaration promising "not to resort to arms to resolve the differences" but did not build on the agreement. According to Abkhazia's de facto foreign minister, Sergei Shamba, the Abkhaz side was closer than the Georgians to signing a full peace plan. He said, "In 1997 we had a Common State agreement that Primakov wrote. Several ministers from both sides reviewed and adjusted the document, which we signed. It would have given us international recognition and common borders."[51]

Life in the postwar years was miserable for the Georgians who had fled Abkhazia. Tens of thousands of IDPs were given only the most rudimentary assistance by the Georgian government. Many felt like "double strangers," having fled Abkhazia to live in parts of Georgia they found quite alien. They occupied sanatoriums, schools, and hotels; as of this writing, the majority have found permanent homes, but many are still there. For more than a decade, Tbilisi's main tall Soviet-era hotel, the Iveria, was home to hundreds of refugees, its windows a web of clotheslines. In 2005, Georgia still officially had 245,000 IDPs, more than 232,000 from Abkhazia and more than 12,000 from South Ossetia, comprising around 5 percent of the population. The new conflict of 2008 added almost 40,000 more.

Life was only marginally better for the remaining population in Abkhazia itself. The sanctions regime meant there was virtually no international aid and travel was difficult. Crime was rampant. Politically, the most difficult test for the Abkhaz was how they could make a legitimate claim to the republic when they had been a minority community before the war. Georgian critics have consistently argued that because less than half of a prewar population of 525,000 in Abkhazia remains, these people do not have a moral claim to represent an entity named Abkhazia. An "Abkhaz government in exile" of ethnic Georgians was set up in Tbilisi, asserting the Georgian version of reality, complete with minor municipal posts for a virtual Sukhumi. The situation inside postwar Abkhazia was even more complex than this suggested. Tens of thousands of ethnic Armenians and Russians remained, and many of those who left did so for economic reasons. Today, other ethnic groups still live and work freely in Abkhazia. Yet Abkhaz are certainly "more equal than others" in Abkhazia, in the sense that they dominate the government and the republic's parliament, and ensuring ethnic harmony is still a process of careful negotiation.

Within a year of the war, as many as 50,000 Mingrelians had also begun to return to cultivate their lands in Abkhazia's southern district of Gali (known as Gal by the Abkhaz), which had a majority Mingrelian-Georgian population before the war. They were caught up in a low-level insurgency waged by small Georgian guerrilla groups—covertly backed by the Georgian security forces and known as the "White Legion" or "Forest Brothers"—against the Abkhaz. In

May 1998, the Georgian guerrillas mounted a sustained campaign in the Gali region in which many Abkhaz were killed. The Abkhaz armed forces brutally swept through the region, forcing more than 20,000 Georgians to flee once again across the border. Russian peacekeepers did not intervene.

In October 1999, the Abkhaz leadership said it had given up on negotiations over a "common state" with Tbilisi, toughened its line, and called a referendum on independence. Abkhaz leader Vladislav Ardzinba, who was running for a second term as Abkhazia's de facto president on the same day as the referendum, used the vote to reassert his claim to be the republic's national leader. Unsurprisingly, a result of 97 percent of participants in favor of independence was declared—although no international body endorsed the result. The Abkhaz démarche deepened the rift with Tbilisi. But what really changed the situation was the change of administration in Russia the following year. Vladimir Putin came to power and gradually instituted policies to punish Georgia, end Abkhazia's isolation, and change the balance of power in the conflict.

6

Caspian Energy and Caucasian Corridors

The World's Oil Capital

Azerbaijan can lay claim to being the oldest oil-producing region in the world. For a time at the beginning of the age of commercial oil, Baku was the world's energy capital, and in the years 1898–1901 it produced more oil than the United States. Travelers had recorded the oil seeping through the ground on the shores of the Absheron Peninsula by the Caspian Sea for centuries. Azerbaijan's ancient Zoroastrian fire-temples burned on flammable gas issuing from oil deposits underground. Oil-impregnated sand, scraped off the beaches, was a valuable fuel sent by camel for hundreds of miles around.

Oil was first exploited commercially in the mid-nineteenth century. The industry took off in 1871, when the Russian government allowed in private enterprise and the first wells were drilled. Two of the Swedish Nobel brothers, Robert and Ludwig, invested in the new industry and by the end of the decade had the biggest refinery in Baku and were shipping barrels of oil across the Caspian Sea to the Russian port of Astrakhan in the world's first oil tanker, the *Zoroaster*. By the 1880s, oil fields such as Balakhany had sprouted hundreds of brick wells extracting the oil from the ground, and Baku's new northern industrial suburb was nicknamed the Black Town because of the clouds of dark oil smoke hanging over it from 200 refineries. In one generation, Baku turned from a forgotten desert citadel into a modern metropolis. The population skyrocketed from 14,000 in 1863 to 206,000 forty years later. "Baku is greater than any other oil city in the world. If oil is king, Baku is its throne," wrote the British author J. D. Henry in 1905. You could become a millionaire literally overnight if an "oil gusher" appeared on your land. One man who got lucky was Haji Zeynalabdin Tagiev, the illiterate son of a shoemaker, who turned into one of Baku's richest and most famous businessmen and benefactors after a gusher appeared on his land. Tagiev was unusual in being a native Azeri. Most of the businessmen were European, Russian, or Armenian. Tensions between the Armenian bourgeoisie and Azeri workers were an underlying cause of the brutal "Tatar-Armenian" war in Baku in 1905 in which hundreds were killed and thousands of oil wells destroyed.[1]

Henry asked rhetorically, "Why is Baku rich? The answer is simple—because it produces a commodity which has a market wider than the civilised world, for it is carried on camels into the innermost parts of the Asian Continent, and on yaks into the wild regions of the Himalayas."[2] But camels and yaks were insufficient to export a major new world commodity to the wider world. Baku faced the same problem that it would a century later—how to export the oil from the landlocked Caspian basin to European consumers. In the 1870s, the geography of the Caucasus was such a barrier that Tiflis imported more American kerosene by ship than it did Baku oil. The Caspian Sea was stormy and dangerous for several months of the year, limiting how much could be sent to Russia. So in 1883 the new oilmen, with financing from the Rothschild family, built the first cross-Caucasian railway from Baku to Batum on the Black Sea. In 1906, Baku oil made another leap forward when the world's longest "kerosene pipeline" was completed, running for 519 miles along the same route to Batum.[3]

In the years 1914–21, oil wealth was a major factor in the international scramble for the Caucasus. In World War I, German commander Erich von Ludendorff saw Azerbaijani oil and its route via Georgia as a key motivation to intervene in the South Caucasus. At the end of the war, the British took control of Baku, and in 1919 British foreign secretary Arthur Balfour identified its oil as Britain's major priority in the region. He said, "I should say we are not going to spend all our money and men in civilizing a few people who do not want to be civilized. We will protect Batum, Baku, the railway between them and the pipe-line." When the British had gone, the oil-starved Bolsheviks made Baku their first target in the Transcaucasus. Having captured the city in April 1920, Trotsky declared that the new oil resources would win the Civil War for the Reds and would be "our hope for restoring

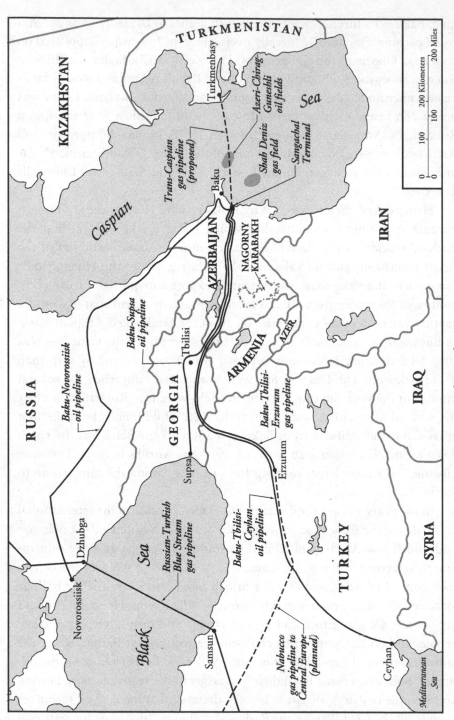

Caucasian pipelines and energy routes.

the economy, for ensuring that old men and women and children do not die of cold in Moscow."[4]

Baku remained a major oil-producing center in the early Soviet era. In 1941 the city was vital to Stalin's war effort against Germany and produced around three-quarters of the Soviet Union's oil. When Hitler's Germany invaded the Soviet Union, the Germans again identified Baku oil as a vital asset. In August 1942, the Germans occupied the western side of the North Caucasus and planned a push south to Azerbaijan. Saying, "Unless we get the Baku oil, the war is lost," Hitler diverted divisions away from the battle for Stalingrad toward the Caucasus. That summer, Hitler's staff famously had a cake made for him that had the shape of the Caspian Sea in the middle. Film footage shows a delighted Hitler taking a slice of the cake, which had the letters B-A-K-U written on it in white icing and chocolate made to look like oil spooned over it.[5]

The debacle at Stalingrad in the winter of 1942–43 meant that Germany never invaded the South Caucasus, but even the threat of attack was a death-sentence for the Baku oil industry. Stalin, who knew the Baku oil fields from his revolutionary days of in 1905, had the oil wells shut down so they would not fall into German hands. Almost the entire Azerbaijani oil industry and its experts were transferred to the oil wells of the Volga and the Urals. After the war, Russia's oil fields received the major part of Soviet investment, and Azerbaijan suffered. The on-inland fields had dried up, and in order to reach the trickier offshore fields, a small town named Oily Rocks was built thirty miles out in the sea—reached across a causeway built on sunken ships. Cramped and polluted, Oily Rocks eked out what could still be drilled of Azerbaijan's oil within the capacity of Soviet technology. But increasingly, the existing expertise was not up to the challenge. By the time the Soviet Union collapsed, Azerbaijan was producing only 3 percent of its oil output.

The Contract of the Century

In July 2006, the Baku-Tbilisi-Ceyhan (BTC) pipeline, linking the Caspian and Black seas, was inaugurated at its final point, the Turkish Mediterranean port of Ceyhan. The presidents of Azerbaijan, Georgia, and Turkey, the three countries along the route, were there to celebrate what Lord Browne, head of British Petroleum (BP), the company operating the pipeline, called "the first great engineering project of the 21st century." The first tanker had already left Ceyhan a month before, carrying 600,000 barrels of Azerbaijani oil to Western markets.

The opening of the BTC pipeline was the culmination of the second act of the story of Azerbaijan's role as a major world energy producer. It could never be as dramatic as the first act, but it emphatically put Azerbaijan back on the world energy map for the first time in a century. At just under 1,100 miles (1,768 km) long, the BTC pipeline was the second-longest oil pipeline in the world, after Russia's Druzbha pipeline, and cost almost $4 billion to build. Its completion was a great political as well as technical achievement. The construction of a major export route from the Caspian gave Western markets an important new source of energy from a new area of the world. At the same time, it transformed a small, fragile country of eight million people into a medium-level world oil producer. Once the pipeline started pumping at full capacity, Azerbaijan stood to receive revenues of around $20 billion—and initially even more than that as oil prices hit record highs. From 2006–8, Azerbaijan's budget revenues went up by around a third every year, making it the fastest-growing economy in the world.

In 1991, newly independent Azerbaijan was fighting the Karabakh war with the Armenians and its economy was collapsing; the new country's GDP fell by 60 percent in the period 1992–95. So the government saw the revival of the oil industry as a strategic imperative. It was free to call on Western expertise for the first time in two generations. The first Western oilman to do deals in Azerbaijan was Steve Remp, a fearless American, head of a tiny company based in Aberdeen, who arrived in Baku in 1989 and was later rewarded with a 2 percent stake in the new international oil consortium. Remp said later, "Everywhere we could see the signs of the great oil boom of the turn of the century. . . . Hundreds and hundreds of rigs, all in disrepair. But no Western presence at all. It was a time warp."[6] The atmosphere was chaotic and tense. Setting up offices in the decrepit Hotel Intourist on Baku's main square, the Westerners looked out for spies, intrigued against each other, and tried to forge relationships with often venal officials in governments that collapsed every few months. In 1994, one local intermediary, who brandished a pistol at meetings, demanded—but did not get—an upfront "fee" of $300 million from the Westerners to secure the right to develop the new oil fields.[7]

Soviet analysts had already identified a rich source of oil that their technology was unable to exploit, an offshore oil field that had been known as "Twenty-six Commissars" and was now renamed Azeri. Two other adjoining fields, Chirag and Guneshli, made for a complex that came to be known as ACG and had estimated reserves of up to five billion barrels of oil—enough for 15–20 years of development. The British oil giant BP, the biggest company in town, first drafted an agreement with nationalist president Abulfaz Elchibey and then, when he was deposed, with his successor, Heidar Aliev. In 1994, Aliev's government signed a deal to develop the ACG fields that was estimated at the time to be worth $10 billion and was proudly called the "contract of the century." The nine foreign companies involved came from six different countries and formed the new Azerbaijan International Operating Company (AIOC). AfterBesides the State Oil Company of Azerbaijan Republic (SOCAR), the major stakes in developing the oil fields were taken by BP, Amoco, Unocal, and the Russian company Lukoil.

The "contract of the century" and Azerbaijan's new energy status had big political ramifications. For the Baku government, in the words of Ilham Aliev, a senior executive of SOCAR, son of the president, and eventually president himself, "We used oil for our major goal . . . to become a real country."[8] President Heidar Aliev, who had run Azerbaijan on and off since 1969, saw it as a way of giving Western governments a stake in Azerbaijan's statehood. Even before Aliev came to power, a relationship had been forged between Britain and Azerbaijan, thanks to BP, which brought former British prime minister Margaret Thatcher to Baku to clinch its first deal in 1991. Aliev kept up that link but set his sights on a bigger goal, the global superpower, the United States. As presidential advisor Vafa Guluzade put it, "the Kremlin is now in Washington."[9] The interest was mutual. US oil companies dispatched a series of Washington heavyweights to the Caspian region, among them Henry Kissinger and Brent Scowcroft, to lobby on their behalf. Four years after coming to power, in August 1997 Politburo veteran Heidar Aliev was received in the White House.

The point, however, was not to replace Moscow with Washington. Aliev was a master negotiator who calculated that his country would be best served by balancing different interests. In the end, American, British, Russian, Norwegian, Turkish, and Saudi companies joined the AIOC consortium. He also wanted to forge better relations with his southern neighbor, Iran. An Azerbaijani-Iranian deal was signed in Baku in November 1994, and the Iranians were promised a 5 percent stake in the consortium. This turned out to be Aliev's only blunder. The U.S. government told Aliev that this was unacceptable, as American companies were barred by law from collaborating with Iran, and he was abruptly forced to withdraw the offer.

(The Iranians were later compensated with a 10 percent stake in developing the Shah Deniz gas field.)

Getting the Russians on board was also of key importance. Russia had the capacity to be a wrecker and was already trying to play a card that could jeopardize the new contract altogether. The issue was legal ambiguity about the status of the Caspian, which until very recently had been jointly shared by the Soviet Union and Iran—was it an inland sea or in fact a lake whose resources should be divided equally, with Russia being entitled to an equal share of all the spoils? If it was not a sea, there was no "Azerbaijani sector" in the Caspian Sea at all, and the ACG fields were not Azerbaijan's to sign away. Russian officials made threatening noises that the offshore production was operating illegally, but they backed off after being overruled by then Russian prime minister and former energy boss Viktor Chernomyrdin.[10] In 2001, Iran used the issue as a pretext to send a navy boat to threaten two Azerbaijani survey vessels with BP experts on board on an inspection trip in the sea. In 2018 the five nations of the Caspian announced that they had finally reached a deal on its legal status, but the challenge of how to divide up its oil- and gas- fields still looked daunting.

As in the early twentieth century, extracting the oil was only the beginning of the story; there was also the challenge of how to transport it efficiently to Western markets. Railway transport was slow and expensive, and pipelines would be needed. Some of the Western oil bosses argued that an oil swap with Iran in which Iran would take Azerbaijani oil and export its own would be the most efficient option, but this was quickly vetoed by Washington on political grounds. Another favored solution among the AIOC shareholders was for the oil to flow to the Russian Black Sea port of Novorossiisk. This fit with the Russians' agenda—in the Soviet era all oil pipelines had run through Russian territory, and for post-Soviet Russia to renounce that advantage meant relinquishing a key lever of control over its former Soviet neighbors. But for that reason, Western and Azerbaijani politicians worried about using this as the only route.

A new plan then emerged to build a new $250 million pipeline (the cost was eventually double that) to the Georgian port of Supsa, not far from Batumi, following most of the same route as the 1906 pipeline. In American eyes, the virtue of this was that not only would it free Azerbaijan from dependence on Russia as an export route, but it would also give a helping hand to their beleaguered ally, Georgian leader Eduard Shevardnadze. Shevardnadze lobbied strongly for the project and patched up his poor relationship with Aliev, which had been difficult when they were both in Gorbachev's Politburo. In September 1995, both the AIOC consortium and the Baku government endorsed the concept of "multiple pipelines," and work began on making both export routes viable. The pipeline to Novorossiisk opened in 1997, and the one to Supsa was completed in 1998. Eventually, only SOCAR crude oil went through the "northern route," which needed a bypass to go around war-ravaged Chechnya, while the AIOC's oil went via Georgia. The capacity of the two lines was relatively modest—they currently carry 100,000 and 150,000 barrels of oil, respectively—but they were a good solution to the challenge of how to export Azerbaijani "early oil" while exploitation of the new Caspian oil fields proceeded.

"Great Game" Politics

Although the first phase of the pipeline dispute was concluded peacefully, it immediately polarized Moscow and Washington on two sides of a geopolitical quarrel. Most officials in the administration of President Bill Clinton, who had invested a lot in Yeltsin's Russia, were careful to stress in public that they wanted to see the Russians as partners, not rivals, in the Caspian and cooperate over pipeline routes. That was not how it was seen in Moscow. One Kremlin advisor declared plainly, "Russia is interested in controlling the oil pipeline." Russian officials accused the Americans of encroaching into their backyard."

These differences were magnified by an atmosphere of hype that was generated about the Caspian in the West in the mid-1990s. Caspian geopolitics became a fashionable topic, leading Dick Cheney, then chief executive of the oil services company Halliburton, to comment in early 1998, "I can't think of a time when we've had a region emerge as suddenly to become as strategically significant as the Caspian. It's almost as if the opportunities have arisen overnight."[12] The intense interest gave birth to two popular ideas. One was that Central Asia and the South Caucasus were an east-west corridor that was the "new Silk Road," the successor to the famous medieval caravan route that had connected China and Europe across Central Asia. The other was that the pursuit of Caspian Sea energy resources was a "new Great Game" analogous to the ruthless struggle for influence between the British and tsarist empires in Asia in the nineteenth century.

In February 1998, making an opening statement to hearings in the U.S. Congress on Central Asia, Congressman Doug Bereuter used the "Great Game" metaphor expansively, setting the tone for a debate on how the United States could seize an opportunity to move into the Caspian region. He said,

> One hundred years ago, Central Asia was the arena for a great game played by Tsarist Russia, Colonial Britain, Napoleon's France, and the Persian and the Ottoman Empires. . . . the collapse of the Soviet Union has unleashed a new great game, where the interests of the East India Trading Company have been replaced by those of Unocal and Total, and many other organizations and firms.[13]

Both concepts sounded attractive but had potentially harmful associations. This kind of talk, with its dramatic vista back into history, prompted overblown predictions about the strategic importance of the region to the West. "Within the next 15 years, the Caspian region will become the planet's second largest source of petrol and gas after the Middle East," wrote the French scholar Olivier Roy in 1997. In the same year, a Washington expert on the region, Ariel Cohen, proposed "a new Silk Road to prosperity" and estimated Caspian oil reserves at 200 billion barrels. He wrote, "Along the shores belonging to Azerbaijan, Kazakstan, Turkmenistan, and possibly Russia and Iran, are oil and natural gas reserves exceeding those of Iran or Iraq. Caspian Sea hydrocarbon resources are equal to those of Kuwait and represent two-thirds of Saudi Arabia's energy riches."[14]

Both of those estimates were wildly optimistic. Current estimates suggest that the Caspian Sea oil resources, both onshore and offshore, are likely to be around sixty billion barrels, or around 5 percent of the world's proven reserves. That means it is still a significant oil-producing region, but more on the level of the North Sea than the Persian Gulf—Iraq alone has twice that amount of oil. Moreover, it is Kazakhstan rather than Azerbaijan that stands to be the big Caspian Sea energy power, with reserves estimated to be more than five times greater than Azerbaijan's. Two vast oil fields in the northeast Caspian, Tengiz and Kashagan—which are being developed by all of the world's major private oil companies except BP—almost certainly contain more oil than Azerbaijan's entire reserves. This glut of oil could last Kazakhstan at least fifty years and in 2015 puts it twelfth place in BP's list of countries ranked by proven oil reserves. Azerbaijan came twentieth in the list, just behind Ecuador.[15]

Some in Washington, such as Clinton's main Russia strategist, Strobe Talbott, disliked the Great Game analogy. "We were big on deleting any references to the Great Game" from briefing papers and talking points, said one of his deputies.[16] But the idea of a new struggle for a major source of world energy stuck—it even invaded a 1999 James Bond film, *The World Is Not Enough,* in which Bond thwarted an attempt to blow up a new oil export pipeline from Baku through Turkey.

As a result of these predictions, some Washington strategists argued that pursuit of American influence in the Caspian basin should be a major goal of U.S. foreign policy, with the explicit aim of outflanking both Russia and Iran. Sheila Heslin, who served in the U.S. National Security Council and then lobbied for this Caspian policy outside it, wrote, "The United States simply cannot afford to allow Russia and Iran to dominate the energy resources of the Caspian, with the enormous political leverage that would confer in the region and even in Europe. . . . Increasingly, the Caspian region is emerging not only as a critical component of Western energy security, but also as a linchpin in the evolving balance of power in Eurasia, Asia and the Middle East."[17]

In 1998, the main practical issue to be solved for Azerbaijan was what should be the route of the Main Export Pipeline should be when large quantities of oil from ACG came onstream. The U.S. government became heavily involved. President Clinton appointed U.S. diplomat and former business executive Richard Morningstar to a new post, special advisor to the president and the secretary of state for Caspian Basin energy diplomacy.[18] On behalf of the administration, Morningstar endorsed plans for a pipeline from Baku to the Turkish Mediterranean port of Ceyhan. The idea originally came from Turkey. The Turkish government made the case that because this route would bypass the Black Sea it would reduce the environmental threat posed by oil tankers sailing down the narrow Bosphorus Strait through the middle of Istanbul. The route could also utilize a port that had been built to take Iraqi oil but had been virtually shut down because of the Iraq sanctions regime. The Georgian government enthusiastically backed the scheme, as it would make Georgia a link in an energy chain to the West and give it much-needed transit revenues.

The Russian government was hostile to the Baku-Ceyhan scheme, as it threatened decisively to end Moscow's dominance of the post-Soviet pipeline network. A few years later, energy minister Yury Shafranik said bluntly, "It is against Russia." For Armenia and its diaspora the project also looked worrying, as the proposed pipeline would curve around Armenian territory while binding three of its four neighbors more closely together. There had been proposals for a "peace pipeline" via Armenia that would have been a central element of a Nagorny Karabakh peace agreement. These failed because the two sides were too far apart to do a deal over Karabakh, and neither the Azerbaijani government nor the oil companies wanted to link a commercial project to a peace treaty. As the energy expert Robert Ebel pithily said, "Peace can bring a pipeline but a pipeline can't bring peace."[19]

What froze the BTC project in 1998 was the resistance of the oil companies, which would have to bear the cost of building the line because governments would not fund it. They complained that they were being pressurized into a project that did not make commercial sense. Terry Adams, president of the international consortium, wrote later, "The regional cooperation enjoyed by AIOC for its Phase I Early Oil Project was dissipated. 'Trade was now being forced to follow Flag.' "[20] Their main worry was that the oil price had sunk to $10 a barrel, making construction of a major new pipeline at great expense simply unviable. This made an upgrade of the Baku-Supsa pipeline a more attractive option. Kazakh president Nursultan Nazarbayev joined the chorus of those talking down the Baku-Ceyhan idea when he said, "You could get the impression that what is to be built is not a purely civilian structure but something that constitutes the dividing line between good and evil."[21]

By the end of 1999, things had begun to turn around. The major foreign oil player in Azerbaijan, BP Amoco (BP having merged with the U.S. company Amoco), endorsed the Baku-Ceyhan route but expressed concerns about the cost. Negotiations began on what governments could provide in terms of protection and political underpinning. In the meantime, the oil price was rising and estimates of the amount of reserves in the ACG fields were raised. In 2001 BP Amoco formally pledged funding to BTC, and in September 2002, construction began at a ceremony at Baku's Sangachal oil terminal, where the three presidents helped lay the inaugural section of piping. "This project guarantees peace, security and stability in the region, and still further unites three countries and three peoples," said President Aliev. Russian foreign minister Igor Ivanov voiced Moscow's disapproval, saying, "We are ready to cooperate but if there are attempts to squeeze Russia out of these regions, where we have historic interests, we will not accept that."[22]

Once construction of BTC was under way, the controversies around the pipeline turned local. In Georgia there was opposition to the routing of it through the Borjomi valley, near the sources of Georgia's famous mineral water. Even so, most Georgians still backed the project. Over time they came to realize, however, that it was less of an economic panacea than they had expected. Construction created only a small number of jobs, and the annual transit fees of around $50–60 million were modest. Of more importance for Georgia was the parallel construction of the South Caucasus Gas Pipeline running from Baku to Erzerum in Turkey, which gradually made Azerbaijan rather than the more unpredictable Russia the main supplier of its gas.

After the first Azerbaijani oil was exported from Ceyhan in June 2006, BTC's capacity increased to the projected one million barrels a day. (By early 2017 the volume had dropped to less than half of that.) That means that even in its heyday BTC supplied only 1 percent of the world's oil output. But its importance is as much in where the oil does not come from as from where it does. For the United States, it was a "not-Iran- pipeline" that preserved the isolation of the Iranian regime. For Azerbaijan and Georgia, it remains a "not-Russia- pipeline" that physically connects them to Western markets, bypassing Russia. From the point of view of Western governments it could also be called the "not-Saudi-Arabia-not-Iraq- pipeline," in that its oil comes from a reliable source outside the Middle East or the OPEC bloc and is controlled by Western energy companies. As energy expert John Roberts put it, "The Caspian is important not only because it is one of the world's major producing areas, but because it is rapidly becoming one of the biggest producing areas in the world in which actual oil production remains essentially in the hands of market-oriented international energy companies."[23]

That reliability is relative of course. The BTC pipeline shut down for nineteen days after August 5, 2008, because of an explosion in eastern Turkey, attributed to either an action by Kurdish militants or a cyberattack by Russian agents.[24] When war broke out between Russia and Georgia three days later, there was controversy as to whether Russian planes had threatened the pipeline in a bombing raid made in Georgia. Several bombs certainly fell near the pipeline at one point, although both Moscow and BP denied that it had been explicitly targeted. The Russian government would certainly have been reckless to jeopardize its relations with Azerbaijan, Turkey, and BP by attacking the pipeline, even if it wanted to hurt Georgia. The Baku-Supsa pipeline, which passes directly next to South Ossetia, was closed for three months because of the war.

The Not-Russia Pipeline. Georgian president Eduard Shevardnadze at a
ceremony laying a section of the Baku-Tbilisi-Ceyhan pipeline
in 2003—probably his biggest foreign-policy achievement. Georgi Kraveishvili.

Another threat comes from the unresolved Nagorny Karabakh conflict, which looms quietly over the region's pipelines. At its nearest point in
Azerbaijan, the pipeline runs just eight miles north of the Karabakh ceasefire line, the Line of Contact. If, theoretically, fighting were to resume over
Karabakh, it is possible that Armenians would target the pipeline's pumping
stations or Azerbaijan's oil infrastructure in general— either by committing
an act of sabotage or by firing the long-range missiles they are rumored to
have. For the Armenian side to do this would be politically suicidal, but in the
case of a life-and-death fight for Nagorny Karabakh, all bets would be off.
During the fighting over Karabakh in April 2016, an Armenian military commander said anonymously that the Armenian side had long-range missiles
targeting Azerbaijan's oil and gas infrastructure.[25] The overall impact of the
pipeline on the conflict could still be positive. With so many billions invested
in Azerbaijan's oil and gas project, Western governments have an extra incentive not to see a war there, and the Azerbaijani government will be less
inclined to risk the destruction of its energy industry. As one Western diplomat in Baku said of the Azerbaijani leadership, "they are oil guys, they're
cautious, they don't need a war." Yet there is no room for complacency—the

South Ossetian conflict of 2008 showed that the parties in an unresolved territorial dispute can be dragged into conflict through force of circumstance and against their better interests. The risk of another full-scale Karabakh war and the threat it poses to energy infrastructure is another good reason to focus international minds on forging a peaceful solution to the conflict.

One unresolved issue in the historical assessment of the BTC project is whether the way the pipeline was planned and promoted helped provoke Russia into an antagonistic attitude that helped create the current "New Cold War" environment in the South Caucasus—or whether Russia would have behaved aggressively toward Western plans there anyway. The project certainly played a role in polarizing the region. An Azerbaijan-Georgia-Turkey axis, supported by Western backers, formed on the one hand and a Russia-Armenia-Iran axis on the other. A new anti-Russian bloc of post-Soviet states named GUAM—Georgia, Ukraine, Azerbaijan, Moldova—was first mooted at around the same time as BTC, with backing from some of the same strategists promoting the pipeline in Washington and with energy cooperation as one of its objectives. At the same time, Armenia turned even more to Russia for its energy needs and signed a deal with Iran to construct an Iran-Armenia gas pipeline, which was completed in 2006; it is majority-owned by a subsidiary of the Russian gas giant Gazprom. Arguably, however, Russia would have been aggressive and driven a hard bargain over pipeline routes, regardless of who it is was dealing with and in any international context. Russian opposition to the early oil options showed that it was not even happy with the multiple-route option. The Russian government also made life difficult for Chevron in Kazakhstan when it refused to expand the capacity of the Caspian Pipeline Consortium (CPC) pipeline taking Kazakh oil to Novorossiisk.

What is certain is that Vladimir Putin, who became Russia's president in 2000, saw Western intervention in the Caspian region as a zero-sum game and looked for ways to reassert Russia's influence there as soon as he could. Within a month of taking office, he had appointed a new deputy foreign minister for Caspian affairs and visited Turkmenistan to sign a deal to buy Turkmen gas. In January 2001, Putin was the first leader from the Kremlin to visit Baku since Leonid Brezhnev, moving to repair Russian-Azerbaijani relations, which had deteriorated badly in the Yeltsin era. Putin underlined the change in tone by reminding everyone that he and Heidar Aliev had formerly both worked for the same employer. He presented Aliev with his graduation certificate from the Leningrad KGB academy in 1949—it was the first public confirmation that Aliev had even studied in Leningrad.

Over the next few years, Azerbaijani-Russian relations improved on several levels, the importance of the GUAM project faded, and the Azerbaijani government made it clear that, unlike Georgia, it had no ambition to join NATO. In August 2013, a year after his return to a third term as president, Putin made his highest-profile visit to Azerbaijan, arriving in Baku, accompanied by six senior ministers. Russia promised new weapons sales to Azerbaijan and discussed energy cooperation. The visit was a conspicuous signal to the country that Russia could be relied on to support Aliev's leader's reelection for a third term, in contrast to Western concerns about the country's deviation from democratic standards. This did not mean that Baku had abandoned its cooperation with the West on energy and security issues. Rather, it was a sign that Azerbaijan wanted a self-sufficient, diversified foreign policy, that balanced multiple interests.

Azerbaijan's Energy Dilemmas

In February 2015 Azerbaijan's oil boom came to an end with a bump. With oil output already declining, the world oil price fell and the National Bank of Azerbaijan was forced abruptly to devalue the national currency, the manat. Two years on, the manat had suffered one of the steepest devaluations of any world currency: on January 1, 2015, one Azerbaijani manat was worth $1.28; in the New Year of 2017 it would buy only 55 cents. The effects of devaluation were felt nationwide in the form of closing banks and, defaulted loans on apartment purchases, and higher food prices that caused demonstrations in small towns. There is no prospect of a new goose with a golden egg—no new Azerbaijani oil fields have been discovered since 1994. But the Azerbaijani government hopes that it is in a period of transition that it can navigate until about 2020, when it can live well again off another essential commodity, natural gas. In the meantime, its new economic model has come under intense strain.

For almost a decade after the BTC pipeline was inaugurated in 2005, Azerbaijan was a nation with newfound confidence. For three years in succession, 2005, 2006, and 2007, the country had the fastest economic growth rate in the world. Its GDP grew spectacularly from $1.3 billion in 1994 to $75.2 billion in 2014, when it began contracting again. The new wealth put Azerbaijan on the map, as the government opened dozens of new embassies around the world, funded new lobbying campaigns, and won a nonpermanent seat on the UN Security Council in 2011. The state oil company SOCAR, once a junior partner to its Western counterparts, became a big player in its own right. It became one of the largest investors in Turkey, saying it had invested $18 billion in the country, and came to own two-thirds of Greece's gas grid.

Some of the revenues were spent well—for example, to upgrade the country's aging infrastructure or to fund scholarship schemes abroad for Azerbaijani students. An oil fund, the State Oil Fund of Azerbaijan, or SOFAZ, was founded as a "rainy day fund" to enable the government to weather fluctuations in oil revenues. But many billions were spent on what could only be called vanity projects.

Azerbaijan's economy showed classic symptoms of "Dutch Disease," the condition whereby heavy reliance on the export of one product—usually oil or gas—weakens the rest of the economy. In 2014, just 10 percent of Azerbaijan's exports, earning only $1.4 billion, came from the non-energy sector. Moreover, oil and gas are notoriously poor at creating employment, supplying only around 1.5 percent of the jobs in the economy. BP, for example, despite its huge operations in Azerbaijan, had only 2,700 Azerbaijani employees in 2014.

A resource-rich country with an authoritarian political system and few checks and balances is a natural breeding ground for corruption. Even before the rapid influx of oil revenues from the BTC pipeline, government officials bought Mercedes automobiles and villas with values far beyond what their salaries could support. Shiny new offices were thrown up in Baku's medieval old town in clear contravention of regulations for what was supposed to be a UNESCO world heritage site. Foreign businessmen trod carefully, encountering the expectation that they would pay bribes for contracts but risking prosecution at home if they did. This dark subculture was for years the subject of gossip but no more than that; until it was brought to light by the case of the Czech wheeler-dealer Viktor Kozeny, nicknamed the "Pirate of Prague."

Kozeny, who first arrived in Baku in 1997, came up with an outrageous scheme to buy up SOCAR when it was privatized. He impressed a number of American investors with his wealth, charm, and apparent contacts in Baku and amassed investments of more than $200 million. But it was all a mirage: SOCAR was never going to be privatized, and most of the money disappeared. Kozeny retired to his home in the Bahamas, apparently unscathed, but an indictment was served on him and two of his investors in October 2005 by the U.S. Attorney's office in New York for allegedly violating the Foreign Corrupt Practices Act. The indictment alleged that Kozeny and two associates had taken part in a "massive scheme to bribe senior government officials in Azerbaijan" with large cash payments and items worth tens of thousands of pounds from the London jeweler Asprey & Garrard.[26] Kozeny managed to escape extradition, but one of his investors, Frederic Bourke, ended up being found guilty by a New York jury in 2009.

Another foreign investor who tried unsuccessfully to make money with elite Azerbaijani partners in Baku was future U.S. president Donald Trump. In 2012, Trump did a deal with Azerbaijan's transport minister Ziya Mammadov and his family to build a thirty-three-storey Trump Tower hotel in Baku. An investigation by the *New Yorker* into the deal described "behavior that seemed nakedly corrupt," with contractors paid with bags of dollars and officials given envelopes stuffed with cash. At the end of 2016, after Trump had been elected president, the Trump organization announced it was cutting its connection with the deal. But the hotel had still not opened, despite a bill in excess of $200 million, and the deals done with the Mammadov family made the Trump Organization vulnerable to prosecution under the Foreign Corrupt Practices Act.[27]

This restrictive oligarchic system has created more than financial problems. It has also stifled opportunities for a whole professional class that might have been expected to flourish in Azerbaijan's oil boom. Specifically, the system has alienated young, well-educated Azerbaijani professionals who have studied in the West, often on government grants, and who should be the next generation in its energy industry. Many of these people face the dilemma of whether to stay abroad or use their talents at home. An increasingly intolerant political climate and the arrest of many young activists espousing democracy, such as Rasul Jafarov and Anar Mammadli, sends a chilling message to those who would try to build a career in Azerbaijan. As Caspian energy expert Laurent Ruseckas points out, "If things don't change, Azerbaijan may well produce a future generation of technology entrepreneurs who will make their fortunes and generate employment in the United States, in the United Kingdom, in Turkey, or wherever else, rather than in their native land."[28]

Caspian Gas and Europe

The recoverable oil reserves of the Caspian Sea are slowly declining, and those of Azerbaijan may be fully depleted in two decades. In September 2017, Azerbaijan signed a new production-sharing agreement with the international consortium, led by BP, managing the giant ACG oil fields that have produced all its oil since 1994. Production from ACG had by this time dropped by around a third from its peak to a level of about 585,000 barrels per day of crude and stabilized at around that rate.

But with oil reserves in a long-term decline, the importance of the Caspian basin on the world energy map is increasingly shifting to its role as a source of natural gas. By far the biggest gas reserves in the region belong to Turkmenistan on the eastern shore of the Caspian, and China is becoming their chief buyer. Following the success of its oil exports via BTC, Azerbaijan plans to sustain itself and keep itself relevant to European consumers by exporting gas via Georgia and Turkey.

Since at least 2006 the European Union (EU) has been keen to lessen its dependence on Russia as its main provider of gas. That was the year in which Russia shut down supplies to Ukraine in the middle of winter, reminding the countries of the EU that they were reliant for at least half their gas supply on the giant Russian supplier Gazprom and Ukrainian transit routes. The perception that Russia was an unreliable supplier was reinforced by the August 2008 war in Europe and the subsequent Russia-Ukraine crisis of January 2009. With Iran, the country with the world's largest natural gas reserves along with Russia, still inaccessible to Western markets, many argued that it was time for European consumers to draw on the gas resources of the Caspian Sea, and particularly on those of Azerbaijan.

Azerbaijan became a world gas player almost by accident. In 1994, BP won the right to exploit a fifteen-mile-long oil field named Shah Deniz in the Caspian south of Baku. Instead, the engineers struck natural gas and condensate, a high-quality oil. It was the largest gas field BP had discovered in a century and had the potential to keep on producing for forty years. As a result, the South Caucasus or Baku-Erzerum gas pipeline was constructed to run along alongside the BTC oil pipeline for most of its route. In 2016, Azerbaijan was estimated to have reserves of 1.1 trillion cubic meters of natural gas, putting it in twenty-third place in BP's ranking of world gas reserves. That means that it has only about one-fifteenth of Turkmenistan's resources—but it does have the advantage of a Western-run gas pipeline already connecting the Caspian Sea to Western markets.

In 2002, plans were made for a new gas pipeline that would take Caspian Sea gas from Erzerum in Turkey to Austria. The five partners in the project—from Austria, Hungary, Bulgaria, Romania, and Turkey—all attended the Vienna State Opera and heard a production of Verdi's *Nabucco*; as a result, they named their projected pipeline Nabucco. Five European prime ministers formally endorsed it in 2009. However, Nabucco never became a viable project. Stepping down as the United States' coordinator for Eurasian energy diplomacy in 2009, senior diplomat Steve Mann warned of "Nabucco hucksterism" and the dangers of repeating some of the errors of the BTC saga. He said, "There have been quite a number of officials who know very little about energy who have been charging into the pipeline debate. Nabucco is a highly desirable project, don't get me wrong. But there are other highly desirable projects besides Nabucco. And the overriding question for all these projects is, Where's the gas?"[29]

Nabucco suffered from competition with Russia's rival project, the South Stream pipeline, projected to run across the Black Sea to Bulgaria. But South Stream also foundered in 2014, after legal objections from Bulgaria and the EU. The bigger problem was upstream, where, as Mann noted, Nabucco needed gas to fill it. Iran and Iraqi Kurdistan were both politically problematic. The most attractive option was Turkmenistan, where a relatively short connecting pipeline was needed to make the Trans-Caspian Pipeline across the Caspian Sea. But, despite much lobbying from Washington, this idea has never made much progress. In 2018, one of the project's major obstacles—international disputes over the legal status of the Caspian Sea—was close to being finally overcome, but other issues remained unresolved, such as doubts as to whether the highly authoritarian Turkmen government could be relied on to sign legally enforceable contracts. Furthermore, the Central Asia-China gas pipeline, inaugurated in 2009 and later expanded, connected Turkmenistan to China and made China the country's most valued customer.

A scaled-down version of Nabucco took shape to ship the additional gas from Azerbaijan's Shah Deniz II field. This involved expanding capacity of the Baku-Erzerum pipeline and building two more pipelines, one across Turkey up to the Greek border known as the Trans Anatolian Natural Gas Pipeline (TANAP), and the other, the Trans Adriatic Pipeline (TAP), running through northern Greece, Albania, and across the Adriatic Sea to Italy's southeastern coast. The declared plan is that from 2019 Azerbaijan will sell 10 billion cubic meters (bcm) of gas to Turkey, and that from 2020 a further 6 bcm will go to Greece, Italy, and the Balkans. In 2016 the EU was consuming about 300 bcm of gas a year, so Shah Deniz gas would cover only 1.5 percent of that demand. Talk of a "Southern Gas Corridor" is overblown when the volumes of gas in question are so modest.

The international gas market is increasingly crowded. In the European market, Azerbaijan will be competing with liquefied natural gas (LNG) from Qatar, the United States, and other countries; shale gas production in Europe itself; and new gas fields being exploited in the eastern Mediterranean by Cyprus, Egypt, and Israel. Moreover, even before the completion of the new pipelines, Azerbaijan's supply was already squeezed, with most of it going to meet domestic demand and the country forced to import gas from Russia. In the winter of 2015–16 Georgian officials held talks with Russia's Gazprom about resuming imports of Russian gas. This caused an outcry domestically, especially as the talks had been conducted in secret. But it later appeared that the main reason for the negotiations was a shortage of gas from Azerbaijan, and the problem was solved in March 2016, when Georgia concluded a new deal to buy Azerbaijani gas at reduced prices.[30] That is an early warning to Azerbaijan as it seeks to earn revenues and a reminder that every country, even friendly Georgia, will try to strike a hard deal to get gas at the cheapest possible rate.

7

Modern Georgia:

Rebirth, Rose Revolution, and Conflict

Shevardnadze's Georgia

In the summer of 1992 Georgia was admitted to the United Nations but could barely be called a state. Abkhazia, Ajaria, and South Ossetia were running their own affairs, independent of Tbilisi, while there was a low-level civil war in the western region of Mingrelia. Shevardnadze, the unelected head of the State Council, was the country's leader more or less by default. The Georgian intelligentsia accepted him only grudgingly—unhappy, so soon after independence, to have invited back the former Communist Party boss they had known since 1972. One Tbilisi intellectual who had entered politics recalled that Shevardnadze had simply had more stamina than Georgia's other would-be leaders and that in a series of long meetings "he out-sat" them and got what he wanted. The veteran of world politics sat impassively in the parliament chamber, like a teacher in an unruly classroom, sipping endless glasses of green tea as voices were raised and occasional punches were even thrown.

Over the next few years, Shevardnadze edged Georgia out of an abyss. Twice, in 1995 and 1998, he narrowly escaped assassination; there were many suspects, but most Georgians blamed the Russian security services. He moved slowly, being elected speaker of parliament in October 1992 and then president in 1995. He gradually curtailed the power of the two warlords who had been running the country. By the end of 1995, both Kitovani and Ioseliani had been put in jail and the armed groups they ran disbanded.

Shevardnadze called in favors he had earned as Soviet foreign minister, especially in the United States and Germany, and used his name to secure billions of dollars of international aid. His biggest successes were undoubtedly in foreign policy. He won Georgia useful friends in the West; he saw through the approval of the BTC oil pipeline route, which made Georgia a link in a new energy chain from the Caspian Sea to Europe; and in 1999 he secured a commitment from Russia to close its military bases in Georgia.

In the West, there was a widespread perception that Georgia was the most progressive post-Soviet country outside the Baltic states. The face of reform was Zurab Zhvania, a former leader of the Georgian Green Party, who became speaker of parliament in 1995 at the age of only thirty-one. Thoughtful and intelligent, if rather portly and slow for someone his age, Zhvania impressed Western interlocutors with his ideas expressed in fluent English and was talked about as a potential successor to Shevardnadze. In 1996–2000, Zhvania and a team of "young reformers" helped give Georgia double-digit economic growth rates.

But this positive picture was very superficial. Georgia remained a weak state captive to powerful political factions. Its basic services were chronically underfunded, with a paltry 1 percent of GDP, or less than $20 million, being spent on state health care. There were so many vested interests holding back reform of the power sector that the country suffered from chronic electricity blackouts. Shevardnadze's feat of breaking the grip of Georgia's warlords was achieved at the cost of Faustian power-sharing deals with businessmen and local governors. The newly powerful interior ministry turned into a semicriminalized monster, which at one point owned Georgia's most famous football club, Dynamo Tbilisi.[1] The leader of the Black Sea region of Ajaria, Aslan Abashidze, bought Shevardnadze stability in return for total control of his home patch. Clever, vain, and somewhat paranoid, Abashidze never traveled to Tbilisi and kept most of the local shipping revenues within Ajaria.

Had Shevardnadze stood down in 2000, he would have been remembered as the savior of the new Georgia, but his last three years in office were characterized by drift and corruption. The president himself was generally perceived to be honest, but there was widespread resentment of his relatives; his nephew Nugzar was one of the richest men in Georgia. The presidential elections of April 9, 2000, confirmed the cynical mood: Shevardnadze was elected for a second time, amazingly, against the man who had succeeded him as party leader in 1985, Jumbar Patiashvili. It reflected badly on Georgia that the two main candidates were former Communist Party bosses.

The second war in Chechnya, waged by Moscow from the end of 1999, exposed how weak the Georgian state was. Thousands of Chechen refugees fled over the mountains into Georgia, and many settled in the Pankisi Gorge area, which was home to the Kists, a small ethnic group related to the Chechens. Among them were many armed fighters and several Arab *jihadi* militants. The valley turned into a center of drug trafficking and kidnapping carried out in collaboration with corrupt Georgian policemen. Two Spanish businessmen, the brother of a famous Georgian footballer, and a British banker were all abducted and held captive there.

The Russian government denounced Georgia for giving refuge to Russia's enemies, making exaggerated claims about the threat they posed to Russia—Russian foreign minister Igor Ivanov even suggested that Osama bin Laden was living in the gorge. The Russian air force staged several intimidatory bombing raids on the area, and Moscow imposed visa requirements on Georgians. Calls for Tbilisi to regain authority grew louder after the September 11, 2001, terrorist attacks in the United States, when Russia depicted Chechnya as a front in the "war on terror." In May 2002, Shevardnadze turned a public relations disaster into a success by inviting U.S. troops onto Georgian soil for the first time as part of a project entitled the Georgia Train and Equip Program. The 150–200 American soldiers involved in the program trained Georgian troops in a support role for a police "anticriminal operation" in the Pankisi Gorge. Within a few months, the gorge was free of armed Chechens—most of them actually moved on themselves after being tipped off—but the U.S. troops stayed on.

The Rose Revolution

In 2002, there was already a distinct end-of-regime mood in Georgia. Zurab Zhvania, the former leader of the "young reformers," had resigned as speaker of parliament and formed his own opposition party, but he was not especially liked by the wider public. Among a crowd of opposition politicians, one of Zhvania's own protégés emerged as the new star. Mikheil Saakashvili, universally known as "Misha" even to those who did not know him, had studied in Kiev, in Strasbourg, and at Columbia University in New York. Tall, charismatic, multilingual, and married to a Dutch wife, he seemed to represent a new post-Communist generation in Georgia. He was appointed justice minister at the age of just thirty-two and got the attention of the public with such actions as riding the Tbilisi metro to work. A year later, he resigned in dramatic fashion, accusing government colleagues of corruption, and set up an opposition party, the National Movement. In November 2002, Saakashvili won election as chairman of Tbilisi's municipal assembly and used the position as a showcase to enact popular reforms.

Georgia's parliamentary elections in the autumn of 2003 were seen as a dress rehearsal for the presidential vote slated for 2005, when Shevardnadze was due to step down. Georgia's chaotic pluralism gave space for lively political debate. The pro-opposition television channel Rustavi-2 broadcast freely despite one clumsy attempt to shut it down. Georgian nongovernmental organizations also benefited from Western aid programs. A new youth movement was formed named Kmara ("Enough"). Kmara's activists cleverly stoked people's dissatisfaction with the status quo by painting their one-word message "Kmara" on walls, street signs, and fences across the whole country.

As the elections approached, Shevardnadze lost some key allies. In June 2003, Nino Burjanadze, whom opinion polls gave the most positive rating of any public figure in Georgia, resigned her post as speaker of parliament and joined up with Zurab Zhvania. Their new movement, "Burjanadze-Democrats," allied her calm demeanor with Zhvania's political acumen. However, the charismatic Saakashvili ran the most successful election campaign.

The elections of semidemocratic Georgia came under much closer international scrutiny than those of other post-Soviet countries. At the end of a chaotic polling day on November 2, Rustavi-2 broadcast the results of a big exit poll and the dramatic news that Saakashvili's National Movement had won first place, with an estimated 26 percent of the vote. The Central Electoral Commission then began to release its own official results, putting the progovernment party in first place. The impression of falsification was obvious. From November 5, diverse antigovernment groups began to hold protest rallies in central Tbilisi. The opposition was divided on tactics, but Shevardnadze refused to compromise and kept its factions united. Then, on November 14, suspiciously late, the Ajaria region released its voting returns, giving the official Revival Party almost 100 percent of the vote there. This manifest theft of votes threatened to give the leader of Ajaria a central role in the new parliament and strengthened the determination of the opposition in Tbilisi.

From this point, momentum shifted behind the crowds on Rustaveli Avenue. Saakashvili was the popular favorite and was lent gravitas by being one member in a triple leadership along with Zhvania and Burjanadze. The protestors waved the red-and-white flag of Saakashvili's National Movement and red roses, which they had adopted as a symbol of resistance. Rustavi-2 provided around-the-clock coverage. The protests were well organized and peaceful and reminded foreign journalists of the democracy movements that had swept aside Communist regimes in eastern Europe in 1989.

On November 22, Shevardnadze tried to legitimize the elections by convening the new parliament in its building in central Tbilisi, just yards from the opposition demonstrations. As he began a rambling speech, Saakashvili led a crowd in a march against parliament. Police cordons simply parted and let the protestors through. Saakashvili dramatically swept into the parliamentary chamber, clutching a single red rose and shouting, "Gadadeki, gadadeki!" ("Resign, resign!") Shevardnadze stopped reading his speech and was hustled from the chamber by his bodyguards. Saakashvili strode onto the podium, theatrically finishing the cup of tea that Shevardnadze had been drinking, and declared the new parliament invalid. Shevardnadze retired to his residence and tried to declare a state of emergency.

Georgia's rising star. Mikheil Saakashvili addressing a rally at the beginning of the Rose Revolution, Tbilisi, November 2003. Georgi Kraveishvili.

The next day was November 23, Saint George's Day. Russia's Georgian-born foreign minister, Igor Ivanov, a former protégé of Shevardnadze, flew in to mediate. He surprised the crowds on Rustaveli Avenue by giving them an impromptu speech and then went to see Shevardnadze. Ivanov's plan, it later transpired, had been for Shevardnadze to stay on for several months but to agree to early presidential elections; the Russians may have hoped that they could thereby influence the choice of the next leader. However, after Ivanov had left Tbilisi, Shevardnadze received Zhvania and Saakashvili for a short meeting and told them he had changed his mind. The two men emerged looking slightly shell-shocked and told journalists that Shevardnadze had announced his resignation with immediate effect.

The Rose Revolution briefly electrified the world. It was a rare example of popular democracy in action and a compelling spectacle pulled off with Georgian flair. Georgia's bloodless revolution was also the first of three so-called Color Revolutions that removed presidents in Ukraine and Kyrgyzstan. A myth gained currency, especially in Russia, that the revolutions had been planned by the U.S. government and executed by organizations such as the National Democratic Institute and George Soros's Open Society Institute. In 2008, the Russian government officially referred to "the regime of M. Saakashvili, who came to power in Tbilisi with the active collaboration of the USA as a result of the so-called 'Rose Revolution.' " In fact, the events that swept away Shevardnadze were extremely improvised, and Russian foreign minister Igor Ivanov was the most senior foreign official involved in them. U.S.–funded nongovernmental organizations played at most a supporting role.

What chiefly transformed a disputed election into the Rose Revolution was the miscalculation of the man at the center of it, Eduard Shevardnadze. Had Shevardnadze agreed to a substantial recount of votes or a new parliamentary election, he would probably have defused the crisis: bad though they were, the polls were far from being the most flawed in the former Soviet Union. By refusing to compromise, the Georgian leader turned an electoral dispute into a street referendum on his presidency. Then, as key allies deserted him, he evidently decided to bow out rather than pick a fight. When it came to the crunch, Shevardnadze also knew that he could expect a peaceful retirement. In the Caucasus, losing office carries the risk of exile or prosecution: in October 2003 in Azerbaijan and in February 2008 in Armenia, official leaders violently suppressed opposition to disputed election results with that in mind. But Shevardnadze knew that he could trust his former protégés Zhvania and Saakashvili to leave himself and his close family in peace. Most

important, Shevardnadze had made the Rose Revolution possible through
his own style of rule. A master of equivocation, he was responsible not only
for Georgia's weak government but also for the lively nongovernmental
sector and free media that the opposition used as weapons to oust him.[2]

Saakashvili in Power

At the beginning of 2004, the three leaders of the Rose Revolution masked
their differences and rode a wave of domestic and international goodwill.
Within a few months, Saakashvili had been elected president virtually un-
opposed, with 96 percent of the vote. Zhvania was appointed prime minister, and Burjanadze was again made speaker of parliament. On January
24, 2004, the day before his presidential inauguration, Saakashvili traveled
to the monastery of Gelati and swore an oath to unite Georgia on the tomb
of the twelfth-century king David the Builder. He said, "At the grave of King
David we must all say: Georgia will be united, strong, will restore its whole-
ness and become a united, strong state."[3] Saakashvili's speech summed up his
coming presidency in a nutshell. It displayed his usual flair for public relations and theatrical presentation and was full of bold promises that would be
all but impossible to realize. The new president also made it clear that his priority was more to build a strong state than to forge democratic institutions,
a point many Western observers missed. Saakashvili later said, "People compare my style to that of JFK, but in terms of substance, I feel much closer
to Ataturk or Ben Gurion, or General de Gaulle—people who had to build
nation states. Shevardnadze had a chance to become a founding father of the
nation, but he missed that chance, so now I have this honor to become one,
along with my friends."[4]

In this spirit, Saakashvili set himself the goal of strengthening the
Georgian state. Within a month of becoming president, he had pushed radical constitutional amendments through parliament that turned Georgia from
a semiparliamentary republic into a strongly presidential one. The changes
stripped parliament—and therefore also Nino Burjanadze—of many of its
powers and gave the president the right to appoint most key state officials.
Saakashvili then appointed new regional governors and began to impose
government control over television stations. In his bid to remodel the entire state, he even had the flag of his own National Movement, a medieval
banner with five red crosses on a white background, made into the national
flag. Saakashvili also kept to his promise to crack down on corruption. He

radically cut and reformed both the regular and traffic police so that bribe-taking became virtually impossible. Former ministers and businessmen accused of enriching themselves under the old regime were detained, often with television cameras filming the arrest. They were put into pretrial detention and forced to pay "bail" or "fines" of millions of dollars directly into the state treasury. Associates of Shevardnadze's son-in-law Gia Jokhtaberidze paid up a staggering $15.5 million. The arrests were wildly popular and enriched the state treasury but fell a long way short of the rule of law.

The biggest achievement of Saakashvili and his first prime minister, Zhvania, was the transformation of the economy. The customs service and tax police were overhauled, tax rates were simplified, red tape was slashed, and companies were forced to declare their incomes. The result was that in July 2006 the president was able to claim that the state budget had increased from $350 million to $3 billion. This in turn funded the construction of new roads, hospitals, and schools. Wages and pensions went up. Foreign investment also shot up, aided by a public relations campaign waged by the president himself. Saakashvili traveled incessantly, presenting the story of Georgia's Rose Revolution and its successes to foreign audiences. He brilliantly courted the Western media, winning positive profiles that portrayed Georgia as a democratic success story.

Saakashvili's other big success was to oust the corrupt regime of Abashidze in Ajaria. Saakashvili ignored warnings about the danger of bloodshed and gave an ultimatum to Abashidze to step down, sponsoring street demonstrations against him. On May 6, Abashidze buckled under pressure and fled to Russia. There was great relief and rejoicing in Batumi, although this was tempered with dismay a month later when Saakashvili trimmed the powers of Ajaria's autonomous government and parliament, reducing them to a more or less decorative status.

Many of these moves led to criticism that the Saakashvili administration was more neo-Bolshevik than democratic. In October 2004, in an open letter, a group of civil society activists and intellectuals chided the president for being intolerant of criticism. In a newspaper article, one of the signatories, the political analyst Ghia Nodia, said the Georgian leadership had a "permanent revolutionary syndrome." Two months later, a report by the Parliamentary Assembly of the Council of Europe concluded: "Today Georgia has a semi-presidential system with very strong powers to the President, basically no parliamentary opposition, a weaker civil society, a judicial system that is not yet sufficiently independent and functioning, undeveloped or non-existing local democracy, a self-censored media and an inadequate model of autonomy in Ajaria."[5]

A big problem was that power was highly personalized in Saakashvili himself. The president personally made most of the government's decisions. He intervened in every aspect of policy in long, rapid-fire, fluent monologues. One Western interlocutor said, "After you've had a discussion with him, you need to lie down. You need a drink."[6] He relied on five or six members of an inner circle who sat in his office late into the night. It was a more extreme example of the "sofa government" for which Britain's Tony Blair was criticized at the time. At the same time, the incessant gossip about his allegedly erratic personal life made comparisons with Bill Clinton and Boris Yeltsin more apt. The youthful Saakashvili had no elder counselors around him and ran Georgia with what was probably the youngest government in the world. In 2008, Georgia went to war with Russia with a forty-year-old president, thirty-six-year-old prime minister, thirty-one-year-old foreign minister, and twenty-nine-year-old defense minister.

All these tendencies took a turn for the worse in February 2005, with the tragic death of Zurab Zhvania, Saakashvili's prime minister, wisest advisor, and rival. Zhvania died of apparent poisoning from a faulty gas heater at the apartment of a friend. Many people suspected foul play, and many questions about his death are still unanswered, although an official Georgian investigation conducted jointly with the FBI concluded that it was probably an accident. The death of Zhvania at the age of only forty-one robbed Georgia of its most level-headed politician and of a calm counterbalance to the impulsive Saakashvili.

Putin's Russia, Abkhazia, and South Ossetia

Relations with Russia were an immediate priority for the new Georgian president. It is easy to forget now, but for six months after the Rose Revolution there was optimism that Georgian-Russian relations were improving. The day after Shevardnadze's resignation, President Putin said he hoped the change in leadership would "restore the tradition of friendship" between the two countries.[7] Saakashvili, in his first press conference after the Rose Revolution, told a Russian journalist in Russian: "For us the main strategic priority is to build normal relations with all countries and first of all Russia. Shevardnadze didn't have good or bad relations with Russia, he had abnormal relations with Russia." Georgia's integration into Europe, Saakashvili went on to say, should take place "together with Russia."[8]

Saakashvili traveled to Moscow for his first foreign trip as president on February 10–11, 2004. His first meeting with Putin got off to a bad start.

Saakashvili spent too much time in the swimming pool of his hotel and arrived at the Kremlin in such a hurry that his suit jacket did not match his trousers.[9] But the two men had a serious and respectful conversation. Afterwards, his foreign minister, Tedo Japaridze, who was not in the meeting, found Saakashvili brimming with optimism:

> He came out of it very much excited and thrilled with that encounter and the man himself: "He's real leader, a resolute and strong man who controls everything—Duma, the mass media and so forth." ... These were his first words when we were driving back to the airport. It's interesting that Saakashvili also called [his main friend in the U.S. administration] Matt Bryza and sort of shared his emotions with him and he did that on his regular cell phone and it looked that some Moscow circuits were pleased to be part of that exchange.[10]

The thaw in relations continued as the Russians acquiesced to the peaceful removal of their protégé in Ajaria, Aslan Abashidze, in May. Later that month, senior Russian businessmen and officials attended a Russian-Georgian business forum in Tbilisi. This led to the appointment as minister of economics of Russian-Georgian businessman Kakha Bendukidze, who then set out a program of radical libertarian economic policies for Georgia. Before their next round of talks, Saakashvili said of Putin: "As opposed to many politicians in this world, he never forgets his promises."[11] The two presidents agreed to ease visa restrictions.

However, less than two weeks after his trip to Moscow, Saakashvili traveled to Washington and received an even more friendly welcome. President George W. Bush said of Saakashvili, "I'm impressed by this leader. I'm impressed by his vision, I'm impressed by his courage. I am heartened by the fact that we have such a strong friend, a friend with whom we share values." Throughout Saakashvili's first term, an impressive string of U.S. politicians from both main parties, from Richard Holbrooke to Joe Biden to John McCain, expressed support for Georgia. This encouraged Saakashvili to bargain hard with Moscow on two of the difficult issues between them: the status of Russian bases in Georgia and Georgia's NATO ambitions. But the main neuralgic issue between Moscow and Tbilisi was once again Abkhazia and South Ossetia.

On the first day of his presidency, Saakashvili said he intended to achieve the "restoration of Georgia's territorial integrity" by the end of his first term. In his speech at the tomb of David the Builder, he said he hoped to hold his next inauguration ceremony in Sukhumi in Abkhazia. After the drift of the Shevardnadze years, it was a clear statement of his intent to shake up the status quo.

Georgia's two breakaway territories were still both poor and isolated: Abkhazia labored under an economic sanctions regime, and South Ossetia lived on agriculture and smuggled goods. But after Putin became Russia's president in 2000, Moscow began quietly to exploit the situation in both regions. The first sign of a new policy came at the end of the year when Russia introduced visas for Georgians but exempted residents of Abkhazia and South Ossetia. The following year, Moscow offered residents of the two territories Russian passports instead of their useless Soviet passports. The Abkhaz and Ossetians were naturally delighted to seize a chance to break out of international isolation—the Georgian government had insisted they needed to apply for Georgian passports in order to travel.

In December 2001, Eduard Kokoity, a businessman and former wrestler with a rather dubious reputation, was unexpectedly elected president of South Ossetia. Kokoity had been the candidate of the Tedeyev brothers, businessmen who controlled the criminalized postwar economy in South Ossetia. But two years later, he ordered them out of South Ossetia and began to invite in a series of former KGB officers from all over Russia to take up posts in his government. Kokoity took a tougher line on the framework agreements that his predecessors had negotiated with the Georgians.

Abkhazia also experienced a shock in 2001, with a bizarre episode that reflected the worst of the late Shevardnadze period in Georgia. A group of 100 Chechen fighters led by commander Ruslan Gelayev were put under pressure to leave the Pankisi Gorge area. In the late summer of 2001, they were suddenly transported to another mountainous valley, the Upper Kodori Gorge, the only part of Abkhazia not under Abkhaz control. There they were joined by a mixed group of armed Georgians and other Caucasian volunteers, bringing their total numbers to around 400. The fighters attacked a village and looked poised to make an attack on Sukhumi, which was less than fifty miles away. The Abkhaz mobilized their troops and halted the attack. Several of the fighters were captured; others melted away. The episode was very murky. The Georgian government denied involvement, which meant that senior leaders either were lying or had acted on their own initiative. If the operation had been a genuine attempt to invade Abkhazia, then the numbers of men were insufficient; if there had been another goal, it never became clear. The events cost the lives of several dozen people, including nine people in a UN helicopter that almost certainly was shot down by the Chechen fighters. The Abkhaz emerged from the crisis distrustful and much less inclined to negotiate with Tbilisi.[12]

This was the environment Saakashvili inherited in 2004. Although the problems he faced were deep-seated, the new Georgian president had a number of advantages. He was a politician from a younger generation that had not been involved in the war, he had a strong public mandate, and he had the hope of forging better relations with Putin than his predecessor had maintained. There was also weariness among the populations in both Abkhazia and South Ossetia that could be exploited by a leader in Tbilisi, so long as he was prepared to be diplomatic and patient.

There were important differences between Abkhazia and South Ossetia. Crudely put, Russia had much more at stake in Abkhazia because of its location and resources. Russians also had a strong emotional attachment to Abkhazia from Soviet times. The army and KGB had had some of their best sanatoria there. Putin said in an interview that he had twice been on holiday in Abkhazia as a student, recalling that he had bought a favorite overcoat in the town of Gagra that he wore for fifteen years afterward.[13]

The same could not be said of poor landlocked South Ossetia. In his first meeting with Saakashvili in February 2004, Putin reportedly said that he was prepared to do a deal over the territory that would restore it to Georgia with large powers of autonomy if Saakashvili would wait a year or eighteen months while he worked with his own bureaucracy and the South Ossetians themselves. Putin indicated that other issues, such as Georgia's NATO bid, were more important to Russia than South Ossetia.

THE ERGNETI MARKET

After the conflicts of the early 1990s ended in the South Caucasus, two markets sprang up more or less spontaneously in which trade transcended ethnic hostility. One was the Sadakhlo market on Georgian territory just across the border from Armenia and not far from Azerbaijan. For a decade, its main traders were thousands of Armenians and Azerbaijanis exchanging goods and produce, with barely a Georgian in sight. The market was eventually shut down in 2005 by the Georgian authorities.

The other trading center, near the village of Ergneti on the border of South Ossetia, was probably the largest wholesale market in the Caucasus. Thousands of Georgians and Ossetians gathered there every day, and it was so large that buyers used motorcycles to get around. The Ossetians sold the Georgians wheat, petrol, cigarettes, and consumer goods from the Russian side of the mountains, while Georgian farmers sold the Ossetians their agricultural produce. The cut-price goods helped impoverished people make ends meet, but the economic downside of the market was that none of the goods were taxed, and there were also reports of stolen cars and illegal alcohol passing through it.[1]

The new government in Tbilisi closed the Ergneti market down in June 2004 on the grounds that it was undermining the state budget. Three months later the Georgian customs department announced that monthly revenues from the legal customs checkpoint with Russia at Kazbegi had increased fourfold to around $2.5 million, as traders were forced to declare goods they would have previously offloaded customs-free at Ergneti.

But the closure of the market was a disaster at a deeper level. It threw thousands of Georgians and Ossetians into unemployment, and a precious and complex web of Georgian-Ossetian people's diplomacy, woven through trade, was destroyed. As one Georgian peace negotiator said later, "If Ergneti didn't exist, it should have been invented." South Ossetia had effectively been part of the Georgian economy for the previous ten years, but after the closure of the market Ossetian traders began to orient themselves toward Russia. The Georgian government launched an antismuggling operation in South Ossetia in the summer of 2004 that led to the worst fighting there in twelve years and prepared the ground for the wider war of 2008. In retrospect, the Georgian government would have been well advised to try to take control of the Ergneti market and keep it open as an investment in peace in South Ossetia.

1. See International Alert, *From War Economies to Peace Economies in the South Caucasus* (London: International Alert, 2004).

On the ground, South Ossetia was in many ways still part of Georgia. Most of its large Georgian population were still living there. The Ergneti market on the border of South Ossetia was the most flourishing trading entrepôt in the Caucasus (see "The Ergneti Market" box). South Ossetians traveled freely into the rest of Georgia. Although Georgia officially forbade dual citizenship, many residents of South Ossetia actually held both Georgian and Russian passports and crossed the border freely.

Saakashvili pursued several tracks at once. He made some characteristic public relations gestures such as inserting declarations of friendship in the Abkhaz and Ossetian languages into his speeches. More practically, he moved to disarm the Georgian criminal groups that had been terrorizing locals in eastern Abkhazia. In 2004 Saakashvili appointed Irakli Alasania as his main official dealing with Abkhazia. Alasania's father had been one of the Georgian officials who had stayed in Sukhumi in September 1993 and had been captured and killed after the Abkhaz took the city. Alasania won respect among the Abkhaz for his nonconfrontational approach and began to get the peace process back on track.

However, at the same time, Saakashvili also decided that he could replicate the quick success he had won in Ajaria in South Ossetia, despite the fact that the Ossetian problem was much deeper and had already caused one war. In summer 2004, the Georgian authorities shut down the Ergneti market, cutting off grassroots Georgian-Ossetian relations at a stroke. Around the same time, conflict resolution minister Giorgi Khaindrava went into the office of Gigi Ugulava, a member of Saakashvili's inner circle and then deputy security minister, and to his horror saw maps of South Ossetia all over the wall with plans for a military campaign. "All the days were mapped out—they wanted to do an exact copy of what they had done in Ajaria," Khaindrava said.[14]

In March, the situation in South Ossetia had been sufficiently calm for Khaindrava to be able to drive through South Ossetia to the Russian border and back again in his own car. Now Tbilisi's antismuggling operation provoked the worst violence in twelve years. Georgian armed police moved into South Ossetia and set up checkpoints. Both sides seized captives. In late July and early August, there were exchanges of gunfire and mortars, and the region approached the brink of war. On August 5, U.S. secretary of state Colin Powell gave Saakashvili a stern warning not to pursue the military option in South Ossetia. On August 19 a truce was agreed, and Georgian troops were pulled back. The hawks had lost ground—and at least seventeen Ossetians and five Georgians had been killed. The crisis boosted Kokoity, who had been an unpopular leader in South Ossetia until that point, and wrecked the grassroots rapport that had grown up between the two communities since 1992. "The remilitarisation of the zone of conflict reversed a decade of progress," concluded the International Crisis Group.[15]

Less than two weeks after the truce, North Ossetia was hit by a greater tragedy. More than thirty Chechen militants seized School No. 1 in Beslan, took more than 1,000 people hostage, and killed many of them. When Russian special forces stormed the school on September 3, more than 330 hostages died, half of them children. Most of the anger in Ossetia was directed against Chechens and their ethnic kin, the Ingush. But there was also fury against the authorities in Moscow, as many local people believed that President Putin had not done enough to save their children. With regard to South Ossetia, the irony is that this low point in Russian-Ossetian relations came too late for the Tbilisi government to make use of it. Had there been no fighting in South Ossetia in June–August, the fall of 2004 might have been a promising moment for Saakashvili to offer a deal to end the conflict peacefully.

Descent into Conflict

On May 10, 2005, President Bush visited Georgia. He was given an ecstatic welcome, and the main highway from the airport to the center of Tbilisi was renamed after him. Bush thanked Georgia for supplying troops to Iraq and Afghanistan—at the peak of its deployment, Georgia's 2,000-strong peacekeeping contingent in Iraq was the second-largest deployment there on a per capita basis after the United States. But his main objective was to praise Saakashvili's Georgia as a triumphant example of democratization in action. Standing next to Saakashvili, Bush made a speech in Freedom Square in Tbilisi in which he told the crowd, "You gathered here armed with nothing but roses and the power of your convictions, and you claimed your liberty. And because you acted, Georgia is today both sovereign and free, and a beacon of liberty for this region and the world."

President Bush also transmitted the message in private that he wanted to see Georgia's conflicts resolved peacefully. This helped breathe some new life into the negotiations. The two new Georgian mediators made some progress. Importantly, Abkhazia soon gained a new leader, who won his position despite Russian opposition and received a popular mandate.

The presidential election in Abkhazia in October 2004 turned into a political marathon that stretched into the following year. The two main candidates were Sergei Bagapsh, a Soviet-era official with an easy avuncular manner and good diplomatic skills, and a younger man, former defense minister and prime minister Raul Khajimba. The two men reflected two different strains within Abkhazia. Khajimba represented a group that was identified both with the outgoing (and extremely ill) leader Vladislav Ardzinba and with the security establishment in Moscow.[16] Bagapsh, whose wife was Georgian, drew support from officials frustrated with Ardzinba's rule and from Abkhazia's other ethnic communities, such as Armenians and the Georgians of the Gali region. Bagapsh pressed for a line that would keep Russia friendly but separate. Moscow heavy-handedly backed Khajimba, organizing a series of pop concerts that backfired badly. At one of them, the famous Russian pop star Oleg Gazmanov made the spectacular blunder of greeting the crowd with the words "Hello, Ajaria!" perfectly summing up Russia's ignorance of local realities.

Because of Abkhazia's unrecognized status and the nonparticipation of its Georgian population, the election was entirely self-organized and was declared invalid by the international community. Yet it turned into a tense constitutional drama, with each side claiming victory and bringing its supporters into the streets. Bagapsh was declared the official victor, but the Russian government began to apply pressure to try to halt his inauguration, set for December 6, by closing the Russian border and railway line. An aide to the Russian prime minister called Bagapsh's team "criminal." Eventually a compromise deal was brokered under which the election results were suspended and Bagapsh ran for a new election with Khajimba as his vice-presidential candidate. The two rivals duly agreed to this unlikely alliance and were elected to their new posts on January 13, 2005. On being elected, Bagapsh was careful to offer his unwavering support for Moscow, but the drama showed that there was a strong undercurrent of suspicion in Abkhaz society toward Russia.

In 2006 there were active negotiations in the peace process for both conflicts. Yet Saakashvili continued to pursue two lines at once. Alasania was making progress on a "road map" document to present to his counterparts in Sukhumi and on May 15 received the main Abkhaz negotiator, Sergei Shamba, in Tbilisi for talks, which both sides greeted as a step forward. But on the very same day, Saakashvili chose not to receive Shamba and traveled instead to the border with Abkhazia, where he inspected a newly built military base in the town of Senaki. By doing so, he delivered an entirely different belligerent message to the Abkhaz and undermined the work his mediators were doing. Two weeks earlier, Saakashvili's young hawkish defense minister, Irakli Okruashvili, a native of the South Ossetian capital Tskhinvali, had disparaged the peacemakers for South Ossetia, saying, "If we fail to celebrate New Year in Tskhinvali on January 1, 2007 I will no longer be the defense minister of Georgia."[17]

As the summer marched on, Saakashvili chose the hawks of his inner circle over the doves. In June, Alasania lost his position as mediator and was made Georgia's ambassador to the United Nations. In July, the Georgian government sent troops into the Upper Kodori Gorge in the mountains of Abkhazia. The pretext was to arrest a local warlord, Emzar Kvitsiani, but he could have been detained when he had spent several weeks in Tbilisi. The real goal was evidently to establish firm control of a strategically important piece of territory that was under no one's full control. As if to emphasize the point, Saakashvili renamed the region Upper Abkhazia and installed his Georgian-staffed "Abkhaz government in exile" in the remote gorge. The Abkhaz side said this was a violation of the 1994 ceasefire agreements and withdrew from negotiations, which never subsequently got back on track.

In parallel, the quarrel between Moscow and Tbilisi had taken a turn for the worse. In March 2006, in what looked like an act of spite, Russia officially banned the import of Georgian wine and mineral water on the grounds that it did not meet health standards—but exempted wine from Abkhazia from the ban. In September, a full-blown crisis erupted. In an apparent act of retaliation, the Georgian government announced it had caught four Russian military spies. President Putin denounced the detention as "state terrorism" and "hostage-taking." Five days later, the men were paraded in front of the media and handed over to international diplomats to be repatriated to Moscow. The Russian response was savage. On October 3, Russia suspended all rail, road, sea, and postal links to Georgia and stopped issuing entry visas to Georgian citizens. Hundreds of ethnic Georgians alleged to be illegal immigrants were summarily deported from Russia. The quarrel showed Russia reverting to its worst bullying instincts, while the Georgians could not resist provoking Russian dignity. Perceived honor and pride took precedence over strategic interests. Sergei Mironov, the speaker of the upper house of the Russian parliament, tellingly let slip the phrase, "We won't forgive those who spit at us."

The countdown to war can be dated to the end of 2006. Russia closed its army bases in Georgia two years ahead of schedule in what may have been a pragmatic decision or a calculation that it did not want Russian soldiers to be potential hostages in Georgia if fighting were to break out. Saakashvili came up with a new strategy to take over South Ossetia. He persuaded a former Ossetian prime minister and defense minister, Dmitry Sanakoyev, to run in a Georgian-administered election to be the alternative "president" of South Ossetia. Sanakoyev was later made head of a pro-Georgian "interim administration" and was presented as a progressive alternative to the main South Ossetian leader Kokoity. The "Sanakoyev project" might have been more successful, and he might slowly have won the trust of Ossetians disaffected with Kokoity, if the environment had been peaceful. But in an environment of looming confrontation, many people on the other side identified him as Tbilisi's stooge or as an outright traitor. Moreover, Georgian leaders were in a hurry. They invited Sanakoyev to meetings with diplomats in Tbilisi and even in Brussels, making clear he was their man. They engaged in a series of bizarre publicity stunts, building an amusement park in one of Sanakoyev's villages and inviting those who joined the pro-Georgian leader to free holidays on the Black Sea. Musicians claiming to be the 1970s pop group Boney M (famous for the song "Ra Ra Raputin") were invited to perform in the small Georgian village of Tamarasheni in the heart of South Ossetia. In a mirror of the Kokoity-Sanakoyev split, other members of the band claimed that the musicians were not the real Boney M but imposters.

It was especially risky to install Sanakoyev in Kurta, one of the Georgian villages in the heart of South Ossetia just five miles north of Tskhinvali. This put the two rival governments right next door to one another. South Ossetia turned into a closely intertwined tangle of alternative administrations for its Georgian and Ossetian communities, using different roads and water supplies. Russia built a gas pipeline from the north to connect with Tskhinvali. Confidence-building projects faded. A smart new lime-green railway terminus built with European Union money stood in Tskhinvali, but with no railway line to connect it anywhere, it proved a memorial to the failure of European goodwill initiatives.

In 2007, all parties in the conflicts felt increased pressure to act. Although many commentators still misleadingly called the disputes "frozen conflicts," they were in fact melting fast. Two international issues began to affect the situation. One was the proposed further expansion of NATO. Georgia (as well as Ukraine) was hoping to be awarded a Membership Action Plan, the first formal step toward membership of NATO. It received strong support for its ambitions in Washington and from central and Eastern European countries, although France and Germany in particular were much cooler—and Georgia was still a long way from meeting NATO's entry criteria. Russian officials said the NATO question was a "red-line" issue for them, saying Georgia's aspirations were a direct threat to their security and citing the opposition of Abkhaz and Ossetians as their main argument. The second issue was Kosovo's drive for independence as talks with the Serbian government on its final status broke down. Western governments insisted that the internationally recognized secession of Kosovo without the consent of Serbia was "not a precedent." But people on the ground in the Caucasus disagreed, and this in itself was enough to change the rules of the game. As Kosovo won international backing for seeking independence, the leaders of Abkhazia and South Ossetia (and Nagorny Karabakh) declared they could accept nothing less than that for their own peoples.

Saakashvili still insisted that he wanted to resolve the conflicts by the end of his first term in January 2009. He sent menacing signals on how he might do this by vastly increasing his military budget. In June 2007, Georgian defense spending doubled almost overnight to $575 million. The Georgian leadership argued that it was building an army from scratch and needed to professionalize the military to take part in peacekeeping operations in Iraq. But Abkhaz and Ossetians said that this looked like rearmament for war and was proof that they needed to rely on Russian support.

Within Georgia, Saakashvili's popularity had fallen. The economic benefits of the new reforms had been spread unevenly, and the government's clean image suffered as senior officials were accused of corruption. In the fall of 2007, a diverse group of opposition politicians who had in common only their rejection of the Saakashvili government held the biggest street demonstrations since the Rose Revolution. On November 7, riot police in black balaclavas were sent in to shut them down. They used teargas, truncheons, and water cannon and chased the opposition activists through the streets. Dozens of people were hurt. The police then moved on to the headquarters of the opposition television station, Imedi. They pulled it off the air midbroadcast and smashed or disabled its equipment. Saakashvili declared a state of emergency.

The violence drew international condemnation and badly tarnished Saakashvili's reputation. His brutal suppression of the protests contrasted badly with the way the Shevardnadze government had treated Saakashvili's own peaceful demonstrations in 2003. On November 8, Saakashvili tried to reclaim the initiative by calling presidential elections for January, a year ahead of schedule. The government was replaced. The election on January 5 showed that Georgians had lost faith in Saakashvili, but also that the opposition had failed to find a credible alternative candidate. In the end, their agreed candidate, businessman and member of parliament Levan Gachechiladze, failed to articulate a coherent message. After the first round of voting, Saakashvili was declared the outright winner with 53 percent of the vote, while Gachechiladze was awarded 25 percent. Some allegations of manipulation looked well-founded, suggesting that Saakashvili would have needed a second round to win a fair contest. As it was, he suffered the set-back of losing the popular vote in Tbilisi.

During the campaign, Saakashvili had again used the issues of Abkhazia and South Ossetia to woo voters. He made a strong and improbable pitch to recover the two territories. He told the audience at a pop concert that the elections would give them "a ticket on a train taking us to Sukhumi" and later promised a group of students, "The regime in Tskhinvali is like a loose tooth ready for removal and I am sure—if the January 5 [presidential elections] are held normally—this is a matter of, if not weeks, then at the very most, months."[18]

As he returned to office, the conflicts were more delicate than ever and were increasingly complicated by the Western-Russian arguments over Kosovo and NATO. On February 17, 2008, Kosovo made a choreographed declaration of independence, and the would-be new state was immediately recognized by most major Western countries. Russia condemned the Kosovo move and explicitly linked it to the Caucasus and NATO. A month later, the loyal Russian parliament, the State Duma, passed a resolution that hinted to Georgia that any further move toward NATO would carry the risk of Georgia losing Abkhazia and South Ossetia altogether. The Duma stated, "The deputies of the State Duma are unanimous in the opinion that the path taken by the Georgian authorities towards full integration in NATO deprives Georgia of the right to consolidate its territory and the peoples living on it."[19]

At the NATO summit in Bucharest on April 2–4 Georgia and Ukraine were not offered Membership Action Plans, but the summit's final communi-qué backed their eventual membership. It said, "NATO welcomes Ukraine's and Georgia's Euro-Atlantic aspirations for membership in NATO. We agreed today that these countries will become members of NATO."[20] The Russian authorities duly took their next step, announcing they were authorizing direct governmental relations with Abkhazia and South Ossetia. Earlier, Russia had withdrawn from its sanctions regime on Abkhazia.

Both sides were edging toward confrontation. Georgia's ambassador to Moscow, Erosi Kitsmarishvili, later recalled that in February, as he and the president flew back from Moscow, Saakashvili said he was planning to relocate the capital of Georgia to Sukhumi—a statement Kitsmarishvili understood as indicating a plan to launch military action against Abkhazia. The Georgians built up their troop numbers in the Kodori Gorge region of Abkhazia. In April, Russian aircraft shot down several Israeli-built Georgian unarmed reconnaissance planes over Abkhazia. Russia sent extra troops to Abkhazia, some of them equipped with artillery. A Russian officer who had stepped down as chief of staff of the peacekeeping force in Abkhazia in 2007 suddenly reappeared as Abkhazia's deputy defense minister. In July, the Russian Fifty-eighth Army held extensive exercises across the North Caucasus, just across the border from both Abkhazia and South Ossetia.

There were also peace initiatives. Irakli Alasania, Georgia's former negotiator for Abkhazia, was drafted from New York and traveled to Sukhumi for talks. The Abkhaz bargaining position was tougher now that they had explicit Russian support behind them, and they insisted on Georgian withdrawal from the Upper Kodori Valley. On July 18, German foreign minister Frank-Walter Steinmayer brought new European proposals to Bagapsh. They contained some new ideas that the Abkhaz side liked, and they asked for more time, but unfortunately time was running out.

There were plenty of warning signs throughout 2008 that war might break out. How was it allowed to happen? Part of the answer is that concerned outsiders picked the wrong conflict zone. They concentrated most of their efforts on Abkhazia—where arguably their diplomacy was effective—but fighting eventually broke out in South Ossetia. While the political dispute was sharper in Abkhazia, the security situation was actually more precarious in the checkerboard landscape of South Ossetia, where Georgian and Ossetian villages were situated side by side. Moreover, direct negotiations had recently broken down in South Ossetia for the first time. The Georgians had long been unhappy about the negotiating forum for the conflict, the four-sided Joint Control Commission, which was weighted against them. In March 2008, they announced they were withdrawing from the Commission unilaterally and called for a new negotiating format that would have a place for their friendly Ossetian leader, Sanakoyev. The Russians and Ossetians rejected this, and the international mediators initially agreed that it was better to have the Commission, imperfect as it was, than no negotiating format at all. On May 30, however, Finnish foreign minister Alexander Stubb, speaking in his capacity as chairman-in-office of the OSCE, said, "I am concerned that the existing negotiating format in the South Ossetian conflict has not been conducive to the resolution of the conflict. It is time to explore possibilities for a new negotiating format that would be acceptable to the parties to the conflict."[21] Stubb's statement effectively killed off the Joint Control Commission without an alternative format being in place.

By July, several Ossetians were forecasting a war in their region. On July 14, for example, an Ossetian commentator, Zaur Alborov, predicted a Georgian offensive and wrote, "Russian peacekeepers on the territory of the Abkhazia and South Ossetia have the right to use force to expel the aggressor from the conflict zones. Proof that Russia will use force to preserve peace and defend its citizens in the case of Georgian aggression comes from the large-scale 'Caucasian Border-2008' exercises, which took place this week in the North Caucasus military district."[22] Comments like this can be interpreted either as a smokescreen for a planned Russian intervention or as a well-founded fear of Georgian intentions. In a sense, which they were does not matter: both standpoints reinforced each other, and each side was increasingly persuaded that it was advantageous to move first.

Throughout July, Georgian and Ossetian villages fought a small-scale conflict. On the night of August 1–2 the exchange of fire was the worst that OSCE observers could remember in four years. Thousands of Ossetians evacuated their families to North Ossetia. Large numbers of Russian journalists started arriving in South Ossetia to cover the violence. On August 6, there were exchanges of fire between many Georgian and Ossetian villages. There were no direct talks, as the Georgian side still refused to use the Joint Control Commission and the Ossetian side rejected the offer of direct Georgian-Ossetian talks.

Georgia's August War

The war that reshaped the South Caucasus in August 2008 lasted only five days. Although the conflict ended in a Russian show of aggression and a painful Georgian defeat, the first of those days was dominated by Georgian nationalist euphoria. Throughout Friday, August 7, the Georgian army deployed large numbers of men and artillery to the border with South Ossetia north of the town of Gori. At seven o'clock that evening, President Saakashvili announced a ceasefire on Georgian television. He said the Russian peacekeepers had informed his government that they had lost control of the South Ossetian side. He told the Russians, "I have been proposing and I am proposing Russia act as a guarantor of South Ossetian autonomy within Georgia."[23] He said that despite extreme provocation, the Georgian side would exercise restraint and not retaliate. Both Georgians and Ossetians in South Ossetia saw or heard about Saakashvili's broadcast, and many were reassured that war had been avoided. But shortly after eleven o'clock, a senior Georgian military leader telephoned the head of the Russian peacekeepers, Marat Kulakhmetov, and told him that a Georgian assault was about to commence.

At 11:35 Georgian time on the night of August 7, the first explosions were heard over Tskhinvali as Georgian artillery fired smoke-bombs. At 11:50, the army opened up a full-scale artillery assault, and Grad missiles rained down across Tskhinvali. Georgian television showed pictures of rockets flying through the night sky. Three OSCE monitors who were sheltering in a basement estimated that the artillery rounds and rockets fell at intervals of fifteen to twenty seconds. Many of the city's residents had been evacuated, but several thousand people remained, huddled in basements that they had used as bomb shelters in the conflict of 1991–92. Amnesty International later recorded that "many missiles that missed their target consequently landed in civilian areas causing considerable damage to private houses and resulting in numerous civilian casualties." Dozens of buildings were hit, and the wounded were in a desperate state. A doctor later told Amnesty International, "The injured were taken to the basement; they arrived not one by one, but in groups of five or fifteen, fighters and civilians. The most serious cases we started to operate right in the corridor. Blood loss was the most serious problem. During the shelling, there had been no possibility to bring the injured here, they had been sitting somewhere for many hours, bleeding. Many people died because of this."[24]

At around half past midnight, Mamuka Kurashvili, a Georgian military official who oversaw peacekeepers in the conflict zone, told journalists that Georgia had "decided to restore constitutional order in the entire region" of South Ossetia. The bombardment continued for much of the night. At around half past six o'clock in the morning, Georgian troops and tanks began a ground assault and battled their way into the center of Tskhinvali, pushing back outnumbered South Ossetian fighters. Initially there was optimism in the Georgian leadership and widespread public excitement about the operation. Just after ten o'clock in the morning, the Rustavi-2 television station reported that around 600 Georgian troops had occupied large parts of Tskhinvali and captured eleven Ossetian villages. In a public television address Saakashvili said, "A large part of Tskhinvali is now liberated and fighting is ongoing in the center of Tskhinvali."

At around four o'clock in the afternoon of August 8, the first Russian tanks entered Tskhinvali, having entered South Ossetia that morning. The small Russian peacekeeping contingent had reported at least twelve dead. Fighting raged over the city for two days. The Georgians hung on, at one point managing to halt a Russian army column and wounding the commander of the Fifty-eighth Army, Anatoly Khrulyov. Overall, Tbilisi had committed around 9,000 troops to the operation, but by the afternoon of August 10, they were exhausted and outnumbered. They retreated, now pursued by Russian forces. Georgian reservists were called up but did not fight, while the country's most effective fighting unit, the First Battalion, based in Iraq, was flown back to Georgia on August 11 but did not engage in combat.

The Russians now moved the war into Georgia proper. A Russian bombing campaign had begun on the morning of August 8. Airfields and military bases were hit across the country. The next day, there was carnage in the town of Gori. A British journalist saw Russian aircraft, apparently aiming for a military barracks, miss their target. Just one of their bombs struck the base. At least two others fell into a compound of long, low-slung apartment blocks, five of which were quickly reduced to blackened shells. A third hit a small secondary school, which crumbled to the ground in a pile of rubble and twisted girders. From the gutted buildings, survivors began to emerge, some hobbling, others bleeding from shrapnel and flying glass, and all covered in a cloak of soot and dust. Then they brought out the dead. In front of a row of garages, a corpse, covered in a chalk-like film, lay on the ground.[25] Georgians said that sixty people died in these air raids, which continued for four days.

The world was taken by surprise by the events, partly because the start of the conflict coincided with the start of the Olympic Games in Beijing, attended by President Bush, Prime Minister Putin, and other world leaders. The initial Western reaction was shaped by the fact that the only television images of the violence were of the bombing of Gori, not of Tskhinvali; this set the tone for much of the Western media coverage of the war, which told the "Russia invades South Ossetia" half of the story and not the "Georgia attacks South Ossetia" half. Western leaders did not explicitly condemn the Georgian attack and were strong in their condemnation of the Russian bombings. The UN Security Council met at Russia's request but failed three times to pass a resolution, because Western countries objected to Russian wording condemning Georgia's use of force.

The Russian government had already swung into action. On August 9, Putin arrived home from Beijing and flew to Vladikavkaz to take charge of the Russian operation, making it clear that it was he, not President Dmitry Medvedev, who was running the show. Putin was stern, blaming Georgia for making "an attempt to involve other countries and other peoples in its bloody adventures."[26] He visited Ossetian refugees from the bombing of Tskhinvali and expressed sympathy with their plight—something that was hard to watch for anyone who recalled Russia's own far more extensive bombardment of civilians in the Chechen capital, Grozny.

On August 11, Georgian forces abandoned Gori and set up defensive lines south of the town to try to halt a Russian advance on Tbilisi. Most of the civilian population of Gori fled. Local Georgians reported that the Russian troops behaved with surprising levels of discipline, but that was not true of the South Ossetian fighters or the North Caucasian volunteers from North Ossetia, Chechnya, and other places who followed in the wake of the Russian army. These armed militias drove the Georgians out of the villages north of Tskhinvali. A villager named Nina told Amnesty International,

> Men in military uniform were going through the gardens. They were Russianspeaking but not Russian soldiers. I took them to be Ossetians, Chechens, some Asians, maybe Uzbeks and Cossacks. They were all wearing the same military uniform and they were armed with Kalashnikovs. They burnt about fifteen houses in Kurta, and took the livestock away on trucks. As we were leaving Kurta we saw two neighbours being abducted, they were pushed into a car boot by the marauders.[27]

As she fled through a series of Georgian villages, Nina said she saw many dead bodies, all of them civilians, not soldiers.

These fighters spread the same terror and destruction to Gori. An Azerbaijani journalist, Idrak Abbasov, who made it into the city saw Russian soldiers stand by and allow the irregular fighters to go on the rampage. "They are doing just what you did in Tskhinvali and we cannot stop them," one officer told Abbasov. An unshaven North Caucasian fighter with white armbands on both arms told him, "The Georgians say we are raping women in Gori—but there aren't any here! If they had been here, we'd have done it with pleasure!"[28]

War in Georgia. A burning apartment block hit by Russian planes in Gori, Georgia, August 9, 2008. Leli Blagonravova.

From August 8, the Abkhaz and Russians opened a second front in the west, aimed at the Upper Kodori Gorge region of Abkhazia. After three days of bombing, Georgian forces and most of the local population—around 3,000 Georgian Svans—fled. The Abkhaz and the Russians took this strategically situated territory virtually without a fight. Russian forces then crossed the border of Abkhazia into western Georgia, destroyed the military base at Senaki, and occupied Georgia's main port, Poti, wrecking its harbor and infrastructure. They blew up the Grakali railroad bridge in central Georgia, effectively cutting the country in two. It was a campaign of humiliation aimed not just at Georgia but at Georgia's main ally, the United States. Few people were killed, but the invading forces demonstrated their power to rampage through the country at will and took especial delight in destroying any U.S.-built military infrastructure. Later, in Sukhumi, the Abkhaz government exhibited hundreds of U.S.-made weapons they said they had found in the Kodori Gorge.

Russian forces halted south of Gori on the road to Tbilisi—to have gone farther was no doubt tempting to Russian generals but risked a real battle with the hardcore of Georgia's armed forces and a much bigger confrontation with its Western friends. Moscow's victory was real enough. Tbilisi had filled up with visiting Western dignitaries expressing solidarity with the Georgians, but the West made it clear it would not intervene militarily. It fell to French president Nicolas Sarkozy to fly to Moscow on August 12 and negotiate a six-point truce very much on Russia's terms. It stipulated that each side should withdraw to the positions it had held before the conflict—a point Russia subsequently did not honor. "International discussions" were convened on the disputed territories, but without a clear agenda. A crucial passage of the plan on "additional security measures" was vaguely worded and was interpreted by Moscow as a cover for it to hold onto a buffer zone outside both Abkhazia and South Ossetia for almost two months until an EU monitoring mission arrived in October. The truce effectively left the Russians in de facto control of Abkhazia and South Ossetia and reinforced the dividing lines between Tbilisi and the two breakaway entities.

Postwar Georgia: The Reckoning

The August 2008 conflict in Georgia was a disaster not only for those who suffered directly in it but for the whole of the Caucasus. The effects of the "five-day war" will be felt for years to come.

The final casualty figures were lower than first suggested but still substantial. Around 850 people lost their lives, and several thousand were wounded. Around half the dead were Georgian and Ossetian civilians; the rest were soldiers. About 138,000 people also fled their homes, of whom 100,000 were able to return over the next two months. That left just under 40,000 Georgian refugees still displaced several years later. Many of their villages in South Ossetia had been burned to the ground. The effort to rehouse them was more professional than in the 1990s, but their chances of returning home look very remote.

The war did catastrophic damage to the overall development of the region. The Georgian economy was badly hit. Not only was infrastructure damaged, but foreign investment fell sharply. The conflict also hurt Georgia's South Caucasian neighbors. The blowing up of the Grakali railroad bridge in central Georgia cost Armenia an estimated half a billion dollars as imports from the Black Sea were halted for a week. Azerbaijan's energy pipelines through Georgia were shut down, losing Azerbaijan huge amounts of revenue.

The fundamental bone of contention in the postwar inquest was over who had started the war and therefore bore the moral responsibility for the

War in South Ossetia. Buildings hit by Georgian artillery in Tskhinvali, South Ossetia, August 16, 2008. Rena Effendi.

tragedy. This centered on two main questions: "Who fired the first shot on the night of August 7?" and "Who started planning for war and when?" The European Union established the Independent International Fact-Finding Mission on the Conflict in Georgia specifically to provide answers to these and other questions. Its report, eventually published on September 30, 2009, confirmed the broad expert consensus that had formed in the meantime, concluding, "The shelling of Tskhinvali by the Georgian armed forces during the night of 7 to 8 August 2008 marked the beginning of the large-scale armed conflict in Georgia, yet it was only the culminating point of a long period of increasing tensions, provocations and incidents."[29]

On the issue of the first shots, no one, including President Saakashvili, disputed that the Georgian army had launched an assault on the city of Tskhinvali shortly before midnight on August 7. The Georgian government later justified its attack on two grounds. The first was that after the Georgian ceasefire at seven o'clock in the evening, the South Ossetians had shelled Georgian villages, chiefly Nikozi, Prisi, and Tamarasheni, and that the Georgian army had to intervene to defend them. This version of events was challenged by the three international monitors in Tskhinvali who had been able to hear from their office what was happening around the city. One of the three reported: "Nikozi, Prisi and Tamarasheni are so close to Tskhinvali, that we would have heard the explosions, but the situation in the area was calm up until 11:35 P.M., when Georgia started firing on Tskhinvali."[30]

The Georgian leaders' other justification for the assault was that they launched it on receiving information on the evening of August 7 that Russia had begun an invasion first and that hundreds of soldiers and pieces of Russian military hardware were entering South Ossetia from Russia through the Roki Tunnel. Journalists who saw the Georgian leaders at this time recall that they were in an intensely nervous state, with many rumors flying around, and some such report may have reached them. But the claim has not been backed up by evidence. It looked implausible at the time, if only because Saakashvili did not refer to it on August 8 and focused on condemning Russian bombing raids. The allegation began to gain currency only a few days later. It also seemed illogical that the Georgians would respond to an incursion in the north of South Ossetia with an attack on Tskhinvali rather than an operation to halt the column itself.

On this issue the EU report concluded, "The Mission is not in a position to consider as sufficiently substantiated the Georgian claim concerning a large-scale Russian military incursion into South Ossetia before 8 August 2008."[31] The available evidence suggests that the units of Russia's Fifty-eighth Army in North Ossetia in fact only moved after the Georgian assault had already begun. The Georgian authorities themselves agreed with this version of events on August 8 when they presented a document to the UN Security Council session saying, "At 5:30 A.M. [on August 8], the first Russian troops entered South Ossetia through the Roki Tunnel." This timeline fits with an Ossetian radio report that Russian units were moving toward the Roki Tunnel around half-past one o'clock in the morning and with the report of a South Ossetian eyewitness in the Java region who said she saw the first small

Russian armored column at around eight o'clock in the morning on August 8—and a major Russian intervention only later in the day.[32]

It is fairly clear, then, that the Georgian side attacked first on the night of August 7–8 and that these two claims were a smokescreen put up to disguise this. The decision to attack may have been made only a few hours earlier in a situation of near panic. Certainly, neither side was fully ready for war on August 7–8. The entire Russian leadership was out of Moscow, with Putin having just arrived at the Olympic Games in Beijing. President Saakashvili had only just returned from a trip to a Tyrolean health farm five days before. The first sign that international observers saw of a Georgian military buildup was on the morning of August 7.

Some kind of operation had been discussed many times before, however. Georgian sources have reported that Saakashvili had made plans long before to launch a reconquest operation in either Abkhazia or South Ossetia. His former defense minister Irakli Okruashvili, one of the hawks who favored this option, said later from exile in France, "Abkhazia was our strategic priority, but we drew up military plans in 2005 for taking both Abkhazia and South Ossetia as well. . . . The original plans called for a two-pronged operation entering South Ossetia, taking Tskhinvali, the Roki Tunnel and Java. Saakashvili's offensive only aimed at taking Tskhinvali, because he thought the U.S. would block a Russian reaction through diplomatic channels."[33]

An important component in the thinking of the Georgian leaders was that—strange as it sounds—several officials apparently believed that Russia would not intervene because it did not care sufficiently about South Ossetia. Two weeks after fighting broke out, Georgian deputy defense minister Batu Kutelia told the *Financial Times*, "I didn't think it likely that a member of the UN Security Council and the OSCE would react like this."[34] The impression that Russia would not fight for South Ossetia may have dated back to Saakashvili's first meeting with Putin in February 2004, when Putin indicated he could be flexible on South Ossetia but not on Abkhazia. Even on the evening of August 7, Saakashvili in his ceasefire speech was pointedly respectful toward Russia, presenting the conflict as a Georgian-Ossetian one, not a Georgian-Russian one.

If there was a belief that the Russians would hesitate to intervene, that could explain why Saakashvili was tempted to launch a lightning operation to take Tskhinvali. Having captured the city by force, he could present Russia and the world with a fait accompli and offer to negotiate a new deal on South Ossetia from a position of strength. He would have triumphantly fulfilled his pledge to voters to return South Ossetia to Georgian sovereignty. On the evening of August 8, Saakashvili was asked by the BBC if he would pull his forces out of Tskhinvali and replied rhetorically, "Pull forces from out of the Georgian territory?" He went on, "This is Georgian territory and we need to have immediate ceasefire; I am willing to have international mediation; I am willing to have international separation of forces; we have to establish a normal regime under international supervision."[35]

Saakashvili almost certainly had an exaggerated belief in American support. American officials were very firm in private with their Georgian counterparts that they would not support them in any kind of military action, but their public stance sent a less stern message that fed the illusions of the Georgian hawks. For example, in Tbilisi on July 10, Secretary of State Condoleezza Rice, having delivered a severe warning in private, warmly endorsed Saakashvili in public, beginning her comments with a strong statement of support for Georgian territorial integrity. One U.S. official told the *New York Times* four days after war began, "The Georgians figured it was better to ask forgiveness later, but not ask for permission first. It was a decision on their part. They knew we would say 'no.' "[36]

The other half of the story is one of Russian aggression. The Russians were already planning something and then intervened with overwhelming force. Moscow had been covertly sending both men and equipment into South Ossetia in the months prior to the war. Russian advisors and military officers had taken up residence in the village of Java, and local workers were helping them construct some kind of military base there. In 2009, the general in charge of the Russian campaign in South Ossetia, Vyacheslav Borisov, let slip in a radio interview: "Our forces had received complete practice, doing exercises a week before [the war] in exactly the same places. And we had only just got out of there so were able to perform our march on Tskhinvali much better." As we have seen, the units of the Fifty-eighth Army had been training just over the other side of the mountains in July. They were in a state of combat readiness and were able to cross into South Ossetia almost instantly.[37]

The Russian buildup in both Abkhazia and South Ossetia after the NATO summit in April was consistent with their effort to step up their covert annexation of both territories so as to keep their strategic foothold in the South Caucasus and weaken the Saakashvili government. It is quite likely that in South Ossetia they had plans to remove the pro-Georgian administration of Dmitry Sanakoyev from the Georgian villages north of Tskhinvali.

That would have rid the South Ossetian government of what it saw as its main irritant and humiliated President Saakashvili as Georgians fled from Sanakoyev's villages. If this was the case, the Russians simply "got lucky" on August 7–8—after being caught by surprise for a few hours, they were able to execute a much more ambitious operation to oust the Georgian presence entirely from both South Ossetia and Abkhazia, rampage through Georgia proper, and humiliate Saakashvili and his Western backers. A Russian documentary on the war entitled *A Lost Day*, released in 2012, filled in some of these details. The film had an evident domestic political agenda, as several senior Russian military figures interviewed for it criticized Medvedev for his alleged hesitation on August 7 and praised Putin for taking decisive action a day later; as such, it was fuel for a campaign to replace Medvedev and restore Putin to the Russian presidency. But it also revealed that there were comprehensive plans on the Russian side to be ready to intervene in South Ossetia.

This is the view from the ground. In a broader sense, the war was the culmination of several years of bad politics in the Caucasus. The Russian strategy is easiest to understand: Russia simply exploited all opportunities to maximize its presence in Abkhazia and South Ossetia. This was consistent with Moscow's policy to reassert a sphere of influence across the former Soviet Union and block the ambitions of any neighbors to join NATO, which it still saw as a hostile alliance. Russia's actions against Georgia looked all the more menacing six years later when it forcibly annexed Crimea from Ukraine in contravention of many international agreements it had signed. Georgia's two small breakaway territories were less important in themselves than as an instrument of influence against Tbilisi and the West. Russia used the two disputes to fire criticism at the West for "double standards" over Kosovo and as bargaining chips over other issues, such as NATO expansion. Once the war was fought, priorities changed, and Russia used the conflict to score points against the West for the grievances it bore over issues such as Iraq and Kosovo. Russia's ambassador to NATO, Dmitry Rogozin, said of the outcome of the conflict: "Everyone here [in Brussels] understands what we did, when we carried out such a large-scale operation and literally in three days not only shattered the Georgian army built on the money and under the leadership of the USA but stopped any opportunity for a third country to intervene quickly. This is not just a very serious military, psychological and moral victory for Russia—it is a gauntlet openly thrown down to the global leader of the modern world."[38]

On the Georgian side, Saakashvili's strategy for four years had been to change the status quo on the ground in both Abkhazia and South Ossetia and mobilize as much Western support as possible behind this shift. That meant challenging the peacekeeping formats, with their reliance on Russia; raising the issue at the highest levels in the West and at international summits; and rebuilding the army so as to have the military capacity to intimidate or defeat the separatists. It was a dangerous and ultimately self-destructive game, but one also born out of fear that the situation on the ground was slipping away from Georgia. Again, once war broke out, priorities changed, and Saakashvili argued that the defense of Georgia against Russia was essential to the new world order. He wrote, for example: "If the international community allows Russia to crush our democratic, independent state, it will be giving carte blanche to authoritarian governments everywhere. Russia intends to destroy not just a country, but an idea."[39]

The stakes had got so high in August 2008 that one can almost excuse the Georgian and South Ossetian sides, culpable as they were, for stumbling into conflict. Both were politically inexperienced and operating in a situation of extreme stress and fear. They knew that in the geography of South Ossetia, one false step or the severing of one road could end in catastrophe; the temptation to attack first as a form of self-defense—and grasp victory over the other side—was therefore very great. Likewise, the actions of Russia were brutal and extreme but also should have come as no surprise: they were a logical continuation of the strategic commitment Russia had made to Abkhazia and South Ossetia in the preceding few years.

In that sense, the main culpability for the conflict lies, strangely enough, with the one actor that did not fight and that sought to stop the violence: the West. The West's sin was in promising more than it could deliver. In the 1990s, Georgia had lost wars in Abkhazia and South Ossetia largely because of terrible mistakes by its own leaders. Georgia had moved on since then, but there was still a strong reflex to regard the two territories as "Georgian land" first and to consider the wishes of their indigenous peoples later. To many Westerners, it was clear that Abkhazia in particular was all but lost, and that it would require a titanic effort to bring it back. Often sympathetic to Georgia for other reasons, Western officials consistently delivered the easy part of the message—that they supported Georgia's territorial integrity—but they did not sufficiently convey the hard part—that recovering the two territories would be a very long haul that would require building a new state and rethinking many old attitudes.

Several Western-funded nongovernmental initiatives in Abkhazia explored more creative and long-term ways of bridging the conflict between the communities on the ground, drawing on experience from places like Northern Ireland, but the prevailing mood was against them. The default policy of isolating the separatists persisted and only drove them further into the embrace of Russia.

In the meantime, Moscow began to advance its own strategic agenda, although it was still constrained by its official support for Georgian sovereignty over the two territories. Again, the Western reaction was weak. If the West did not want to see a new Pax Russica in Abkhazia and South Ossetia, it needed to offer a strong alternative; otherwise, it had to factor Russian interests into the equation. In the end Western governments did not act robustly enough to restrain the Georgian side from playing a game it ended up losing badly. The strategic winner was Moscow, which skillfully played on Abkhaz and Ossetian insecurities and Western hesitations. Russia was able to set the terms of the new realities on the ground.

The United States in particular gave many confusing signals. The fact that U.S. troops were in the region supposedly to train Georgian troops for peacekeeping and antiterrorism functions, not for combat against Abkhaz and South Ossetia, was a distinction lost on most observers, including most Georgians. President Bush consistently praised Saakashvili, yet the U.S. commitment to Georgia was only rhetorical. When Bush said in Freedom Square in Tbilisi in May 2005 that "the path of freedom you have chosen is not easy but you will not travel it alone," he had not meant it literally.

Under the Obama administration, a line was drawn under the previous Georgian policy, and the Caucasus, unsurprisingly, was given a lower priority in world affairs vis-à-vis issues such as nuclear proliferation, Iran, Afghanistan, North Korea, and climate change as Washington declared its new "reset" policy with Russia in 2009. Vice-president Joe Biden was sent to Tbilisi as President Obama himself traveled to Moscow, underlying where priorities lay: Georgia would still get economic and rhetorical support, but its grievances would not be allowed to jeopardize a new relationship between Russia and the United States.

Lost in the middle somewhere were the ordinary Georgians and Ossetians who were the chief victims of the war. It is important to remember that Georgian-Ossetian relations still remained relatively good on a grassroots level right up until the fighting began. Georgian workers were still working in Tskhinvali until August 7, and some were even trapped there by the fighting. There are still multiple mixed marriages and shared businesses across the conflict divide. Two settlements on either side of the South Ossetian border, the Georgian village of Meghriskhevi and the Ossetian village of Grom, for example, had shared an agricultural market for years. In 1991, the Georgian villagers saved Grom from being ravaged by Georgian fighters. In 2008 the Ossetian villagers repaid the favor, and the Georgian village was spared from revenge attacks after its inhabitants had fled. Now, however, the big internationalized dispute is throwing up a frontier between these two villages. In December 2008, a Georgian villager named Zakharia complained that he missed his Ossetian friends and trading partners. "I don't know who was right and who was wrong, but this didn't need to happen," he said. If it had been up to these villagers, there would never have been a Georgian-Ossetian conflict. They were not to blame, but it was they who suffered the most.

8

Conclusion:

A Modern Tour of the South Caucasus

Baku, A Post-Russian City

In 2018, ten years after the cataclysm of the five-day war between Georgia and Russia, the South Caucasus is as diverse as it has been at any time in its modern history. Its different territories—the three recognized states of Armenia, Azerbaijan, and Georgia and the three unrecognized statelets of Abkhazia, Nagorny Karabakh, and South Ossetia—are growing apart from one another as they all seek their own place in the modern world.

Concluding the updated version of this book in 2018, I take the reader on a brief tour of the region. For the traveler who came here in the 1990s, one thing is striking: it no longer makes much sense to call the region "post-Soviet." An entire new generation has grown up since the end of the USSR in 1991, and no one below the age of thirty-five now remembers life as a Soviet citizen. The Soviet Union's legacy recedes year by year, and with it so does use of the Russian language and the influence of Moscow. Russia is still important, but not as important as it thinks it is. This region is still "Russia's neighborhood," but it is also the neighborhood of many other countries, including Iran, Turkey, and the European Union. This is a reality that many commentators who still see the countries of the former USSR through a Russian lens or, even more narrowly, through the lens of Vladimir Putin fail to grasp.

The fact of this diminishing influence has also largely escaped the Russian elite itself and makes them inclined to overestimate their power in this region. To give one example, one of Putin's closest friends from his college days in Leningrad in the 1970s is an Azerbaijani, Ilham Rahimov. When Putin came to power, Rahimov used his top-level connection to become an intermediary in Russian-Azerbaijani relations and for many years was co-owner of Moscow's massive Ukraine Hotel. But the next Russian leader will not have those connections to another country, forged in a time when they were part of the same state.

The skyline of Baku, the first stop on our tour, describes a very different place from the city that first became the capital of independent Azerbaijan in 1991. Oil wealth has pushed up a forest of skyscrapers and made the city a Dubai-on-the-Caspian. The tallest buildings, the three glass "Flame Towers," rising to a height of 182 meters, are so called because of their sinuous shape, which is illuminated at night.

In the 1980s, Baku was a multiethnic Soviet city and a major industrial center. In 1918, it was the location for the short-lived Bolshevik-led Baku Commune, whose supporters later welcomed the conquest of the Red Army in 1920, marching down from the north. The city's many different nationalities spoke Russian as a lingua franca. You still hear plenty of Russian on the streets of Baku, spoken with a charming distinctive local accent in which the intonation rises at the end of the sentence. But nowadays you mainly hear the Azeri language. A poll by the Caucasus Research and Resources Center in 2013 found that 64 percent of the population had "no basic knowledge of" or were beginners in the Russian language. (In Georgia, the corresponding level of ignorance of Russian in 2018 was much lower, at 33 percent, while in Armenia, which maintains a close alliance with Russia, it was 19 percent.) Young educated people may speak better English than Russian. Many ordinary folk are monolingual.

Russia now competes for influence in Azerbaijan with the EU, Iran, Turkey, and—increasingly—China, which is one of the three top investors in all three South Caucasus countries. The much-delayed opening of the Baku-Tbilisi-Kars railway in October 2017 not only linked Azerbaijan, Georgia, and Turkey by rail but gave China a new rail route to Europe, bypassing Russia.

Many of the billions Azerbaijan earned from oil consolidated the country's statehood. The "tent camps" housing refugees and internally displaced people from the Nagorny Karabakh conflict were closed down and their residents rehoused. Azerbaijan put itself on the international map. It opened several dozen new embassies around the world and was elected a nonpermanent member of the UN Security Council in 2011. The State Oil

Company of the Azerbaijan Republic, SOCAR, became one of the biggest investors in Turkey and acquired a two-thirds stake in the operator of Greece's natural gas grid.

Much of the money, however, also went into the pockets of a few who bought private jets, apartments in Mayfair in London, and villas in the south of France. One of the Flame Towers opened a dealership for the luxury car maker Lamborghini. Below the three towers, a cascade of new shopping malls and hotels flows downhill to the Caspian Sea in a wave of marble. This luxury began to look like hubris when the country's oil revenues went into sharp decline in 2015. Billions were also spent on prestige projects that delivered brief fame at fantastic cost. They included the Eurovision Song Contest (2012), the inaugural European Games (2015), and the Formula One race (2016) in Baku. In 2010, the government spent $32 million on building the world's tallest flagpole (at 162 meters), flying the world's biggest flag. The Crystal Hall arena for the Eurovision events reportedly cost $350 million. The cost of the opening ceremony for the European Games was $95 million, and for the Olympic stadium, where its main events were held, it was $400 million. A year after the games the stadium was being so little used that it was hired out for weddings.

The government spent less on long-term development. Despite much talk of developing a non-oil sector of the economy, around 90 percent of Azerbaijan's revenues still came from oil and gas. New infrastructure was built, but there was little investment in education. State education spending fell to 2.7 percent, lower than the European average of 4.5 percent.

In parallel, Azerbaijan took an authoritarian turnand turned into something more akin to a Central Asian–style dictatorship than the politically pluralist country it had briefly resembled in 1992 or had been during the First Republic of 1918. In 2009, President Ilham Aliev held a referendum to amend the constitution and change presidential term limits, enabling him to run for a third term in 2013. He did so and was duly elected, getting a predictably massive 84.5 percent of the vote. In 2018, he won a fourth term, now extended to seven years, facing virtually no opposition.

Beginning in 2013, the ruling regime cracked down on dissenting and opposition voices. It began by jailing Ilgar Mammadov, leader of the pro-Western opposition Republican Alternative (REAL) Party, who had been planning to run in the presidential elections. (Mammadov was released in August 2018 after several rulings by the European Court of Human Rights opposing his detention.) Later, more than a dozen pro-Western civil society leaders, human rights activists, and journalists were arrested and imprisoned on dubious charges. These included human rights defender Leyla Yunus; her husband, historian Arif Yunus; lawyer Intigam Aliyev; journalist Khadija Ismail; and youth activist Rasul Jafarov. (All four were later released, but other lessknown activists were subsequently arrested.) At the same time, Western organizations, including the National Democratic Institute, the Peace Corps, the International Research and Exchanges Board (IREX), Radio Liberty, and Oxfam, were shut down or forced to leave the country.

Azerbaijani relations with the West were limited to energy and security cooperation. At the same time there was a new rapprochement with Russia, ahead of the October 2013 presidential vote. Two months before the Azerbaijani election President Vladimir Putin visited Baku, accompanied by senior officials. A large part of Russia's Caspian Flotilla conspicuously followed him and was docked in the bay of Baku for the duration of his stay.

Why the lurch toward dictatorship in a country that was stronger and wealthier than ever before, whose elite should have felt eminently secure? Because, it seems, the Azerbaijani elite does not feel secure. President Ilham Aliev and members of his ruling circle reportedly said in private conversations that they feared the popular revolts of the Arab Spring of 2011 or the Maidan in Ukraine in 2013–14. As in Russia, Western pro-democracy organizations were seen as dangerous agents of "regime change." A close relationship with Putin's Russia (along with an increasingly authoritarian Turkey), rather than the West, provided a strong insurance policy against any revolt.

To consolidate power, the constitutional referendum of 2016 not only extended the presidential term to seven years but also created the institution of the vice presidency, with First Lady Mehriban Alieva becoming first vice president. This cemented the status of her family, the Pashaevs, as Azerbaijan's de facto first family, with an unmatched political influence and wealth. The Pasha Holdings company, whose CEO is first cousin of the first lady, owns hotels, ski resorts, banks, and insurance, travel, and construction companies.

Throughout the South Caucasus, informal centers of power are more important than public institutions. In Azerbaijan, informal "neo-patrimonial" power is everything. Jobs, resources, and favors are bestowed through personal connections, flowing down from one or more patrons to a network of clients below. Public office means little. From 1996 to 2018, for example, Azerbaijan had a prime minister, Artur Rasizade, who had no political influence, who was unknown outside the country, and whose departure barely merited any commentary.

Real power lay elsewhere. The minister of emergencies Kamalacklin Heydarov—owner of, among other things, the Gabala football club—and the minister of taxes Fazil Mammadov had far greater wealth and influence than one would expect for such minor political positions and even had their own rudimentary private armies. In the phrase of Audrey Altstadt, the best historian of modern Azerbaijan, President Ilham Aliev is the "keystone" of this system. He is the indispensable central figure, who holds things together and is the arbiter of disputes—but one also gets the sense that he is crushed by the weight of the system.[1]

Sources of Discontent

In 2015 Azerbaijan's system tottered. Oil prices fell, and the hasty devaluation of Azerbaijan's currency, the manat (see chapter 6), badly hurt the urban middle classes of Baku and brought "boomtown Baku" to a lurching halt. Even worse effects of the crash were felt out in the provinces. The divide between the prosperous capital city and the struggling provinces is a miserable feature that all three countries of the South Caucasus have in common, and one the casual visitor who only sees the capitals can easily miss. In Azerbaijan, the contrast between wealthy Baku and the rest of the country is striking. Even Azerbaijan's rather sleepy second city Ganja(formerly Kirovabad and Elizavetpol) looks like a miserable poor cousin in comparison to the capital.

Small Azerbaijani towns in the era of Ilham Aliev typically have the same look. They have a newly built highway, an "Olympic Center" for public sports activities, and a smart statue of Heidar Aliev in a well-tended park, where local citizens can revere the deceased father of the nation. Real economic life is limited, however. Hidden unemployment and underemployment is the curse of the South Caucasus, especially in the provinces—even though official unemployment levels are quite low. At the height of the oil boom in 2013, the Caucasus Barometer—the annual survey of the polling organization CRRC—found 60 percent of Azerbaijani respondents reporting that they had no job and more than half reporting a monthly income of less than $250. Across the region, villages are half empty, with those of working age having left for Russia or Turkey as guest workers and older people staying behind.

In the years of plenty, these towns and villages were sustained by remittances from the departed guest workers. But the falling oil price also hit Russia hard, and many Azerbaijanis working there came home, inflicting a double blow on the economy. In January 2016, a string of street demonstrations flared up in a dozen locations across Azerbaijan. The protests died away after the government promised to reverse some price rises. Video footage on social media showed that many of the protestors were returnees from Russia sporting leather jackets and speaking Russian.

The regime had regained a more stable footing by 2018, thanks to a higher oil price. The opening of the Baku-Tbilisi-Kars railway and the new contract extending the life of the ACG oil fields promise more stability. Yet the government still has limited capacity to spend its way out of trouble. The 2016 protests revealed an inescapable truth to the Azerbaijani elite: most of the country's society looks very different from them. In 2018, most of the Azerbaijani public is young; around 40 percent of the population is under twenty-five years of age. They are poor, with the vast majority earning less than $400 a month. They are also more religious. According to a Pew Forum survey in 2012, more than 96 percent of Azerbaijanis say they are Muslim, both Shia and Sunni, and 70 percent of those who identify as believers say they pray more than once a day.[2]

A secular elite still holds sway in Baku. A visitor to the capital of this Muslim country might wonder where all the Muslims are. On the streets of Baku, you never hear the call to prayer. President Aliev did go on pilgrimage to Mecca in 2015, but the lavish lifestyle he and his family enjoy and their fashionable Western outfits don't speak very loudly of a religious commitment. Outside the center of Baku, a different picture takes shape. The extreme corruption of the regime as well as its close relationship with Israel have fueled the antagonism of pious Muslims toward the country's leaders.

Shias are still the majority, representing around two-thirds of the country's Muslims. In the south of the country near the Iranian border, and especially among the Talysh minority, who speak a language related to Farsi, the Iranian influence is strong; in this region, Iran funds mosques and medressahs. Sunnis, many of them in the north, near Russia's turbulent region of Dagestan, are gaining in number. One positive aspect of Azerbaijan, however, is that the country has so far not suffered from the Shia-Sunni antagonism and violence that has torn apart Iraq and Syria. This is mainly because Shia-Sunni differences were blurred under Communist rule, so many Azerbaijanis do not strongly identify as belonging to one faith or the other.

Government repression of both Shias and Sunnis and a zero-tolerance policy toward those who sport beards or wear headscarves are fostering radicalism. According to Audrey Altstadt, "The Azerbaijani government is conflating real threats to secular statehood with the lesser challenges of regime critics who use Islamic rhetoric, posters of [Ayatollah] Khomeini, and/or have beards. As both faith and practice of Islam have grown, the state has behaved as if the only 'non-threatening' displays of piety or observance are those controlled by state institutions."[3]

The government has targeted Shiite religious leaders. The moderate cleric Haji Ilgar Ibrahimoglu (Allahverdiyev), leader of Baku's Juma Congregation and a self-identified human rights activist, was harassed by the authorities and his mosque closed in 2004. The more radical leader of the Islamic Party of Azerbaijan, Movsum Samadov, was jailed in 2011.

Since the start of the war in Syria, there has been a much bigger crackdown on Sunnis believed to be extremist Salafis. Several hundred Azerbaijanis are thought to have gone to fight in Syria, many recruited from the poor industrial town of Sumgait. Azerbaijan's northern regions bordering the unstable Russian region of Dagestan, which are home to the Lezgin minority, are also a recruiting ground for extreme Sunni militant groups, such as the so-called Islamic State in Iraq and Syria. If detained, their members face a policy of zero tolerance. It is reported that in 2017, 151 people were stripped of their Azerbaijani citizenship for fighting in the ranks of terrorist organizations. Rabiyat Aslanova, chairperson of the parliament's Committee on Human Rights, declared that alleged former fighters must "face the law, because whatever they were doing was completely unlawful."[4]

The true extent of radical Islamic sentiment in Azerbaijan is so hidden that it is hard to judge properly. The only thing that can be said with certainty is that the younger generation is more devout than their elders. For better or worse, the end of the Soviet Union also marked a retreat from a value system that was more secular and multinational.

Smoldering Karabakh

Azerbaijan has a mass of new problems to deal with at home and abroad. One problem, however, was three decades old in 2018 and more dangerous than ever before: the unresolved Nagorny Karabakh conflict.

Out in the west of Azerbaijan, a long way from Baku, the roads lead into plains, which are a dustbowl in summer and covered by a crust of snow in winter. There are small villages, each with a single pinnacled minaret. Military vehicles in grays and greens proliferate. Eventually the roads peter out at a tangle of roadblocks and army camps. The next stop on our tour is the 160-mile scar that still runs across Azerbaijan, known as the Line of Contact. This is the ceasefire line established in May 1994 to halt the Karabakh conflict that left large areas of Azerbaijani territory under Armenian military control. Intended to be a temporary arrangement before a proper peace deal was made, it has stayed in place ever since .

The unresolved Armenian-Azerbaijani conflict over Karabakh rarely flares into levels of violence that make international headlines, but it casts a great shadow over the Caucasus. More than any other single factor, the conflict has held back the forward development of the region. It pits two of the three countries in perpetual confrontation with one another, poisons politics, hurts economies, and diverts billions from public services into military spending. For Azerbaijan it means that one-seventh of its de jure territory is under the control of foreign forces. Armenia's two longest borders, with Azerbaijan and Turkey, are closed; its trade routes east and west are blocked; and it must rely on a military alliance with Russia to feel secure.

In the 1990s the trenches that form the Line of Contact outside Nagorny Karabakh were relatively quiet and manned by lightly armed conscripts. The trenches have barely moved since then. The international presence is still limited to a small number of unarmed observers from the Organization for Security and Cooperation in Europe who make inspection visits to the frontline twice a month.

Since then, however, the conflict zone has turned one of the most dangerous patches of geography in the world, a fearsome militarized zone bristling with heavy weapons. There are 20,000 soldiers on each side of the line. Both armies now possess heavy artillery and long-range missiles. The Azerbaijanis, the losing side in the conflict of the 1990s, have spent billions on armaments to secure military superiority, buying fearsome weapons such as Russian-made attack helicopters, Sukhoi fighter planes, and Israeli "suicide drones," which were used with deadly effect in the fighting of April 2016. Instead of rifle fire, the two sides routinely break the ceasefire, both along the Line of Contact and along the length of the international border between Armenia and Azerbaijan, with long-range snipers and mortars. In July 2017, a two-year-old Azerbaijani girl and her grandmother were killed in the village of Alkhanly by an Armenian artillery shell.

Armenian-controlled territory begins on the other side of no-man's land, a zone that has become a jungle of thistles. Although the world recognizes

Aghdam and other towns as being the sovereign territory of Azerbaijan, the city has lain empty and ruined, and has been run by Armenians since it was captured in 1993. Our Armenian tour begins not in the capital of Yerevan but in the occupied territories to the east of Karabakh. This is somehow appropriate, as the logic of "absolute security" in the Karabakh conflict—the need to defend the lands won in 1994 and to keep Nagorny Karabakh as an Armenian territory at the expense of any Azerbaijani claims—is still the primary driver of all Armenian state policy. It is also a major reason whyfor two decades after 1998, two Karabakhi Armenians served as presidents of Armenia. In 2016, a new phrase was coined in Armenia to instill the same patriotism in the younger generation: Armenia, in a state of suspended war with Azerbaijan, was an "army-nation."

The Karabakh conflict is so intractable in large part because the Armenians still hold, in whole or in part, not just Nagorny Karabakh itself but the seven Azerbaijani regions surrounding it (see chapter 4). In the 1990s, the Armenians said they had captured these regions as a buffer zone that would then be traded away in political talks and returned to Azerbaijan. That is still the basis of international talks, but the temporary has become semipermanent. Every year that there is no peace deal, the boundary blurs between Nagorny Karabakh—the Soviet-era autonomous region the Armenians claimed for themselves in 1988—and the surrounding territories. In the Aghdam region the Armenians opened to visitors the archaeological site of what they say is the ancient Armenian city of Tigranakert—a none-too-subtle message that this is ancient Armenian land. A newly refurbished road connects Karabakh and Armenia via the large occupied Azerbaijani region of Kelbajar.

In Stepanakert, the capital of the "Nagorno-Karabakh Republic," there is no trace of the ruins and war damage that still scarred this city in the late 1990s. Armenian diaspora money has made the town look respectable—smart even. Armenians from California and France have spent millions on the roads and monuments of this land and come here in the thousands each year. They can sit on the terrace of the Hotel Armenia, gazing across at the new parliament building with its splendid white dome, sip an espresso, and access Wi-Fi before boarding a bus to tour the beautiful medieval churches of Amaras and Gandzasar, now heavily restored. For many, "Artsakh," as it is now officially called by the Karabakh Armenians, is the ideal Armenian territory that the Republic of Armenia failed to become after independence, a statelet built from the bottom up, which they hope the world will eventually recognize as a sovereign state.

All this is deceptive, of course. This is still a war zone that every year draws thousands of young Armenian and Azerbaijani men as conscripts to stand in trenches facing one another. Armenian Karabakh is a little Sparta in which every young man serves in the army, and most of the economy is geared toward supporting the military. Every spring, as the snows thaw in the mountains around the Line of Contact, watchers of the Karabakh conflict wonder if this is the year when the two sides will go back to war. With no international peacekeeping presence on the frontline and the peace process all but moribund, some Azerbaijanis call for the military option to reconquer lost territory. That in turn makes the Karabakh Armenians a population ready to go to war at any moment. Three decades from the start of the conflict in 1988, it is as unfinished and dangerous as ever.

Electric Yerevan

Of the big cities of the Caucasus, the Armenian capital Yerevan seems most unchanged since the breakup of the USSR in 1991. The city center still has the look of the Soviet 1950s, with monumental buildings in pink and purple, constructed from the local volcanic stone known as tuff. It is not a flashy city. This bolsters the perception of Armenia as the most serene, stable, and unchanging of the three countries of the South Caucasus—or, as others would say, the most isolated and stagnating of them. Ethnic homogeneity—98 percent of the population is ethnic Armenian—and two closed borders with Azerbaijan and Turkey also seem to make for predictability. In early 2018, an unchanging elite and the continuation of the same leadership in power promised more of the same, with at best some modest economic improvements. Yerevan was apparently the city where nothing changed.

In April 2018, the people of Yerevan overthrew that stereotype. The biggest crowds Armenia had seen since the Karabakh demonstrations of early 1988 brought the city to a standstill. A few weeks earlier, Nikol Pashinian, an opposition member of parliament, had begun a protest march across the country with just a few dozen supporters. Slowly his peaceful protest caught the imagination of the Armenian public, who were sullenly unhappy with the status quo but did not believe they had a voice to say so.

Pashinian had picked the moment at which Armenia's ruling regime was at its weakest. On April 9, on the completion of Serzh Sargsyan's second and final term as president of the country, a new constitution came into effect. The position of president was downgraded to a mostly ceremonial post, as in

Germany or Italy. Armen Sarkissian (no relation to his predecessor, bearing the same surname but spelled differently), a respected diplomat, scholar, and businessman, was inaugurated as president. Serzh Sargsyan made a sideways move to become prime minister, a position now endowed with the same powers as that of a British head of government, in control of the economy, foreign policy, and security. So everything changed, but everything stayed the same. Sargsyan kept the country's top job—and even the same offices he had occupied for the past ten years. As in Russia, Turkey, and Azerbaijan a constitutional fix enabled the same group to retain control.

When he reached Yerevan on April 13, Pashinian's demonstrations grew. Public opinion in the modern South Caucasus is not a monolith but a wave. Most of the population supports its rulers—and confirms this in elections and opinion polls—out of a mixture of inertia, instinctive loyalty, the influence of state media, pressure exerted by bosses, and the threat of repression. But once the public sees change is coming, the ruling regime can quickly be swept away. In Armenia, Pashinian's protest movement to "Reject Serzh" (*merjinserjin*, a phrase that in Armenian rhymes) became that wave. Hundreds of thousands of ordinary Armenians began to join.

Young revolutionaries. Protestors in Armenia's nonviolent revolution of April 2018 in Yerevan wave placards calling for the resignation of Serzh Sargsyan. Vahram Baghdasaryan.

The Armenian protest leaders had learned hard lessons from the violence of 2008 and also from the bloodshed of the Maidan in Ukraine in 2014. A better example was a series of peaceful demonstrations in 2015 called "Electric Yerevan," which were sparked by a rise in electricity tariffs by Armenia's Russian-owned power company. The government caved in and the price rises were canceled—but not before a new generation of young Armenians had got a taste for peaceful protest. The sequel to Electric Yerevan came in 2018, and the electricity now pulsed through street politics. The activists preached nonviolence and told the police through megaphones that they were their friends. They were also careful to make the demonstration all about Armenian domestic politics, not geopolitics. Protestors did not hold EU flags, as in Ukraine, or carry anti-Russian placards. Everyone carried the Armenian tricolor flag and made the demonstration a carnival of patriotism, peaceful protest, and mockery of the government.

The mass carnival put Sargsyan in a dilemma. He could give orders to try to suppress the protests by force, but that would mean mass bloodshed, or he could negotiate. At a brief televised meeting with Pashinian, Sargsyan said that he would not accept an ultimatum to resign and walked out of the room. But his popular legitimacy had crumbled. On April 23, he announced his resignation with the extraordinary words, "Nikol Pashinian was right, I was wrong." His allies in the Republican Party took a little longer to capitulate. After another day of national protest again paralyzed the country, on May 8 parliament agreed to appoint Pashinian as head of a new interim government.

The outgoing leader, Sargsyan, was not so much an autocrat as the CEO of a conglomerate, an elite network that had taken over the country and had representatives in every Armenian town and village. So the street protests were about much more than him. The conglomerate was centered around the Republican Party, which dominated parliament and all local municipalities in elections it was always assured to win. This core group, Armenia's business-political elite, owned or ran most of the country's most lucrative businesses and had every reason to resist longer than its leader. These men owned kitschy fake Roman villas, drove Hummers or Bentleys, and were reviled by the public. One of the most notorious was Samvel Aleksanian (nicknamed "Lifik Samo" after the Russian word for bra—his father had a bra shop in Soviet times), who ran a chain of supermarkets and controlled the import of sugar and butter into the country.

Another, former army commander Manvel Grigorian, ran the cathedral town of Echmiadzin as his personal fiefdom. There were gasps when Grigorian was arrested. Television footage of his country house showed a private arsenal of guns, rifles, and ammunition and a garage full of Hummer and Range Rover cars. More shocking to the public were an ambulance donated to the army and stockpiled donations of food and first-aid kits sent by schoolchildren during the fighting of April 2016, along with their handwritten notes. The authorities said that Grigorian had used the food donations to feed tigers and bears at his private zoo.[5]

Discoveries like these outraged the overwhelming majority of Armenians, who felt themselves the victims of economic inequality. Average incomes in Armenia were a few hundred dollars a month and had not risen appreciatively in a decade. Remittances from guest workers in Russia still contributed to around a fifth of national revenues. Economic underperformance also continued to cause disastrous emigration rates. The International Organization for Migration estimated that 23.7 percent of all Armenian-born citizens lived outside the country in 2015. In total, about half a million fewer people lived in Armenia in 2018 than did during the late Soviet era three decades earlier. The only new sector that had done well was information technology (IT), which employed about 15,000 people. Being borderless, it did not challenge entrenched monopolies. Yerevan now has trendy locations such as the Hub where young professionals can work on startups in open-plan offices. These IT professionals turned out en masse to protest in April 2018.

Armenia's "Velvet Revolution" had its own Armenian peculiarities. Why did Sargsyan, the strongman of the Karabakh conflict and boss of Armenia's security structures, choose to surrender after a decade in power rather than crack down? His decision seems to have stemmed partly from a feeling of patriotism and an understanding that he would not face a vendetta. Moreover, national solidarity—the fear that Azerbaijan might use a moment of national weakness to launch an offensive on the Karabakh front—told him that a violent suppression of the protests might risk the security of the country.

Twenty years younger than Sargsyan, Pashinian, who turned forty-three in June 2018, represented a new generation and a different outlook. He won the support of the crowds with charismatic speeches and a demonstrably modest demeanor. As a parliamentarian, he lived with his wife and four children in the kind of ordinary three-room apartment that most of his fellow protestors inhabited. Throughout his walk across Armenia and the protests, as his beard lengthened, the opposition leader wore the same camouflage

T-shirt and a cap bearing the slogan "Dukhov" (meaning roughly "Resist" or "Courage"). All this marked him and his team—mostly even younger than he was—as men and women who bore almost no imprint of the Soviet Union.

Russia, First among Equals

Armenia's successful Velvet Revolution was first of all about domestic issues, not geopolitics. That did not stop a host of foreign observers, as ever, from writing "Russia" and "Putin" into their headlines. A few referred to Armenia as "Russia's backyard" without evidently looking at the map and noticing that the two countries did not have a common border.

In any event, Moscow was notable for how it kept out of the crisis, from both a wise instinct that Armenia's geopolitical orientation would not change, as Ukraine's had, and also the knowledge that intervention would only trigger an anti-Russian backlash. At his first meeting with President Vladimir Putin on May 14, Pashinian thanked the Russian leader for his "balanced position"—Russia's noninterference—in the crisis. Pashinian, who had advocated Armenia's withdrawal from the Eurasian Economic Union, reassured his host that he actually had no such plans.

The Moscow-Yerevan relationship was too important for both sides to question. Russia kept its main military base in the South Caucasus in the Armenian city of Gyumri. Armenia needs Russia as its main security guarantor—even while knowing that Russia also has a strong relationship with Azerbaijan. By virtue of their joint membership in the Collective Security Treaty Organization, Armenia can buy Russian weapons at a discount. The two countries have a joint air defense agreement, and Yerevan in June 2016 ratified a treaty on the operation of a joint Russian-Armenian anti-aircraft system. In 2015, Moscow provided Armenia with a $200 million loan to purchase Russian weapons, including new Iskander cruise missiles, which were paraded on Armenian Independence Day.

These connections also signify a relationship that has become transactional, based on weapons and money. It was security, not economics, that drove Serzh Sargsyan into joining Putin's Eurasian Economic Union (EAEU) project in 2013. Accession to a union with countries with which it shared no borders and had very different economic profiles made little sense. In September 2013, Sargsyan abandoned a painstakingly negotiated Association Agreement with the EU, flew to Moscow and announced that Armenia was joining the customs union with Russia and Belarus, a forerunner to the EAEU.

Evidently under pressure, Sargsyan had succumbed to an "offer he could not refuse." In Moscow, with Putin at his side, Sargsyan dutifully declared, "I have repeatedly said before that when you are part of one system of military security it is impossible and ineffective to isolate yourself from a corresponding economic space." For Putin, the announcement was as much, if not more, about winning over Ukraine, which was in the grip of the first Maidan protests, as it was about Armenia.

By its actions, Russia demonstrated that it has no strategy for Armenia beyond wanting to keep its military base there and maintain the ownership of economic assets it acquired in the 2000s. A series of steps convinced Armenians that Russia did not have their best interests at heart. Most obviously, Moscow's decision to sell weapons to Azerbaijan showed it had divided loyalties when it came to the Karabakh conflict. This caused a backlash in Armenia against Russia after the four-day war of 2016. Over many years, Moscow also failed to support the main demand of Armenian businessmen trading with Russia, which was to facilitate road traffic across Georgia. The main road border crossing between Georgia and Russia across the Caucasus at Upper Lars was impassable for four or five months of the year, thereby limiting traffic between Russia and Armenia. A Swiss-brokered deal that enabled Russia to join the World Trade Organization in 2011 foresaw the opening of three "transit corridors" for international traffic, two of which would cross the territory of Abkhazia and South Ossetia, with Swiss customs monitors having the right to check cargoes. Both Armenian and Russian businessmen lobbied hard for this deal, and there were signs that it might finally be completed in 2018. But the Kremlin hesitated in giving its final approval. Armenians have concluded from messages such as these that Russia is a partner, not a friend. At a more fundamental level, Moscow is no longer a metropolis for younger Armenians. The only attraction it has is an economic one.

Every post-independence Armenian government has declared a foreign policy based on "complementarity" or "multipolarity"—in other words, partnership with many states, and not just Russia. In 2018, Armenia had a better chance to make this a reality than it had twenty-five years previously. In 2017, the EU and Armenia signed a Comprehensive and Enhanced Partnership Agreement. This was an attempt to rescue the political parts of the draft association agreement abandoned in 2013 while accepting that the economic elements were not compatible with Armenia's membership in the EAEU. The two sides agreed on cooperation on good governance, the environment, antiterrorism, and other measures.

The Armenian diaspora was also beginning to play a different role. Of the more than 10 million Armenians in the world, less than a third live in the Republic of Armenia. The majority are the descendants of Ottoman Armenians who were survivors of the Armenian Genocide of 1915 and whose homeland in eastern Turkey is lost to them. This vast diaspora is a potentially huge resource for Armenia—but one that has not been successfully utilized. "Eastern" Armenians, who live in present-day Armenia, and "Western" Armenians, the majority of the diaspora, have different conceptions of what their Armenian identity means. The primary focus of the diaspora and its organizations has always been the injustice suffered by its people's parents and grandparents in the Genocide, fueled by a drive to get the world to recognize the killings of 1915 as a genocide and marked by the waging of a war of information with Turkey. The Republic of Armenia has been less important to them. In post-independence Armenia, many diasporans chose to fund soft projects, such as church restoration and children's charities, rather than become involved with the difficult business of state-building.

The commemorations of the centenary of the Genocide in 2015 marked a turning point. When they were over, there was a feeling of closure for many influential diasporans, who sought other projects and therefore began to get more involved in Armenia. As one of them, Sara Anjargolian, the CEO and co-founder of Impact Hub Armenia, said in an interview, "The idea is to change the dynamic from post-genocide charity to pro-entrepreneurial investment."[6]

An influx of foreigners has helped revitalize Yerevan. It may still be a bit drab, but it is much more cosmopolitan than it was in the 1990s, being now a city of Indian medical students, a well-funded Chinese-language school, and hordes of Iranian tourists. Syrian Armenian refugees have opened up cafes and shops. Slowly but surely, within certain limits, it is becoming an international city, a place that feels like a capital at last.

Distant Ararat

Despite the mood of optimism in Armenia after the country's Velvet Revolution, some things did not change—among them, the country's political geography. On a clear day in Yerevan you look out at the magnificent twin peaks of Mount Ararat floating above the horizon—and still on the other side of a closed border in Turkey. Armenia's two longest borders, with Azerbaijan and Turkey, remain closed as a direct result of the Karabakh conflict. That leaves only two routes to the outside world. One is over a mountainous border to Iran, a country friendly to Armenia but still living in international semi-isolation. The other route is to Georgia and the Black Sea port of Batumi, which remains Armenia's main outlet to the world. The result of this semi-isolation is that Armenia is often a hostage to the quarrels between its close neighbor, Georgia, and its main patron, Russia.

Isolation and closed borders have exerted visible and hidden costs on Armenia. They have increased Armenia's economic dependence on Russia and allowed oligarchs to control import and export monopolies. More insidiously, they have shaped the thinking of the younger generation, who may be digitally savvy but are also in many ways more inward-looking than their parents. Living in a state of suspended war with Azerbaijan, these young people have internalized twenty years of Armenian nationalist rhetoric, knowing only that Azerbaijan is the enemy, that Turkey is unfriendly, and that their countryrules not just Nagorny Karabakh but the surrounding Azerbaijani regions as well.

Lest it be thought that all Armenians are always as pacific as in Yerevan in 2018, it is worth recalling a more violent protest in Yerevan in July 2016 that also attracted wide public support. A group of radical nationalists, many of them ex-combatants of the Karabakh conflict, seized a police station on the edge of Yerevan, took several hostages, and killed two policemen before they eventually surrendered. Their first demand was the release of Jirair Sefilian, a Lebanese-born veteran of the war who had been arrested the month before on weapons charges. The radicals' group called itself Sasna Tsrer, or "Daredevils of Sassoun," in reference to a medieval Armenian epic poem. They harked back to a tradition of Armenian warriors who are known by the Arabic name *fedayin*. They both railed against corruption and took an unyielding stand on the Karabakh issue, opposing any return of "liberated territories" to Azerbaijan.

One of the first acts of the new government was to facilitate the pardoning of Sefilian. And despite being an apostle of political nonviolence, Pashinian initially took a tough stance on Karabakh in public that made him sound more like a man of the street than a diplomat prepared to do business with Azerbaijan. In contrast to his former patron, Levon Ter-Petrosian, Pashinian said that Nagorny Karabakh was an "inseparable part" of Armenia and that the occupied regions around Karabakh should not be returned to Azerbaijan.

The new Armenian government also declared that it was ready for a new rapprochement with Turkey. But the conditions for that were far less favorable than they had been a decade before. After a period of thaw and liberalization in the early 2000s, Recep Tayyip Erdoğan led an increasingly nationalist and authoritarian regime. Tolerance of Armenians and discussion of the Armenian Genocide were not on the agenda. Despite the differences between the pious Erdoğan and the secular Aliev on a number of issues, especially Israel, Azerbaijan was one of Turkey's few close allies. Erdoğan expressed full support for Azerbaijan during the fighting of April 2016.

A few years before it had all been so different. Armenia and Turkey were on the verge of a historical agreement. In October 2009, the foreign ministers of Armenia and Turkey signed two protocols in Zurich on restoring diplomatic relations and reopening their closed land border; it only remained for the agreements to be ratified by the countries' parliaments. The Swiss government had hosted confidential talks between the two sides. Then Turkish president Abdullah Gül made an extraordinary visit to Yerevan in October 2008 to watch an Armenia-Turkey international football match. Gül was the first ever Turkish leader to visit Armenia. He spent only six hours in Yerevan—the engines of his plane did not stop running—but the symbolic importance of his visit was hard to overstate.

The visit coincided with a thaw in Turkey in which the urban middle classes and historians began to examine the blank pages of their history in the early twentieth century: the expulsion of Greeks, the persecution of Kurds, and—most painfully—the destruction and deportation of almost the entire Armenian population of the Ottoman Empire. Books were written, conferences held at Turkish universities, and untold stories revealed. The hidden histories of the descendants of Armenians left behind in 1915 and adopted by Kurdish and Turkish families, either by force or through kindness, were told at last. The Kurdish municipalities of eastern Turkey went the furthest. In the city of Diyarbakir, the old Armenian church was reopened and restored, and the local government offered an apology to the Armenians. It was a favorable moment for confronting taboos.

For Turkey, the Zurich agreement of 2009 promised to draw a line under the Armenian issue and its international repercussions—if Azerbaijan could be persuaded to swallow it. For Armenia, the economic benefit of opening the border, restoring the closed railway line, and linking Armenia to Europe via Turkey was clear. At a stroke, Armenia's international isolation would end. The document was designed to sidestep both the Karabakh and the Genocide issues. Armenia would have to accept its international border with Turkey as established by the Treaty of Kars in 1921 to be permanent, but this was a fait accompli as far as the world was concerned.

But the protocols were never ratified. Vocal Armenian diasporans objected to the proposed formation of a vaguely worded "sub-commission on the historical dimension" to be staffed by Armenian, Turkish, and international historians. This was the Turkish government's attempt to insert into the process its right to debate the genocide issue—if only to defend itself against nationalist claims that it had sold out. Many Armenians considered that even this vague formulation amounted to a betrayal of their history. President Sargsyan was not deterred, but it certainly dampened his willingness to lobby actively for the rapprochement in public.

The Armenian-Turkish rapprochement would undoubtedly have succeeded, however, had it not been for Azerbaijan's opposition. The documents signed in Zurich did not explicitly mention the Karabakh conflict—the reason Turkey had closed the border in the first place in 1993. There was a tacit understanding that progress on Armenia-Turkey relations would shift the biggest historical boulder weighing down Armenia and galvanize international efforts to resolve the conflict with Azerbaijan. As the International Crisis Group argued, "An open border could help break Armenian perceptions of encirclement by hostile Turkic peoples, making them less adamant about retaining the territories around Nagorno-Karabakh as security guarantees." Baku did not see it that way, however, and Azerbaijani officials lobbied hard in Ankara against the protocols, even threatening to renegotiate Azerbaijan's gas sales to Turkey.

In the end, Turkey's most powerful politician, then prime minister Erdoğan, called for Armenia to withdraw from occupied territories in Azerbaijan the day after the Zurich ceremony. The process stalled, the protocols were not ratified, and Armenian-Turkish relations became even worse than before. Soon after, both Armenia and Azerbaijan doubled down on their traditional military alliances as Armenia and Russia signed a new military agreement and Azerbaijan and Turkey signed a new defense pact. Azerbaijan-Turkish projects bypassing Armenia, such as the new TANAP gas pipeline and the Baku-Tbilisi-Kars railway, forged ahead.

In early 2018, the Armenian government finally formally withdrew its signature from the 2009 Zurich Protocols. The country was thus still caught in the same international tangle of unresolved conflict and closed borders, formed in the 1990s whicheven more tightly knotted in 2018. The country can develop only so far within these constraints. To remove them, Armenia, Azerbaijan, and Turkey would need to work together in concert in the name of a larger strategic goal—a fantastic prospect in a region where historical rivalries are still so intense.

Open Georgia, Closed Georgia

Cross the border from Armenia into Georgia and you come to the country that is, despite many caveats, the undoubted success story of the South Caucasus. Modern Georgia is a real democracy, albeit a flawed one, with contested elections, a lively media, and working governmental institutions. Tbilisi has turned into a vibrant European capital that is a joy to visit, with art galleries, cafes, wine stores, and dozens of small hotels catering to crowds of Russian, Iranian, and European tourists. New pedestrian crossings have even curbed Georgian males' penchant for fast and dangerous driving.

Georgia's government moved in a decisively European direction after two developments. The war of 2008 meant the de facto loss of Abkhazia and South Ossetia and the severing of diplomatic relations with Russia. The coming to power of the Georgian Dream government in 2012 replaced Mikheil Saakashvili, who had made relations with the United States a priority and declared that he wanted to make Georgia into "Singapore." In 2014, Georgia and the European Union signed an association agreement, which came into force in 2016. In 2017, Georgians won the important concession of visa-free travel to the Schengen zone in the European Union.

Yet it would be misleading to call contemporary Georgia a fully European country. It still has a complex identity and is subject to many opposing forces, which coexist uneasily in the same space. In the modern era, the country has become both more open to the world and more conservative. Religious piety, support for "family values," and anti-Muslim sentiment have increased—and so has a culture of tolerance toward lesbian-gay-bisexual-and-transgender (LGBT) rights and minorities in the capital.

These two worlds collided on the night of May 11, 2018. Hundreds of riot police with machine guns raided Café Gallery and Bassiani, two popular Tbilisi nightclubs, dragging young people off the dance floors and into detention. The ostensible reason was a crackdown on drug dealers, but none were arrested. Instead it appeared to be an act of intimidation against young people with an alternative lifestyle. The next day thousands of young people staged a rave in broad daylight to protest police brutality. Inevitably, they held it on the stage of all Georgian protests of the previous three decades, Rustaveli Avenue. A group of far-right activists held a counter-rally, with the police in between. The interior minister issued an unprecedented apology for the police raids. A few days later, another march was held by conservative Georgians carrying icons and singing hymns to celebrate a "day of sanctity and strength of the family."

The immediate issue was harsh legislation that criminalized the possession of even the tiniest amount of drugs. This snared hundreds of young people and kept Georgia's prison population unreasonably high—the fourth highest in Europe per capita. It also exposed the wide cultural gap between different Georgians as the country opened up to the world. A tension between "open Georgia" and "closed Georgia" has run through the country's entire post-independence history.

A further wave of protests against "closed Georgia" hit the country a few weeks later. This time the cause was the country's problematic justice system. The spark was the acquittal of two teenagers accused of murdering a sixteen-year-old, Davit Saralidze, in a knife fight. Television viewers were moved by the sight of the grieving father of the murdered boy demanding justice. The court ruled that neither of the two accused had stabbed the boy, and there were claims that a leading prosecutor had been shielding his nephew from being charged.

All three South Caucasus countries suffer from what the Turks call a "deep state." This term refers to a hidden nexus of security and law enforcement officials who commit abuses with impunity and are beyond the scrutiny of the media and the courts. In a legacy that dates back to the Russia of Peter the Great, state prosecutors are often used as instruments of this deep state, empowered to punish the disloyal and the inconvenient.

In Georgia, this kind of abusive behavior by security organs has been a constant of all post-independence administrations, especially that of President Mikheil Saakashvili, who was always more pro-Western than he was liberal. In 2012, Saakashvili, who had opened Georgia up to the world in an unprecedented way a few years before, was displaying ever greater illiberal and authoritarian tendencies. The draconian justice system meant that less than 1 percent of the accused were acquitted in a Georgian court, and the prisons were full. The tax police harassed businessmen who refused to contribute

to government infrastructure projects. Public officials gave interviews sur-
reptitiously, fearful of surveillance by the powerful interior minister Vano
Merabashvili.

Georgian Dream

In 2011, with a year until the next elections in Georgia, Mikheil Saakashvili
appeared to have weathered the postwar crisis that had left him tarnished
both at home and abroad. His party still dominated parliament, the main
television channels gave him uncritical coverage, and the opposition
was weak.

Saakashvili's second presidential term was due to end in 2013. He had
the constitution changed to establish a system in which the prime minister and parliament had greater powers and the president's authority was
downgraded—as Armenia was to do a few years later. The expectation was
that Saakashvili would seek the prime minister's post and stay in power. But,
as in Armenia in 2018, the plan did not go according to script.

Unexpectedly, a new opposition figure emerged whom it was much
harder to crush. Bidzina Ivanishvili was Georgia's richest man, having made
his money in Russia in the 1990s. *Forbes* estimated that he was worth $5.5
billion. Ivanishvili's eccentric personality defied easy characterization, although it made good and exotic journalistic copy. He came from a small
village in western Georgia but lived in a soaring glass-and-steel futurist castle
designed by the Japanese architect Shin Takamatsu overlooking Tbilisi. For
years he had been the country's biggest benefactor for cultural and humanitarian projects, supporting Georgian theater and children's charities and the
construction of the country's biggest church, Trinity Cathedral in Tbilisi. He
also kept a private zoo with penguins and zebras and amassed a vast art collection. In 2006, Picasso's *Dora Maar with Cat* was sold in New York for
$95 million, making it the second most expensive painting ever auctioned.
For years, the name of the buyer remained a mystery, until it was finally revealed to be Ivanishvili.

Ivanishvili stayed on the sidelines until 2011. In another bizarre chapter
of the family's tale, his son Bera, who had moved to Los Angeles, was more
celebrated than his father as Georgia's most famous rapper. In October 2011,
Ivanishvili made his move, declaring that the Saakashvili government was
discredited and he was ready to head the opposition. In an interview, he
called contemporary Georgia "a façade economy, façade everything, just a

Potemkin village." He gave his new movement the name Georgian Dream, the title of a song by his rapper son.[7]

Even Ivanishvili may have been surprised by how quickly almost the whole Georgian opposition hitched itself to his bandwagon, from the pro-Western liberals of the Republican Party and former ambassador to the United Nations Irakli Alasania to the conservatives of Industry Will Save Georgia. Now they had a sponsor and protector. The authorities reacted swiftly and clumsily, stripping Ivanishvili and his wife of their Georgian citizenship on dubious grounds, a move that only won him more public sympathy, including from Patriarch Ilya II, the head of Georgia's Orthodox Church.

The election, nominally one for parliament, turned into a contest between two very different big personalities whom Georgians called by their first names: Misha and Bidzina. It was free but not fair. Saakashvili's United National Movement dominated media coverage and controlled municipal administrations. The president had developed a passion for architectural projects, from the new towers of Batumi to a modern glass bridge across the River Kura in Tbilisi, and made this building spree one of the central themes of his campaign. Accompanied rather bizarrely by Hungary's prime minister, Viktor Orban, Saakashvili opened a shiny new airport for the city of Kutaisi the week before election day.

Saakashvili also tried to make the election about Russia, repeatedly accusing Ivanishvili of being an agent of Moscow. (Ivanishvili had made his money in Yeltsin's Russia in the 1990s. That certainly proved that he had been a successful operator in a rough, criminalized environment, but not that he had any ties to the Putin administration. When he went into Georgian politics, Ivanishvili undertook the task of selling his remaining assets in Russia.)

Ivanishvili gained momentum by focusing on a basic bread-and-butter domestic agenda. He drew support from two entirely different social groups. In rural areas, unemployment was high, as the United National Movement, applying its libertarian economic principles, had invested very little in agriculture. These rural voters were enthusiastic about Georgian Dream's promises of job creation and higher spending on social benefits. In the capital, the urban professionals who had supported the Rose Revolution now felt choked by the encroachment of one-party rule, the power of the police, and the lack of freedom of speech. They also backed Georgian Dream in large numbers.

On the evening of September 18, 2012, a scandal broke that turned the tide against Saakashvili. Video footage was released and shown on two small opposition television channels of horrific abuse of prisoners in Tbilisi's Gldani Prison. Prisoners were shown being mocked, physically abused, and, in one case, apparently sexually abused with a broom. The videos unleashed a wave of protest, mainly led by young people. For many it was highly personal: Georgia's prisons were so full that everyone, it seemed, knew a current or former inmate. Despite sackings and apologies, Saakashvili's government could not shake off the accusation that the abuse was institutionalized and a result of its proudly proclaimed zero-tolerance policy on crime.

On October 1, Saakashvili's team still thought he had won, but the opinion polls got it wrong. Georgian Dream captured 55 percent of the vote and 85 of the 150 seats in parliament. Tbilisi delivered the most emphatic blow to Saakashvili, with two-thirds of voters backing Georgian Dream. Saakashvili proved his democratic credentials by conceding defeat with some gracious words. He remained president for another year, while Ivanishvili became prime minister of a Georgian Dream government.

Looking East and West

In Georgia's election of 2012, even the city of Batumi on the Black Sea, a favored showcase of Saakashvili, voted in large numbers against President Saakashvili. Herein lies a story that says a lot about the history of modern Georgia. For a decade after independence, Batumi had been a sleepy outpost on the edge of Georgia, ruled by a corrupt local feudal lord, Aslan Abashidze, who failed to use the city's potential as a port on the Black Sea next door to Turkey. When Abashidze was ousted following the Rose Revolution of 2003, the new government began to invest in the city. For Saakashvili, it was a chance to indulge his penchant for big new architectural projects and make Georgia into a "new Singapore." A forest of new skyscrapers filled the skyline. Batumi acquired a Sheraton hotel, a Radisson, and a string of new casinos. The president began to spend more time in the city than in Tbilisi, hosting foreign guests such as Hillary Clinton there in June 2012.

Clinton's nemesis, Donald Trump, came to the city two months before she did. Trump and Saakashvili spoke in front of a billboard on an empty lot with the words "Trump Tower Batumi" and a picture of a forty-seven-story skyscraper. Saakashvili's critics noted that Trump had merely lent his name and no money to the project. Others questioned why the city needed more luxury housing and another casino when ordinary residents were still living in poor-quality housing. In any case, Trump withdrew from the project when he became president, and the lot stayed empty.

Batumi represents a different, less European, Georgia, which is a magnet for Armenian, Azerbaijani, Iranian, and—especially—Turkish tourists. Georgian-Turkish trade turnover reached $1 billion under Saakashvili, with nine-tenths of it being Turkish imports into Turkey. Turkish truck drivers, restaurant workers, and holiday-makers followed the money trail into Georgia.

The Turkish influx caused a backlash among some conservative Georgians in the Ajaria region. Although Georgian politicians name Russia as the country's biggest enemy, public antipathy is actually stronger toward Turks. In 2012, complaints covered the spectrum from merely disappointed ("local people aren't getting jobs") to the fully paranoid and xenophobic ("the Turks are buying up the city," "Turkey is working with Saakashvili to recapture Batumi"). Batumi was part of the Ottoman Empire between 1878 and 1918, and the Ottoman influence lives on in large communities of Georgian Muslims in the region. Parts of the Georgian Orthodox Church and nationalist politicians urged these Muslims to "reconvert" to Christianity and railed against Turkish influence in Batumi.

One such xenophobic populist was Murman Dumbadze, Georgian Dream's successful local parliamentary candidate in Batumi. While some of his colleagues spoke up for democracy and European integration, Dumbadze focused his campaign on Turkish immigration. He denounced plans to reconstruct a mosque built by the Ottomans in the mid-nineteenth century and destroyed by the Soviet regime in the 1930s. The project was eventually suspended, but not before the nationalist wing of Georgian Dream had exploited it to win votes.

Managing to look both east and west, Georgian Dream took power in Georgia, and Ivanishvili became prime minister, apparently unprepared for his own victory. For a year there was an extremely cantankerous period of cohabitation between Ivanishvili and his bitter rival Saakashvili before Saakashvili served out his presidential term and went into exile, first in the United States and then in Ukraine. Several unpopular figures of the previous government, including interior minister Vano Merabishvili and Tbilisi mayor Gigi Ugulava, were tried and jailed. There was a strong hint of political vendetta about this, but the charges for abuse of power were well substantiated. In 2018, Georgian courts also handed out two jail sentences in absentia to ex-president Saakashvili.

Continuity of a pro-Western foreign policy was assured under new ministers, who included Irakli Alasania as defense minister. Georgia pressed ahead with forging closer relations with the European Union. Diplomatic relations with Russia remained severed because of the conflicts over Abkhazia and South Ossetia, but the new government unfroze other aspects of the relationship and reopened transport and trade links. In a short while, Georgian wine had recovered its previous dominant position in the Russian market. Tens of thousands of Russian tourists began to visit Georgia once again.

When it came to domestic politics, the new government seemed to be in a perpetual organizational muddle, in which "friends of Bidzina" thrived. Ministers were afraid to make decisions, and there was no discernible economic policy. Those who professed loyalty to the new leader prospered. They included former AC Milan footballer Kakha Kaladze, who served as energy minister and then was elected mayor of Tbilisi in 2017. When Ivanishvili stepped aside as prime minister in November 2013, he left as his successor Irakli Garibashvili, aged just thirty-three, a man who had spent his entire career up until then working for Ivanishvili in business or politics. More independent figures, such as Alasania, departed or were sacked.

Yet political pluralism endured in Georgia. Parliament had a strong and vocal minority group, and the television channel Rustavi-2 still favored Saakashvili's United National Movement. The new constitution also encouraged a healthy division of powers. The president had less executive power but was still head of state and the arbiter of constitutional disputes. The man whom Ivanishvili nominated for the role and who was elected to the position in November 2013 was Giorgi Margvelashvili, who had been education minister and before that rector of the Georgian Institute of Public Affairs. Although the official candidate, the jovial Margvelashvili soon established his credentials as an independent figure, vetoing several parliamentary bills and clashing with the government.

As the elections of October 2016 approached, it seemed no foregone conclusion that Georgian Dream would win another term in office. Voters' enthusiasm had faded as Ivanishvili's government had failed to deliver on his main promise, to lower unemployment and give jobs to the disadvantaged. Yet in the end, Georgian Dream won again and actually increased its tally of seats to 115 out of 150.

Georgian Dream's success was in large part due to the disastrous performance of the opposition. The election became a rerun of the 2012 contest between the current and former governing parties. More simply, it was the same personality clash between the two titans, Ivanishvili and Saakashvili— even though neither man was on the ballot—a repetition of what one author caustically called "the perpetual Tom and Jerry of Georgian politics."

Saakashvili, resident in Ukraine, was still leader of the United National Movement. Banking on the idea that he was still personally popular, he chose to make the election a de facto referendum on his return to Georgia. Three days before polling day, he broadcast live to a rally in central Tbilisi via a giant video screen. He promised an end to the rule of the "Russian oligarch" Ivanishvili and signed off by saying that "three days are left before I cross this sea. . . . [S]ee you in a victorious Georgia!"[8] The message backfired. Georgian society had outlived its former president and opted for stability. Georgian Dream won 48 percent of the vote, the United National Movement garnered 27 percent, and almost all other parties were marginalized. For the third time since independence Georgia had become a de facto one-party state, with one party dominating parliament. When this happened under Shevardnadze and Saakashvili, checks and balances began to disappear and the authorities became increasingly arrogant. This time around, the new Georgian Dream government proposed controversial constitutional changes that would enhance its own powers. Despite all this, for two and a half years, prime minister Giorgi Kvirikashvili, a calm technocratic figure who generally avoided the angry invective of most Georgian politicians, was a stabilizing presence, presiding over an improvement in the economy and deepening ties with the European Union. But the godfather of Georgian Dream, the country's other would-be messiah, Ivanishvili, was still active behind the scenes. Ivanishvili's own popularity had tumbled, especially after he indulged in more eccentric stunts, such as spending a fortune transporting a 135-year-old "tulip tree" across the Black Sea for his private arboretum. In 2018, Ivanishvili returned to be party leader of Georgian Dream. Not long after, Kvirikashvili resigned, apparently after stormy disagreements with Ivanishvili and his close circle over economic policy (including probably the protection of their private interests). Informal power, possessed by men who included Ivanishvili's cousin, continued to be exercised in ways that ordinary Georgians could not control.

In 2018, the gap between "open" and "closed" Georgia had never been so stark. The country was on track to receive a million and a half temporary visitors, most of them tourists. Tens of thousands of ordinary Georgians were making use of opportunities to visit the European Union visa-free. At the same time, ultranationalists organized events such as a "Georgian March" with openly xenophobic slogans. And there was shock when an Azerbaijani opposition journalist, Afgan Mukhtarli, who had been taking refuge in Tbilisi, was suddenly abducted and turned up in detention in Azerbaijan. The most plausible explanation was that he had been snatched in collusion with elements of the Georgian security services. The biggest problem the country had, according to one Western ambassador, was "lack of political oversight of the security services." In Georgia, at least, the country's problems are debated and the government's decisions are openly protested.

Beyond the Boundaries

More than a quarter of a century after the end of the USSR, two territories, Abkhazia and South Ossetia, were still officially recognized as part of independent Georgia but had lived outside control by Tbilisi all that time.

On August 26, 2008, two weeks after the end of fighting in Georgia, Russian president Dmitry Medvedev sprang a surprise by declaring that Russia was formally recognizing the independence of South Ossetia and Abkhazia. He announced that Russia was defending them from Georgian "genocide." Russia's recognition paradoxically closed off Abkhazia and South Ossetia even further from the outside world. The two were now client statelets of Moscow, which stationed approximately 7,000 troops on their territory. South Ossetia, as far as most of the world was concerned, disappeared behind barbed wire. Its economy sank, as apart from farming it now basically served the Russian military base, and many voted with their feet, pushing the population down to as low as 30,000, one-third of the level it had been in the late Soviet era. Most of the remaining Georgians were displaced, and several of their villages were bulldozed and left in ruins. The many Ossetians and Georgians who had shared families because of mixed marriages were now separated by an increasingly hard border.

It was an absurdity that with such a tiny population South Ossetia should be alleged to be a sovereign country while North Ossetia, with a population of 600,000, remained an autonomous republic of the Russian Federation. The absurdity was no secret to most South Ossetians themselves, and in 2015 their leader, Leonid Tibilov, called for a referendum on unification with Russia, only to be politely ignored by the Kremlin. For Moscow, South Ossetia was important only as a geopolitical pawn and a thorn in the side of Tbilisi.

Abkhazia was a different proposition. The roots of the conflict with Georgia went deeper, and the aspirations of the Abkhaz to build their own state were more serious. Abkhazia is surely the most mysterious and melancholy place in the Caucasus, as well as one of the most beautiful. After this little slice of paradise on the Black Sea was struck by calamity in the war of 1992–93, it struggled for years to recover anything resembling a normal existence. The ravages of war were visible in towns and villages, while grand Soviet-era sanatoria and guest houses that had entertained the cream of the USSR's elite, including Stalin himself, crumbled from neglect. More than a decade after the end of the Soviet Union, this author went on a tour of the vast underground caverns near Novy Afon—so big that they are accessed by a Moscow metro train set up specially on site. The guide proudly declared that "this is one of the biggest cave complexes in our country"; by "our country" she evidently meant the USSR.

Russian recognition in 2008 improved the lives of ordinary Abkhaz materially. Thanks to a big influx of Russian money, Abkhazia began to look more like a normal state and less like a postwar disaster zone. The vast, ruined, honeycombed concrete hulk of the Soviet-era parliament building, burned in 1993, still overlooked the city of Sukhumi like an abandoned shipwreck. Elsewhere, however, war-damaged houses that had stood miserably for twenty years were cleared away. Roads were repaired, shops and cafes opened, and Sukhumi (or Sukhum, as the Abkhaz themselves and now the Russians call the city) even had its first traffic jams. Most ordinary Abkhaz were delighted with the fruits of recognition.

In 2012, Russian direct assistance to Abkhazia— paying pensions and social welfare benefits, building infrastructure, and funding the police and armed forces—was worth almost $300 million. This came with strings attached, of course. Russia opened a huge new embassy in the middle of Sukhumi, larger even than the Abkhaz government headquarters, to demonstrate who was in charge. Loyalty to Moscow was expected, and given, on many issues. The 2014 "strategic partnership" treaty with Russia effectively subsumed the armed forces of Abkhazia to the Russian forces and gave Russia joint control of the border with western Georgia. Yet the Abkhaz stubbornly refused to give in to a central Russian demand, which was to legalize the sale of property to foreigners—in other words, to Russians. Although Russian businessmen could always find ways around this if they wanted, this provision stemmed a tide of acquisitions that, Abkhaz feared, would see the prime buildings along the entire Black Sea coast snapped up by their northern neighbor.

The new euphoria of Abkhaz-Russian relations slowly faded. The joke was heard that "we used to have independence, now we have recognition." Russian budgetary assistance declined—especially after 2014, when the bill for annexing Crimea landed in Moscow and the value of the ruble fell. The Abkhaz historian Stanislav Lakoba clashed with Russians over textbooks whitewashing Russia's imperial history in the region. Tourist numbers from Russia surged in the first years but declined somewhat thereafter—reportedly many had come back once out of curiosity or nostalgia for Soviet-era holidays but had been disappointed by the quality of service. In 2014, the Abkhaz hoped to benefit from the Winter Olympics in Sochi just across the border and even see their airport reopen—but nothing happened.

Domestic politics in Abkhazia also became more turbulent. Politics had always been contested—within the constraints that ethnic Abkhaz dominated public life and held almost all official posts, even though the Armenian community was almost as large in numbers. Russian recognition had given the Abkhaz the luxury to fight one another, former de facto foreign minister Sergei Shamba observed: "After the war [of 2008], the main external issue [the conflict with Georgia] was resolved. Our internal fights intensified because the external threat had receded."

In 2011, Abkhaz president Sergei Bagapsh died of a heart attack. Alexander Ankvab, a former policeman and interior minister who vowed to crack down on corruption, was elected as his successor. Ankvab was much less consensual than his predecessor and made many enemies, both inside Abkhazia and in Moscow. In the spring of 2014, opposition leaders organized street protests that called for Ankvab to be ousted, apparently with the encouragement of Vladislav Surkov, the emissary of the Kremlin. Ankvab was forced to resign. Raul Khajimba, who had first tried to be president in 2004, finally achieved his ambition of being elected leader of Abkhazia.

Abkhazia had two faces to the world: the international border with its patron-state, Russia, and its border with western Georgia, recognized by the world only as an "administrative boundary line." The Georgian gate is half-locked, being heavily manned by Abkhaz and Russian border guards. Almost all travelers across this border go on foot or hitch a ride with a horse and cart. The long bridge across the River Inguri, built in 1948 by Soviet Interior Ministry troops, has a magnificent view of the Caucasus Mountains, but it is a miserable long trudge for Georgian villagers making their way back and forth across it, especially when the rain or snow comes down.

After the 2008 conflict, multiple crossing points remained open across the river between the Gali region of Abkhazia and western Georgia. They allowed for continued international access to Abkhazia through Georgian-controlled territory and permitted the 30,000 or so Georgians still resident in Gali to move back and forth. Gali is famous for its hazelnuts, and these people could still make a decent if precarious living by having one foot on each side of the border. In 2017, all but one of these crossings was closed. Simultaneously, the Gali Georgians faced discrimination in Abkhazia, finding it difficult to get Abkhaz documents and having secondary education in the Georgian language restricted.

The Georgian government, it was said by observers of the conflict, half in jest and half in sadness, always offered the right thing to the Abkhaz—but ten years too late. In 2012, Tbilisi came up with a scheme for "neutral passports": these would be issued in Tbilisi but bear no Georgian insignia and would enable Abkhaz to travel abroad. Yet by that point, most Abkhaz had obtained Russian passports and the taboo on accepting any documents from the Georgians was too strong. The 2008 Law on Occupied Territories, adopted by the Saakashvili government after the conflict, sought to control all access by international organizations and limit economic activity.

When the Georgian Dream government took office in Tbilisi in 2012, Paata Zakareishvili, a veteran of civil society dialogue, became the minister responsible for talks with Abkhazia and South Ossetia. Symbolically he changed the name of his ministry to "Ministry of Reconciliation." Despite the respect he enjoyed from Abkhaz and Ossetians, even he enjoyed limited success. One exception was a project that resulted in the exhumation, identification, and reburial of more than 160 sets of remains of bodies left over from the conflict of 1992–93. Abkhaz were also encouraged to cross the border and come and use Georgian healthcare—and many took advantage of it.

Although the temperature of the conflict went down, contacts between the two sides remained painfully limited. Genuine cooperation was possible in principle, and in one case in which both sides had an interest—jointly managing the water resources of the Inguri Hydro-Electric Power Station on the Abkhaz border—they did work together. Elsewhere, the insuperable issue of status—Was Abkhazia part of Georgia and subject to its law or wasn't it?—made most joint initiatives impossible. Even when the two sides were threatened by a devastating pest, the "brown marmorated stink bug" that devastated the hazelnut crop on both sides of the border, with no regard for sovereignty or disputes, teams of experts faced obstacles working with their counterparts on the other side.

Previously there had been many contacts and negotiations, but in 2008, with no agreement on what the two sides' new roles should be, the United Nations mission was forced to leave Abkhazia and the OSCE quit South Ossetia. The Abkhaz and Ossetians did not allow the European United Monitoring Mission, newly established after the conflict, to monitor their side of the boundaries. That left only one international forum for the conflict, the Geneva International Discussions, convened thanks to the six-point ceasefire plan of August 2008. Held four times a year, they brought together Georgian, Russian, Abkhaz, and South Ossetian officials in talks chaired by three co-chairs from the European Union, OSCE, and United Nations. These sessions were called "discussions" because they were not formal negotiations, and the representatives from Tbilisi, Moscow, Sukhumi, and Tskhinvali attended as individuals so as to avoid disputes about their exact titles or affiliations. Even this format did not prevent a theatrical environment of démarches and walkouts, with the Russians pretending that they were merely interested outsiders and not a real party to the conflict. Almost a decade after the conflict, they had established themselves as an occasionally useful participant in messages and discussions, but only on humanitarian, security, and technical issues. The unresolved political issues were buried too deep to merit proper discussion.

Many Abkhaz contend that their conflict was resolved in 2008 and they have no reason to interact with Georgia or Georgia's Western friends. The result is that a good half of their isolation, which is the republic's biggest problem, is self-imposed. The conflicts in Abkhazia and South Ossetia exercise few minds. Almost no one is dying—in contrast to the violence between Armenia and Azerbaijan or in Ukraine. But they are still a tragedy burning on a low flame. They still hurt the lives of tens of thousands of displaced Georgians. They also restrict the lives of Abkhaz and Ossetians, who have the security blanket of Russian recognition and protection but still live in the shadows of the global marketplace.

Back to the Mountains: A Different View

The ancient stone towers of Svaneti, in the highest mountains of Georgia east of Abkhazia, are at least 1,000 years old. Ushguli, a group of four villages, calls itself the highest settlement in Europe to be inhabited year-round. Around seventy families still live there, surrounded by majestic peaks and amid reminders of a much more glorious past in the shape of around 200 stone towers. It is a small miracle that the Svans, who still speak their own language related to but quite distinct from Georgian, have survived in these harsh conditions and through multiple different political regimes into the modern era.

The tour of the South Caucasus in 2018 ends where the book began, in the mountains. The extraordinary natural features of the Caucasus cross all political boundaries, and its extraordinary landscape and outstanding bio-diversity are its often-hidden glory. Foreign visitors are awestruck by these landscapes, still far less developed than the alpine zones of western Europe. The World Wildlife Fund has named the wider Caucasus region—stretching into Russia and Turkey—one of thirty-five "biodiversity hotspots" on the planet, with over 1,650 indigenous plants and animals in nine climate zones. To name but three examples of this biodiversity: the mountains of Georgia and Azerbaijan contain more species of oak than western Europe, as they survived the last Ice Age; a few mountain leopards still prowl the highlands of Armenia; and less than 200 "goitered gazelles" are to be found on the borders of Azerbaijan and Georgia.

Some natural spectacles draw visitors from all over the world. From late August to early October, birdwatchers come to the Black Sea coast of Georgia to see the annual migration southwards of millions of birds of prey through a 10-kilometer-wide corridor between the sea and the Lesser Caucasus Mountains known as the "Batumi bottleneck." On October 2, 2014, after days of rain kept the gates of the corridor closed, an astonishing 271,000 birds were counted flying through and darkening the skies.

This biodiversity is threatened by illegal logging in Armenia's forests, industrial pollution of Azerbaijan's Caspian Sea coast, and a legal but om-inous program to build a network of dams supplying hydroelectric power in the mountainous areas of Georgia, such as Svaneti. In 2018, one branch of the Georgian government—the Roads Department—announced plans to build a new road between the mountain regions of Khevsureti and Tusheti that would cross two protected areas and a "Strict Nature Reserve" despite the objections of locals, environmentalists, and many inside the government. A villager named Levan told one reporter, "I sometimes work as a tour guide. The tourists tell me—'please take me away from the road.' Why do tourists like Tusheti? Because they can run away from asphalt, dust, noise; because they can walk or ride horses."[9]

This is part of a wider competition of values and priorities. As livelihoods of ordinary people improve and the nation-states of Armenia, Azerbaijan, and Georgia modernize, a contest is underway between those who see the region's natural beauty as the greatest asset the Caucasus possesses and those who deem it to be a side issue as the region pursues rapid economic development.

Up until now, those in charge of the tourist industries of the South Caucasus have not heeded messages of this sort. There is still a belief that to aspire to be "Western" means building big hotels such as the new skyscrapers in Baku or Batumi or the monstrous 300-meter, thirty-two-floor Biltmore Hotel that now towers over Tbilisi. The protectors of the environment counter that managed ecotourism would protect naturaltreasures and bring great economic benefits as well.

Several noncommercial internationally backed projects are making a difference. The Caucasus Nature Fund raises funds to protect eighteen national parks in all three South Caucasus countries, fund park wardens, and deter poachers. In Svaneti and in Dilijan in Armenia, another group has started on an even more ambitious project it is calling the Transcaucasian Trail. The plan is to make a 3,000-kilometer hiking trail along and between the Greater and Lesser Caucasus ranges, connecting twelve national parks. Representatives of the Transcaucasian Trail spent a lot of time talking to local communities on the route about their needs and wishes. They started in two areas, using summer camps of international volunteers to build the trails. In the summer of 2018 it was possible to hike for ten days in the mountains of Svaneti or five days in the hills and forests of Dilijan.

Part of the charm of these projects is that they anticipate a day when borders will matter less or even disappear and the South Caucasus will function as a proper region once again. Seen from a satellite photograph, it is evidently a coherent geographic region, crossed by its two big mountain ranges and bounded by two seas. The view from higher in the mountains is very different from that on the ground.

Yet the region still suffers from a lack of inclusive thinking. Most of the big ideas and regional initiatives that have emerged in the last two decades have excluded either one of the South Caucasus countries themselves or a key outside power. Both Iran and Turkey have proposed "security pacts" for the Caucasus that have left out the United States and the European Union. The Commonwealth of Independent States has all but vanished, and Georgia has left it anyway. GUAM excluded Armenia. For a while, Moscow unsuccessfully promoted the idea of a "Caucasus Four" that included it and the three South Caucasus countries. Concentrating on a "Black Sea region" is to the detriment of Azerbaijan. Focusing on the Caspian leaves out Armenia. The metaphor of a "Silk Road," pretty though it is, implies a return to a premodern world in which Russia did not exist. The idea of a "Great Game" unhelpfully casts Russia in a reprised role of a hostile nineteenth-century power.

Rather than add any new metaphors to this list, I offer a concluding thought that all the constituent parts of the South Caucasus—including its unrecognized and partially recognized territories—deserve to have a say in any issue that concerns them, and that the interest of all outside powers without hostile intent has to be factored into any regional projects.

More division and conflict can be avoided if the different parts of the South Caucasus start to think less like individual actors and more like members of a region. Such a shift will not come easily. History has meant that there have never been any successful voluntary integration projects here. The plan for an independent Transcaucasian Federation in April 1918 collapsed after only a month. The only other unions have been colonial ones imposed from above, by the Persian, Ottoman, and Russian empires and by the Soviet Union. The Soviet project is hard to defend, but it did have the effect of bringing people together in a cohesive economic structure that many people still miss. In retrospect, the South Caucasian nationalists of the late 1980s lurched from one extreme to another when they took a bulldozer to the complex Soviet system. They exchanged suffocating integration for extreme disintegration, and you could say that they threw out the Caucasian baby with the Communist bathwater. Many of the economic and cultural links from those times are still there under the surface waiting to be reexploited. Environmental cooperation and cross-border tourism will immensely benefit all parts of the region, if they can only work together.

The one neighbor that could be a facilitator for voluntary integration in the South Caucasus is the region that has itself accomplished such an integration, the European Union. The example of Georgia shows that progress can be made, but there are definite limits. The EU's Eastern Partnership project is a laudable idea but can only do so much when the six countries involved, including the three South Caucasian states, have no membership perspective to join the EU. In the EU itself, there is caution. Partly, it has far too many problems to solve without having to deal with the headaches of the Caucasus. Partly, there is a perception that the governments of Armenia, Azerbaijan, and Georgia need to show a stronger commitment to democracy and reform to deserve that stronger interest. It is a vicious circle.

So the current period may be one of less engagement and greater realism. If that is the case, it may not be all bad news. History has been unkind to the South Caucasus, but there is no shortage of experience or talent there. Independence means responsibility without many of the threats of the past. If the outside powers step a bit further away, local people may remember that they also have the skills, fashioned by the centuries, to solve their own problems.

Chronology

301	Armenia converts to Christianity (some historians say 314)
327–32	Georgia converts to Christianity
639	Arab invasions bring Islam to Caucasus
10th c.	Oghuz Turks settle in present-day Azerbaijan
1099–1125	David the Builder establishes unified Georgian kingdom
1184–1213	Rule of Georgian Queen Tamar
1223–43	Mongols conquer South Caucasus
mid-15th c.	Heyday of Shirvanshah dynasty in Baku
1501	Safavid dynasty begins rule in Persia; adopts Shia faith as official religion
1722	End of Safavid dynasty leads to rule by autonomous khanates
1795	Persian army sacks Tiflis (Tbilisi)
1801	Tsarist Russia annexes eastern Georgian kingdoms
1828	Russo-Persian Treaty of Turkmenchai confirms Russian control of Transcaucasus
1845–55	Reformist Prince Mikhail Vorontsov made viceroy of Caucasus
1864	Russian victory in Caucasian Wars; mass expulsion of Circassians to Ottoman Empire
1871–83	Commercial oil industry begins in Baku; Baku-Batum railroad constructed

1905	"Armenian-Tartar War"; revolutionary uprising in Georgia
1906	Oil pipeline constructed from Baku to Batum
1914 August	First World War begins
1915 Apr. 24	Armenian leaders arrested in Constantinople; beginning of massacres and deportations of Armenians in eastern Anatolia
1917 February	Tsarist regime deposed in St. Petersburg; last Russian viceroy leaves Tiflis
November	Bolshevik revolution in St. Petersburg; Russian army abandons eastern front
1918 Mar. 31	Armenian militias massacre Azerbaijanis in Baku
May 26	Georgia declares independence
May 28	Armenia and Azerbaijan declare independence
Sept. 15	Turks and Azerbaijani government enter Baku; massacre of Armenians
1920 Apr. 28	Bolsheviks take Baku; proclaim Soviet power in Azerbaijan
June	Georgian Mensheviks devastate South Ossetia after uprising
Nov. 29	Bolsheviks take Yerevan; proclaim Soviet power in Armenia
1921 Feb. 25	Bolsheviks capture Tiflis (Tbilisi); depose Menshevik regime
Mar. 31	Abkhazian Soviet Republic established
July 5	Caucasus Bureau declares Nagorny Karabakh part of Azerbaijan
Oct. 23	Treaty of Kars between Turkey and Bolshevik Russia sets borders of South Caucasus
1922 April 29	South Ossetia Autonomous Region established within Soviet Georgia

1924	
Jan. 21	Death of Lenin; Stalin emerges as his successor
1931	Status of Abkhazia downgraded to autonomous republic within Georgia
1931–38	Lavrenty Beria is party boss of Georgia
1936	Stalinist Terror begins; murder of leading Bolsheviks in Caucasus
1941	
June	Hitler's Germany invades Soviet Union in Operation Barbarossa
1942	
August	Farthest point of German advance in North Caucasus; Baku oil fields abandoned
1953	
March 6	Death of Stalin
1969–82	Heidar Aliev heads Azerbaijani Communist Party
1972–85	Eduard Shevardnadze heads Georgian Communist Party
1974–88	Karen Demirchian heads Armenian Communist Party
1978	Status of Georgian language reaffirmed in Soviet Georgian constitution; Abkhazia given own university and television station
1985	
March	Mikhail Gorbachev becomes Soviet leader
1987	
Oct.–Nov.	First interethnic Armenian-Azerbaijani violence reported
1988	
Feb. 20–29	Nagorny Karabakh crisis begins; regional soviet requests transfer of province to Armenia; mass rallies in Yerevan; anti-Armenian pogroms in Sumgait
November	Rallies in Baku; mass flight of Azerbaijanis from Armenia and vice versa
Dec. 7	Devastating earthquake in Armenia
1989	
Mar. 18	Forum in Abkhazia calls for separation from Soviet Georgia

Apr. 9	Soviet troops break up demonstration in Tbilisi; nineteen people killed
Nov. 23	Zviad Gamsakhurdia organizes mass march on South Ossetian capital Tskhinvali

1990

January	"Black January" in Baku; anti-Armenian pogroms; Soviet troops enter city, killing protestors
May	Opposition Armenian National Movement wins election in Armenia
Oct. 28	Opposition wins election in Georgia; Gamsakhurdia becomes speaker of parliament
Dec. 11	Georgian parliament votes to abolish autonomy of South Ossetia

1991

January	Fighting breaks out in South Ossetia
May 26	Gamsakhurdia elected president of Georgia
Aug. 19–21	Failed coup d'état against Mikhail Gorbachev in Moscow
Sept. 8	Ayaz Mutalibov elected first president of Azerbaijan
Oct. 16	Levon Ter-Petrosian elected first president of Armenia
Dec. 31	End of USSR; de facto independence for three countries of South Caucasus

1992

Jan.–May	Azerbaijani siege of Karabakh capital Stepanakert
Jan. 6	Gamsakhurdia flees Georgia after heavy fighting in Tbilisi
Feb. 25–26	Armenians capture Azerbaijani village of Khojali; hundreds killed
Mar. 6	Mutalibov resigns as president of Azerbaijan
Mar. 7	Shevardnadze returns to Georgia to head new State Council
May	Karabakh Armenians capture town of Shusha, then Azerbaijani town of Lachin
June–Aug.	Azerbaijani offensive captures almost half of Nagorny Karabakh
June 7	Abulfaz Elchibey elected president of Azerbaijan

| June 24 | Russian-Georgian agreement in town of Dagomys ends war in South Ossetia |
| Aug. 14 | Georgian National Guard attacks Sukhumi; war in Abkhazia begins |

1993

April	Armenians capture Azerbaijani region of Kelbajar; Turkey closes border with Armenia
June	Rebellion in Azerbaijani city of Ganja; Elchibey flees Baku
June–Oct.	Armenian offensive recaptures most of Nagorny Karabakh and Azerbaijani towns of Aghdam, Fizuli, Jebrail, Kubatly, and Zangelan
Sept. 27	Abkhaz forces capture Sukhumi; mass flight of ethnic Georgians from Abkhazia
Oct. 3	Heidar Aliev elected president of Azerbaijan
Dec. 31	Gamsakhurdia dies in western Georgia

1994

May 12	Ceasefire agreement signed for Nagorny Karabakh
May 14	Formal truce in Abkhazia; Russian-led peacekeeping force established
Sept. 20	"Contract of the century" signed for Azerbaijani oil fields

1995

| Nov. 5 | Shevardnadze elected president of Georgia |

1996

| Sept. 23 | Levon Ter-Petrosian reelected in disputed election |

1997

| Nov. 12 | "Early oil" starts flowing from Azerbaijan's ACG oil fields |

1998

| Feb. 3 | Levon Ter-Petrosian resigns as Armenian president, is succeeded by Robert Kocharian |
| Oct. 11 | Ilham Aliev reelected president of Azerbaijan |

1999

| October | Vladislav Ardzinba elected de facto president of Abkhazia; independence declared |
| Oct. 27 | Shootings in Armenian parliament leave six senior politicians dead |

2000

Mar. 25	Vladimir Putin elected president of Russia
Apr. 9	Shevardnadze reelected president of Georgia
Dec. 5	Russia imposes visa regime on Georgian citizens

2001

Apr. 3–7	Armenian-Azerbaijani peace talks in Key West, Florida
October	Dozens die in Chechen-Georgian operation in Kodori Gorge of Abkhazia

2002

Apr. 29	U.S. government launches Train and Equip Progam for Georgia (GTEP)

2003

Mar. 5	Robert Kocharian reelected president of Armenia
Oct. 15	Ilham Aliev elected president of Azerbaijan; opposition street protests
Nov. 23	Shevardnadze resigns as president of Georgia after "Rose Revolution" protests
Dec. 12	Heidar Aliev dies of heart illness

2004

Jan. 4	Mikheil Saakashvili elected president of Georgia
June–August	South Ossetia's Ergneti market closed; violence in South Ossetia

2005

Jan. 12	Sergei Bagapsh elected de facto president of Abkhazia after lengthy election dispute
Feb. 3	Georgian prime minister Zurab Zhvania dies
May 10	President George W. Bush gives speech in Freedom Square in Tbilisi

2006

July 13	Baku-Tbilisi-Ceyhan oil pipeline inaugurated
July 28	Georgian government takes control of Kodori Gorge; Abkhaz breaks off peace talks
Sept.–Oct.	Russia breaks off communications with Georgia after spy row
November	Parallel elections held in South Ossetia; alternative leaders elected

2007

Nov. 7	Riot police disperse demonstrators in Tbilisi

Nov. 30	"Madrid Principles" document for Nagorny Karabakh resolution filed with OSCE
2008	
Jan. 5	Saakashvili reelected president of Georgia in early election
Feb. 18–Mar. 2	Disputed presidential election in Armenia; ten people die in street protests
April	Escalation of crisis in Abkhazia
Apr. 2–4	NATO summit in Bucharest pledges eventual membership for Georgia and Ukraine
Apr. 9	Serzh SargsyanSargsyan inaugurated as president of Armenia
July	Violence escalates in South Ossetia
Aug. 7–12	Five-day war in Georgia; fighting in South Ossetia, Kodori Gorge, city of Gori, and other areas of Georgia; French president Nicolas Sarkozy negotiates ceasefire plan
Aug. 26	Russia recognizes independence of Abkhazia and South Ossetia
Sept. 6	Turkish president Abdullah Gül visits Yerevan for football match
2009	
April–July	Opposition demonstrations in Georgia
July 13	Intergovernmental agreement signed in support of Nabucco gas pipeline
Sept. 15	Russia signs military cooperation agreements with Abkhazia and South Ossetia
Oct. 10	Armenian and Turkish foreign ministers sign protocols on normalizing relations
2010	
Apr. 22	Armenia suspends ratification of protocols with Turkey, blaming Ankara for lack of progress
Aug. 22	Armenia and Russia sign new military treaty extending lease of Russian military base
2011	
May 29	Abkhaz president Sergei Bagapsh dies
June 24	Presidents Aliev and Sargsyan fail to agree on framework peace deal for Karabakh conflict at meeting convened by Russian president Dmitry Medvedev in Kazan.

| Aug. 26 | Alexander Ankvab elected as de facto president of Abkhazia |

2012

Apr. 8	Leonid Tibilov elected de facto president of South Ossetia
Sept. 18	Big street protests in Georgia after release of video footage of abuse of prisoners
Oct. 12	Georgian Dream declared winner of Georgia's parliamentary election

2013

Feb. 4	Azerbaijani opposition politician Ilgar Mammadov arrested
Feb. 5	Russia lifts embargo on Georgian wine and mineral water
Feb. 19	Serzh Sargsyan elected for a second term as president of Armenia
Sept. 3	Sargsyan announces Armenia will join Russia-led customs union, abandon EU association agreement
Oct. 9	Ilham Aliev elected for a third term as president of Azerbaijan
Oct. 27	Giorgi Margvelashvili elected president of Georgia with reduced constitutional powers
Nov. 17	Mikheil Saakashvili ends presidential term; leaves Georgia soon afterwards

2014

June 1	Alexander Ankvab resigns as president of Abkhazia after street protests
Aug. 24	Raul Khajimba elected as de facto president of Abkhazia
Nov. 24	Abkhazia and Russian sign "partnership treaty"

2015

| Dec. 6 | Armenia's constitution changed in a referendum to transfer powers from president to prime minister |
| Dec. 21 | Azerbaijani manat devalued by a third amid falling oil prices |

2016

| Apr. 1–5 | Four-day war rages between Armenia and Azerbaijan near Nagorny Karabakh, causing hundreds of casualties |
| July 1 | EU-Georgia association agreement enters into force |

| Sept. 26 | Constitutional referendum held in Azerbaijan, extending presidential term to seven years |
| Oct. 8 | Georgian Dream wins increased majority in Georgia's parliamentary election |

2017

Feb. 20	Karabakh Armenians vote to call their homeland "Artsakh Republic" in a referendum not recognized internationally
Mar. 28	Georgians gain visa-free access to EU's Schengen Zone
Apr. 2	Ruling Republican Party wins a majority in parliament in Armenian elections
Apr. 9	Anatoly Bibilov elected de facto president of South Ossetia
July 19	Bako Sahakian elected for a three-year term as de facto president of Nagorny Karabakh
Oct. 30	Baku-Tbilisi-Kars railway is opened

2018

Apr. 9	New constitution comes into force in Armenia, enabling Armen Sarkissian to become new president and Serzh Sargsyan to become prime minister with enhanced powers
Apr. 11	Ilham Aliev elected for a fourth term as president of Azerbaijan.
Apr. 23	Sargsyan resigns as Armenian prime minister in face of big street protests, enabling opposition leader Nikol Pashinian to be elected in his place two weeks later
May 13	Thousands protest in Georgia after raids on two popular nightclubs
June 13	Giorgi Kvirikashvili resigns as prime minister of Georgia

Notes

INTRODUCTION

 1. Lionel Dunsterville, *The Adventures of Dunsterforce* (London: Edward Arnold, 1920), 118–19.

CHAPTER 1

 1. *The Geography of Strabo,* Vol. 2, Book 11, Chapter 21 (London: George Bell, 1903), 226.
 2. Kurban Said, *Ali and Nino* (London: Chatto and Windus, 2000), 13–14.
 3. Adile Abas-oglu, *Ne Mogu Zabyt'* [*I Cannot Forget*] (Moscow: AST), 38.
 4. A. Namitok, "The Caucasus," *Caucasian Review* [Munich] 1 (1935): 7.
 5. August von Haxthausen, *The Tribes of the Caucasus* (London: Chapman and Hall, 1855), 270 n.
 6. Haxthausen, *Tribes of the Caucasus,* 192.
 7. Quoted in Razmik Panossian, *The Armenians: From Kings and Priests to Merchants and Commissars* (New York: Columbia University Press, 2006), 43.
 8. Haxthausen, *Tribes of the Caucasus,* 224 n.
 9. R. W. Thomson, "The Origins of Christian Civilization: The Christian Component," in Ronald Suny, ed., *Transcaucasia, Nationalism and Social Change: Essays in the History of Armenia, Azerbaijan and Georgia* (Ann Arbor: University of Michigan Press, 1983), 35.
10. Alexandre Bennigsen and S. Enders Wimbush, *Muslims of the Soviet Empire: A Guide* (Bloomington: Indiana University Press, 1986), 140.
11. W.E.D. Allen, *A History of the Georgian People* (London: Routledge, 1932), 148.
12. Allen, *History of the Georgian People,* 319.
13. Brenda Shaffer, *Borders and Brethren: Iran and the Challenge of Azerbaijani Identity* (Cambridge, Mass.: MIT Press, 2002), 19–20.
14. Ronald Suny, *The Making of the Georgian Nation* (Bloomington: University of Indiana Press, 1988), 50.
15. On Sayat Nova, see Charles Dowsett, *Sayat Nova: An Eighteenth-Century Troubador* (Leuwen: Peeters, 1997).
16. Quoted in Firuz Kazemzadeh, *The Struggle for Transcaucasia* (New York: Oxford University Press, 1951), 267.
17. Fred Halliday, "Condemned to React, Unable to Influence: Iran and Transcaucasia," in J. Wright, S. Goldenberg, and R. Schofield, eds., *Transcaucasian Boundaries* (London: UCL Press, 1996), 78.
18. Shaffer, *Borders and Brethren,* 23.
19. Muriel Atkin, *Russia and Iran, 1780–1828* (Minneapolis: University of Minnesota Press, 1980), 148.

20. Tadeusz Swietochowski, "National Consciousness and Political Orientations in Azerbaijan, 1905–1920," in Suny, *Transcaucasia*, 213.

21. Osip Mandelstam, *Journey to Armenia*, trans. Clarence Brown (London: Redstone Press, 1989), 19.

22. Philip Mansel, *Constantinople: City of the World's Desire* (London: John Murray, 2006).

23. Charles King, *The Ghost of Freedom: A History of the Caucasus* (New York: Oxford University Press, 2008), 177–80.

24. K. S. Papazian, *Patriotism Perverted: A Discussion of the Deeds and the Misdeeds of the Armenian Revolutionary Federation, the So-Called Dashnagtzoutune* (Boston: Baikar Press, 1934), 24.

25. Richard Hovannisian, *The Armenian People from Ancient to Modern Times II* (New York: Palgrave Macmillan, 2004), 367; John Roy Carlson, *Cairo to Damascus* (New York: Knopf, 1951), 436.

26. John Steinbeck, *A Russian Journal* (New York: Viking, 1948), 150.

27. Odette Keun, *In the Land of the Golden Fleece* (London: Bodley Head, 1924), 179–80.

28. W.E.D. Allen, *A History of the Georgian People* (London: Routledge, 1932), 176.

CHAPTER 2

1. Nikolas Gvosdev, *Imperial Policies and Perspectives towards Georgia, 1760–1819* (New York: Palgrave Macmillan, 2000), 63.

2. David Lang, *A Modern History of Soviet Georgia* (New York: Grove Press, 1962), 38.

3. Muriel Atkin, *Russia and Iran, 1780–1828* (Minneapolis: University of Minnesota Press, 1980), 64.

4. W. Monteith, *Kars and Erzeroum* (London: Longman, Brown, Green and Longmans, 1856), 72.

5. Nikolai Dubrovin, *Istoria voiny i vladychestva Russkikh na Kavkaze* [*The History of the War and Dominion of the Russians in the Caucasus*] (St. Petersburg: n.p., 1871–88), 5:454.

6. Vasily Potto, *Kavkazskaya Voina v Otdel'nykh Ocherkakh: Epizodakh, Legendakh i Biographiakh IV* [*The Caucasian War in Separate Sketches, Episodes, Legends and Biographies IV*] (St. Petersburg: n.p., 1885), 425.

7. Potto, *Kavkazskaya Voina v Otdel'nykh Ocherkakh*, 1:11.

8. Atkin, *Russia and Iran*, 163.

9. Tadeusz Swietochowski, *Russia and Azerbaijan: A Borderland in Transition* (New York: University of Columbia Press, 1995), 26.

10. Ronald Suny, *The Making of the Georgian Nation* (Bloomington: University of Indiana Press, 1988), 86.

11. Oliver Wardrop, *The Kingdom of Georgia: Notes of Travel in a Land of Wine, Women and Song* (London: Sampson Low, Marston, Searle and Rivington, 1888), 15–16.

12. Suny, *Making of the Georgian Nation*, 93.
13. Wardrop, *Kingdom of Georgia*, 13–14.
14. G. G. Moskvich, *Putevoditel' po Kavkazu* [*Guide to the Caucasus*] (St. Petersburg: n.p., 1913), 433–34.
15. I am grateful to Oliver Reisner in Tbilisi for this quotation.
16. Ronald Suny, *Looking towards Ararat: Armenia in Modern History* (Bloomington: University of Indiana Press, 1993), 31.
17. Arminius Vambery, "The Turks in Persia and the Caucasus," *Asiatic Quarterly Review* 4 (1886): 177.
18. Swietochowski, "National Consciousness and Political Orientations in Azerbaijan, 1905–1920," in Ronald Suny, ed.,*Transcaucasia, Nationalism and Social Change: Essays in the History of Armenia, Azerbaijan and Georgia* (Ann Arbor: University of Michigan Press, 1983), 233.
19. J. D. Henry, *Baku: An Eventful History* (London: Archibald Constable, 1905), 3.
20. Swietochowski, "National Consciousness," 215–16.
21. Suny, *Looking towards Ararat*, 49.
22. Lang, *Modern History of Soviet Georgia*, 185.
23. Taner Akçam, *A Shameful Act: The Armenian Genocide and the Question of Turkish Responsibility* (New York: Holt, 2007), 84.
24. Quoted in Akçam, *Shameful Act*, 32.
25. Mansel, *Constantinople: City of the World's Desire* (London: John Murray, 2006), 127–28.
26. Richard Hovannisian, *The Armenian People from Ancient to Modern Times II* (New York: Palgrave Macmillan, 2004), 224.
27. In 2008, the handwritten, seventy-seven-page private notebook of interior minister Talat Pasha, known as the "Black Book," was published. It contains his own detailed calculations on the number of Armenians whose deportation he ordered. He writes in a note: "[The] true number of Armenians in 1914 can be taken as 1,500,000, and the number of Armenians remaining in the provinces . . . to be around 350,000 to 400,000." See Ara Safarian, "Talat Pasha's Black Book Documents His Campaign of Race Extermination, 1915–17," *Armenian Reporter*, March 14, 2009, 4–5.
28. Donald Bloxham, *The Great Game of Genocide: Imperialism, Nationalism, and the Destruction of the Ottoman Armenians* (Oxford: Oxford University Press, 2005), 92.
29. James Harbord, *Conditions in the Near East: The American Military Mission to Armenia, 1920* (Washington, D.C.: U.S. Government Printing House, 1920), 8–9, www.armenianhouse.org/harbord/conditions-near-east.htm.
30. Two rival terrorist groups, ASALA and the Justice Commandos of the Armenian Genocide, both formed in Beirut; the latter, affiliated with the Dashnak Party, carried out the attacks.
31. Ronald Grigor Suny, *They Can Live in the Desert but Nowhere Else: A History of the Armenian Genocide* (Princeton, N.J.: Princeton University Press, 2015), 359.

32. Alfred Rawlinson, *Adventures in the Near East, 1918–22* (London: Dodd, Mead, 1923), 126.

33. N. Zhordania, *Za dva goda: Doklady i rechi* [*Over Two Years: Lectures and Speeches*] (Tiflis: n.p., 1919), 52.

34. Firuz Kazemzadeh, *The Struggle for Transcaucasia* (New York: Oxford, 1951), 74.

35. Quoted in Hovanissian, *Armenian People*, 299.

36. Lionel Dunsterville, *The Adventures of Dunsterforce* (London: Edward Arnold, 1920), 219.

37. Quoted in Stephen Jones, *Socialism in Georgian Colors: The European Road to Social Democracy* (Cambridge, Mass.: Harvard University Press, 2005), 281.

38. C. E. Bechhofer, *In Denikin's Russia* (London: Collins, 1921), 41.

39. Bechhofer, *In Denikin's Russia*, 261.

40. Rawlinson, *Adventures in the Near East*, 184.

41. Merrill D. Peterson, *"Starving Armenians": America and the Armenian Genocide, 1915–1930 and After* (Charlottesville: University of Virginia Press, 2004), 73.

42. Harbord, *Conditions in the Near East*, 14.

43. Artin Arslanian, "Britain and the Question of Mountainous Karabagh," in Suny, *Transcaucasia*, 305.

44. Quoted in Audrey Altstadt, *The Azerbaijani Turks: Power and Identity under Russian Rule* (Stanford, Calif.: Hoover Institution Press, 1992), 106.

45. *Pravda*, November 30, 1920.

46. Reprinted in A. Kvashonkin, ed., *Bol'sheviktskoe Rukovodstvo, Perepiksa 1912–27* [*The Bolshevik Leadership, Correspondence 1912–27*] (Moscow: Rosspen, 1996).

47. Kvashonkin, *Bol'shevitskoe Rukovodstvo*.

48. Cited in G. Galoyan. *Rabochee Dvizhenie i Natsional'ny Vopros v Zakavkaz'e, 1900–1992 gg* [*The Workers' Movement and the National Question in the Transcaucasus, 1900–1922*] (Yerevan: n.p., 1969), 398–99.

49. The full text of the Anglo-Soviet trade agreement of March 1921 is available at http://wwi.lib.byu.edu/index.php/Anglo-Soviet_Trade_Agreement.

50. Kazemzadeh, *Struggle for Transcaucasia*, 326–27.

51. Quoted in Charles King, *The Ghost of Freedom: A History of the Caucasus* (New York: Oxford University Press, 2008), 173.

52. Redjeb Jordania, "Preface," in Stephen F. Jones, ed., *The Making of Modern Georgia, 1918–2012* (London: Routledge, 2014), xxiii–xxvi.

CHAPTER 3

1. *Doklad Obshchemu Sobraniyu Tiflisskoi Oganizatsii Kommunisticheskoi Partii Gruzii* [*Speech to the General Assembly of the Tiflis Organization of the Communist Party of Georgia*], July 6, 1921, available online in Russian at http://stalinism.ru/Tom-V/Ob-ocherednyih-zadachah-kommunizma-v-Gruzii-i-Zakavkaze.html.

2. Quoted in V. Gorny, ed. *Natsional'ny vopros na perekrestke mnenii* [*The National Question at the Crossroads of Opinion*] (Moscow: Nauka, 1992), 162–63.

3. Alfred J. Rieber, "Stalin: Man of the Borderlands," *American Historical Review* 106, 5 (December 2001): 1685–86.

4. Amy Knight, *Beria: Stalin's First Lieutenant* (New Haven, Conn.: Yale University Press, 1993), 34.

5. Quoted in Tadeusz Swietochowski, *Russia and Azerbaijan: A Borderland in Transition* (New York: Columbia University Press, 1995), 104.

6. Arthur Koestler, *The Invisible Writing* (London: Hutchinson, 1969), 109.

7. Ronald Suny, *The Making of the Georgian Nation* (Bloomington: University of Indiana Press, 1988), 233.

8. Ronald Suny, *Revenge of the Past: Nationalism, Revolution and the Collapse of the Soviet Union* (Stanford, Calif.: Stanford University Press, 1993), 87.

9. Terry Martin, "Modernization or Neo-Traditionalism? Ascribed Nationality and Soviet Primordialism," in Martin, *Stalinism: New Directions* (London: Routledge, 2000), 355.

10. Terry Martin, *The Affirmative Action Empire* (Ithaca, N.Y.: Cornell University Press, 2001), 23–24.

11. Adile Abbas-oglu, *Ne Mogu Zabyt'* [*I Cannot Forget*] (Moscow: AST, 2005), 38.

12. Figures for military dead of Armenia: 150,000; Azerbaijan: 210,000; Georgia: 190,000; quoted in Vadim Erlikman, *Poteri narodonaseleniia v XX veke: Spravochnik* [*Population Losses in the Twentieth Century: A Handbook*] (Moscow: n.p., 2004).

13. Rieber, "Stalin," 1691.

14. John Steinbeck, *A Russian Journal* (New York: Viking, 1948), 147.

15. Quoted in Thomas de Waal, *Black Garden: Armenia and Azerbaijan through Peace and War* (New York: New York University Press, 2013), 150.

16. Andrei Sakharov interview in *Ogonyok*, July 31, 1989. The historian Firuz Kazemzadeh used the same phrase in 1951 to describe Georgia in the period 1918–20: "In a year or two Georgia had traversed the long road from a colony of Russia to a small empire of her own. The difference between the Georgian attitude towards Abkhazia, or Ajaristan, and the attitude of Russia towards Georgia, or Armenia, was not one of principle, but of scale. In their own backyard the Georgians proved to be as imperialistic as the Russians." *The Struggle for Transcaucasia* (New York: Oxford University Press, 1951), 203.

17. De Waal, *Black Garden*, 150.

18. Suny, *Making of the Georgian Nation*, 300.

19. G. Mars and Y. Altman, "Managing in Soviet Georgia: An Extreme Example in Comparative Management," *European Journal of International Management* 2, 1 (2008): 612, 66.

20. Georgi Derluguian, *Bourdieu's Secret Admirer in the Caucasus* (Chicago: University of Chicago Press, 2005), 201.

21. Nash "B" Klass [Our Class B], http://14bklass.web-box.ru/klass.

CHAPTER 4

1. Mehmet Zade Azerbaijanli, *Kavkaz* (Paris: n.p., 1935).
2. For a good Armenian source on the history of Karabakh, see Levon Chorbajian, Patrick Donabedian, and Claude Mutafian, *The Caucasian Knot: The History and Geo-politics of Nagorno-Karabakh* (London: Zed Books, 1994).
3. Thomas de Waal, *Black Garden: Armenia and Azerbaijan through Peace and War* (New York: New York University Press, 2013), 154.
4. TASS news agency, February 23, 1988.
5. De Waal, *Black Garden*, 84.
6. De Waal, *Black Garden*, 68.
7. De Waal, *Black Garden*, 68–72.
8. Markar Melkonian, *My Brother's Road: An American's Fateful Journey to Armenia* (London: Tauris, 2004), 185.
9. De Waal, *Black Garden*, 178–179.
10. Melkonian, *My Brother's Road*, 226.
11. Memorial, *Doklad pravozashchitnogo tsentra "Memorial" o Massovykh Narusheniyakh Prav Chelovek, Svyazannykh s Zanyatiem Naselennogo Punkta Khodjaly v Noch' s 25 na 26 Fevralya 1992g Vooruzhennymi Formirovaniyami* [*The Report by the Human Rights Center Memorial on Mass Abuses of Human Rights Connected with the Seizure by Armed Units of the Town of Khojali on the Night of 25–26 February, 1992*] (Moscow: Memorial, 1992), available at www.memo.ru/hr/hotpoints/karabah/Hojaly/Chapter1.htm (in Russian).
12. Melkonian, *My Brother's Road*, 214.
13. De Waal, *Black Garden*, 211.
14. De Waal, *Black Garden*, 212.
15. The best and liveliest account of Azerbaijan's turbulent first few years of independence is Thomas Goltz's *Azerbaijan Diary* (Armonk, N.Y.: Sharpe, 1998).
16. For an excellent collection of essays on the recurring failed dynamics of the Karabakh peace process, see Laurence Broers, ed., *The Limits of Leadership: Elites and Societies in the Nagorny Karabakh Peace Process*, Accord Series no. 17 (London: Conciliation Resources, 2005), http:www.c-r.org/our-work/accord/nagorny-karabakh/contents.php.
17. On the "four-day war" of April 2016, see Laurence Broers, "The Nagorny Karabakh Conflict: Defaulting to War," *Chatham House Russia and Eurasia Programme Research Paper*, July 2016; Thomas de Waal, "Prisoners of the Caucasus: Resolving the Karabakh Security Dilemma," *Carnegie Europe*, June 16, 2016; International Crisis Group Report No. 239, *Nagorno-Karabakh: New Opening, or More Peril?*, July 4, 2016.
18. "Minister: Karabakh Land Will Burn under Occupants' Feet," *News.az*, December 29, 2015.
19. On the Aylisli case, see Mikail Mamedov, "The Stone Dreams Scandal: The Nagorny Karabakh Conflict and Armenian-Azerbaijani Relations in Contemporary Literature," *Caucasus Survey* 2 (2014): 1–2, 42–59.

CHAPTER 5

1. Stephen Brook, *Claws of the Crab* (London: Picador, 2003), 31.
2. The killings were the cause of an investigation conducted under the auspices of the new Soviet parliament, the Congress of People's Deputies, led by the popular independent deputy Anatoly Sobchak, later mayor of St. Petersburg. For the commission's damning findings, see *Zaklyuchenie Komissii S'yezda Narodnykh Deputatov SSSR po rassledovaniyu sobytii, imevshikh mesto v g. Tbilisi 9 aprelya 1989 goda* [*The Conclusion of the Commission of the Congress of People's Deputies of the USSR for the Investigation of the Events that Took Place in Tbilisi on April 9, 1989*], available at http://sobchak.org/rus/docs/zakluchenie. htm.
3. Jonathan Wheatley, *Georgia: From National Awakening to Rose Revolution* (Ashgate, England: Saffron Walden, 2005), 44.
4. David Remnick, "Democracy with a Vengeance," *Washington Post*, October 7, 1990.
5. James Rupert, "Christian Knights Claim Key Role in Georgia," *Washington Post*, January 14, 1992.
6. M. Volkhonsky, ed., *Konflikty v Abkhazii i Yuzhnoi Osetii: dokumenty 1989–2006 gg* [*The Conflicts in Abkhazia and South Ossetia: Documents, 1989–2006*] (Moscow: Russkaya Panorama, 2008), 50.
7. Vasily Potto, *Kavkazskaya Voina v Otdel'nykh Ocherkakh: Epizodakh, Legendakh i Biographiakh IV* [*The Caucasian War in Separate Sketches, Episodes, Legends, and Biographies IV*] (St. Petersburg: n.p., 1885), 85.
8. This is from figures in the 1897 census in the Russian Empire.
9. Kosta Dzugayev, *Yuzhnaya Osetia v Kontekste Rossiisko-Gruzinskikh Otnoshenii* [*South Ossetia in the Context of Russian-Georgian Relations*], 2006, published online at http:www.viu-online.ru/rus/science/center/bulletine/18.html and http://www.viu-online.ru/rus/science/center/bulletine/19.html.
10. Firuz Kazemzadeh, *The Struggle for Transcaucasia* (New York: Oxford University Press, 1951), 192.
11. See Valery Tishkov, *Ethnicity, Nationalism Conflict in and after the Soviet Union* (Oslo: Sage, 1997), 90.
12. Julian Birch, "The Georgian/South Ossetian Territorial and Boundary Dispute," in John Wright, Suzanne Goldenberg, and Richard Schofield, eds., *Transcaucasian Boundaries* (London: UCL Press, 1996), 166.
13. Stuart J. Kaufman, *Modern Hatreds: The Symbolic Politics of Ethnic War* (Ithaca, N.Y.: Cornell University Press, 2001), 111.
14. Volkhonsky, *Konflikty v Abkhazii i Yuzhnoi Osetii*.
15. Nikola Cvetkovski, "The Georgian–South Ossetian Conflict" (Ph.D. diss., Aalborg University, 2000), http://www.caucasus.dk/publication5.htm.
16. In North Ossetia, a stable Georgian community of around 10,000 people remained and persists to this day, again suggesting that where there was no one directly instigating conflict, peaceful interethnic relations were perfectly possible.

17. Alan Parastayev, "North and South Ossetia: Old Conflicts and New Fears," in Parastayev, *The Caucasus: Armed and Divided* (London: Saferworld, 2003).

18. Michael Dobbs, "Nationalists, Minority Battle in Soviet Georgia; Moscow Accused of Arming Ossetians," *Washington Post*, March 21, 1991.

19. Human Rights Watch, "Georgia/Abkhazia: Violations of the Laws of War and Russia's Role in the Conflict," *Human Rights Watch*, March 1995, 15.

20. Quoted in Dzugayev, *Yuzhnaya Osetia*, 20.

21. Vicken Cheterian, *War and Peace in the Caucasus* (London: Hurst, 2008), 183.

22. Akhsarbek Galazov, "Voiny Nachinayutsya Legko i Bystro, Vykhodit' iz Nikh Dolgo i Trudno" [It's Easy and Quick to Start Wars, but Long and Difficult to Get Out of Them], *Daryal* [Vladikavkaz] 4 (2001), available online at http://www.darial-online.ru/2001_4/galazov.shtml.

23. *Nezavisimaya Gazeta*, June 23, 1992, quoted in Alexei Zverev, "Ethnic Conflicts in the Caucasus 1988–1994," in Bruno Coppieters, ed., *Contested Borders in the Caucasus* (Brussels: VUB Press, 1996), available online at http://poli.vub.ac.be/publi/ContBorders/eng/contents.htm.

24. Volkhonsky, *Konflikty v Abkhazii i Yuzhnoi Osetii*.

25. Kaufman, *Modern Hatreds*, 125.

26. Wesley Andrew Fisher, *The Soviet Marriage Market: Mate Selection in Russia and the USSR* (New York: Praeger, 1980), 219.

27. Rachel Clogg, "Religion," in George Hewitt, ed., *The Abkhazians* (Richmond, England: Curzon Press, 1999), 205.

28. Quoted in Stanislav Lakoba, *Abkhazia Mezdu Dvumya Imperiyami* [*Abkhazia Between Two Empires*] (Sapporo, Japan: Slavic Research Center, 2004), 19.

29. William Gifford Palgrave, *Essays on the Eastern Question* (London: Macmillan, 1872), 270.

30. Akaky Mgeladze, *Stalin, Kakim ya ego Znal: Stranitsy Nedavnego Proshlogo* [*Stalin as I Knew Him: Pages from the Recent Past*] (Tbilisi: n.p., 2001), 111.

31. Mgeladze, *Stalin*, 108.

32. Oleg Glebov and John Crowfoot, eds., *The Soviet Empire: Its Nations Speak Out* (London: Harwood, 1989), 79.

33. Georgi Derluguian, *Bourdieu's Secret Admirer in the Caucasus* (Chicago: University of Chicago Press, 2005), 234–35.

34. From *Absence of Will*, documentary film (Tbilisi: Studio Re, 2009).

35. Steven Erlanger, "As Georgia Chief, Shevardnadze Rides Whirlwind," *New York Times*, August 25, 1992.

36. Zerkala Separatizma [Mirrors of Separatism], *Moskovsky Komsomolets*, February 10, 1996.

37. Jon Steele, "Shooting in the Dark," *Guardian Weekend Magazine*, August 10, 2002.

38. Huge Pope, "Georgia's Ill-Disciplined Army Lacks Clout to End Conflict," *Independent*, April 13, 1994.

39. Oksana Antonenko, "Frozen Uncertainty: Russia and the Conflict over Abkhazia," in Bruno Coppieters and Robert Legvold, eds., *Statehood and Security: Georgia after the Rose Revolution* (Cambridge, Mass.: MIT Press, 2005), 214.

40. Shamil Basayev, interview in the documentary film *Battle for Gagra* (Salt Lake City, Utah: Combat Films and Research), available online at http://www.combatfilms.com/cfrtv_archive_0009.asp.

41. See Thomas de Waal, *Abkhazia's Archive: Fire of War, Ashes of History*, July 12, 2007, available online at http://www.opendemocracy.net/democracy-caucasus/abkhazia_archive_4018.jsp.

42. A transcript of this famous interview was reportedly published in the local Georgian press. A video clip of Karkarashvili can be seen on YouTube: *The Georgian Commander-in-Chief on TV Threatens the Abkhazian Nation with Genocide* http://www.youtube.com/watch?v=XzvtaZIMy98.

43. Lyudmila Tarnava, *Abkhazsky Dnevnik* [*Abkhaz Diary*] (Sukhum: n.p., 2008), 125–26.

44. Human Rights Watch, "Georgia/Abkhazia," 5.

45. Human Rights Watch, "Georgia/Abkhazia," 42.

46. The best published account of the fall of Sukhumi—and a fascinating account of Georgia in this period in general—is Thomas Goltz's *Georgia Diary* (Armonk, N.Y.: Sharpe, 2006).

47. Tarnava, *Abkhazsky Dnevnik*, 288.

48. Lawrence Sheets, "Abkhazians Loot Sukhumi as Georgians Flee," Reuters, October 5, 1992.

49. Quoted in Human Rights Watch, "Georgia/Abkhazia," 43.

50. George Hewitt in the article *Abkhazia, Georgia and History: A Response*, August 25, 2009, available online at http://www.opendemocracy.net/article/abkhazia-georgia-and-history-a-response, cites the Georgian writer Guram Odisharia's 2001 book *The Pass of the Persecuted* on this point.

51. Sergei Shamba, interview by Paul Rimple, August 1, 2005. This interview with a now defunct website named *Sobaka* is available online at http://www.abkhaz.org/index.php?option=com_content&task=view&id=122&Itemid=72. The best (but now outdated) book on the Abkhazia peace process is Jonathan Cohen, ed., *A Question of Sovereignty: The Georgia-Abkhazia Peace Process*, Accord Series no. 7 (London: Conciliation Resources, 1999), http://www.c-r.org/our-work/accord/georgia-abkhazia/index.php.

CHAPTER 6

1. J. D. Henry, *Baku: An Eventful History* (London: Archibald Constable, 1905), 5.

2. Henry, *Baku*, 7.

3. Daniel Yergin, *The Prize: The Epic Quest for Oil, Money and Power* (New York: Simon and Schuster, 1991), 56–61. For the history of early European

investment in Baku and Batum, see also Robert W. Tolf, *Russian Rockefellers: The Saga of the Nobels and the Russian Oil Industry* (Stanford, Calif.: Hoover Institution Press, Stanford, 1976).

4. Leon Trotsky, *How the Revolution Armed: The Military Writings and Speeches of Leon Trotsky* (London: New Park, 1981), 256, available online at http://www. marxists.org/archive/trotsky/1920/military/ch58.htm.

5. *Hitler & Co Eating the "Nazi Cake,"* http://www.youtube.com/ watch?v=rGzEs3K66hA.

6. Quoted in Elkhan Polukhov, "Contract of the Century: The Problem in an Historical Perspective," *Caucasian Regional Studies* 2, 1 (1997); online journal available at http://poli.vub.ac.be/publi/crs/eng/0201–00.htm.

7. Steve Levine, *The Oil and the Glory: The Pursuit of Empire and Fortune on the Caspian Sea* (New York: Random House, 2007), 184–85.

8. Dan Morgan and David B. Ottaway, "Fortune Hunters Lured U.S. into Volatile Region," *Washington Post*, October 4, 1998.

9. Brenda Shaffer, *Energy Wars* (Philadelphia: University of Pennsylvania Press, 2009), 54.

10. Polukhov, "Contract of the Century."

11. Polukhov, "Contract of the Century."

12. Tyler Marshall, "U.S. Dives into a Sea of Major Rewards—and Risks," *Los Angeles Times*, February 23, 1998.

13. *Hearing on U.S Interests in the Central Asian Republics*, February 12, 1998, http://commdocs.house.gov/committees/intlrel/hfa48119.000/hfa48119_of.htm.

14. Olivier Roy, "Crude Manoeuvres: The Caspian Region's Oil and Gas Supplies," *Index on Censorship* 26, 4 (July–August 1997): 144; Ariel Cohen, "U.S. Policy in the Caucasus and Central Asia: Building a New 'Silk Road' to Economic Prosperity," *Heritage Foundation Backgrounder*, no. 1132, July 24, 1997.

15. Levine, *Oil and the Glory*, 215.

16. BP Statistical Review of World Energy, June 2016, https://www.bp.com/content/ dam/bp/pdf/energy-economics/statistical-review-2016/bp-statistical-review-of- world-energy-2016-full-report.pdf.

17. Sheila Heslin, "The New Pipeline Politics," *New York Times*, November 10, 1997.

18. Morningstar left to become U.S. ambassador to the European Union in 1999 but in 2009 was basically given his old job back in the new Democratic administration, this time serving as special envoy of the U.S. secretary of state for Eurasian energy. From 2012 to 2015 he served as U.S. ambassador in Azerbaijan.

19. Quoted in, among other places, Inga Saffron, "Black Gold, Once Red, Fuels an Oil Rush," Knight-Ridder Newspapers, July 20, 1997.

20. Terry Adams, *Caspian Hydrocarbons: The Politicisation of Regional Pipelines and the Destabilization of the Caucasus* (Brussels: CEPS, 1998), http://poli.vub. ac.be/publi/crs/eng/Vol5/adams.htm.

21. Nursultan Nazarbayev, interview in *Nezavisimaya Gazeta*, February 24, 2000, quoted in Radio Liberty's *Caucasus Report*.

22. "Caspian Oil Project Forges Ahead," BBC News, September 18, 1992, http:// news.bbc.co.uk/2/hi/europe/2265670.stm.

23. John Roberts, e-mail correspondence with author, October 26, 2009.

24. For evidence of a Russian cyber-operation, see Jordan Robertson and Michael Riley, "Mysterious '08 Turkey Pipeline Blast Opened New Cyberwar," *Bloomberg News*, December 10, 2014.

25. "Karabakh gotov nanesti udar po neftyanym kommunikatsiyam Azerbaidzhana," (Karabakh Is Ready to Strike at Azerbaijan's Oil Communications"), *Newsarmenia.com*, April 5, 2016, http://newsarmenia.am/news/nagorno_karabakh/srochno-karabakh-gotov-nanesti-udar-po-neftyanym-kommunikatsiyam-azerbaydzhana-/.

26. See Will Fitzgibbon, Miranda Patrucic, and Marcos García Rey, "How Family that Runs Azerbaijan Built an Empire of Hidden Wealth," *Panama Papers*, April 4, 2016, https://panamapapers.icij.org/20160404-azerbaijan-hidden-wealth.html.

27. United States Attorney for the Southern District of New York, *U.S. Announces Charges in Massive Scheme to Bribe Senior Government Officials in the Republic of Azerbaijan*, October 6, 2005, http://www.usdoj.gov/usao/nys/pressreleases/October05/kozenyetalindictmentpr.pdf.

28. Adam Davidson, "Donald Trump's Worst Deal," *New Yorker*, March 13, 2017.

29. Steve Levine, "Nabucco Hucksterism, Iran Polyannishness, and a $5 Billion Bribe," *Oil and the Glory*, April 11, 2009, http://oilandglory.com/2009/04/nabucco-huckerism-iran-pollyanishness.html.

30. Simon Pirani, "Azerbaijan's Gas Supply Squeeze and the Consequences for the Southern Corridor," *Oxford Institute for Energy Studies*, July 2016.

Chapter 7

1. Jonathan Wheatley, *Georgia: From National Awakening to Rose Revolution* (Ashgate, UK: Saffron Walden, 2005), 114.

2. On the Rose Revolution, see Lincoln A. Mitchell, *Uncertain Democracy: US Foreign Policy and Georgia's Rose Revolution* (Philadelphia: University of Pennsylvania Press, 2009); and Zurab Karumidze and James V. Wertsch, eds., *Enough! The Rose Revolution in the Republic of Georgia, 2003* (New York: Nova, 2005).

3. "Saakashvili Vows Improvements with Drastic Measures," *Civil Georgia*, January 25, 2004.

4. Arkady Ostrovsky, "How to Be a Founding Father," *Financial Times*, July 9, 2004.

5. Parliamentary Assembly of the Council of Europe, *Report of the Honouring of Obligations and Commitments by Georgia*, doc. 10383 (Strasbourg: Parliamentary Assembly of the Council of Europe, December 21, 2004).

6. Wendell Steavenson, "Marching through Georgia," *New Yorker*, December 15, 2008.

7. Sanobar Shermatova, "Thaw in Ties with Moscow Likely," *IWPR Georgia Alert*, no. 5, November 28, 2003.

8. Thomas de Waal, "Saakashvili Eyes Presidency," IWPR Caucasus Reporting Service, no. 206, November 26, 2003.
9. Clifford J. Levy, "The Georgian and Putin: A Hate Story," *New York Times,* April 18, 2009.
10. Tedo Japaridze, e-mail correspondence with author, October 7, 2009.
11. *Izvestia,* July 2, 2004.
12. Alexander Iskandarian and Alan Parastaev, *Events in the Kodori Gorge, Moscow Defense Brief* 16, no. 2 (2009), http://mdb.cast.ru/mdb/2–2002/ac/ekg/.
13. "Putin Pledges $500 Million for Security Purposes in Abkhazia," *Russia Today,* August 12, 2008, http://www.russiatoday.ru/Top_News/2009–08–12/putin-interview-abkhazia-georgia.html.
14. Giorgi Khaindrava, interview with author, December 2, 2008, Tbilisi.
15. International Crisis Group, *Georgia: Avoiding War in South Ossetia,* Europe Report No. 159, November 26, 2004, 14.
16. Arzdinba spent most of his last years suffering from an undisclosed grave illness and died in Moscow in March 2010 at the age of sixty-four.
17. "Okruashvili Reiterates S. Ossetia Reunification Deadline," *Civil Georgia,* May 1, 2006.
18. "Saakashvili Focuses on IDP Return to Abkhazia in Campaign," *Civil Georgia,* December 1, 2007; "S. Ossetia a Matter of, at Most, Months—Saakashvili," *Civil Georgia,* December 4, 2007.
19. "Gosduma Predlozhila Rassmotret' Prezidentu i Pravitel'stvu Vopros o Nezavimisosti Abkhazii i Yu.Osetii" [The State Duma Asked the President and Government to Consider the Issue of the Independence of Abkhazia and South Ossetia], Itar-Tass, March 21, 2008.
20. Final communiqué of NATO Bucharest summit, April 4, 2008, quoted by Secretary General Jaap de Hoop Scheffer, http://www.nato.int/docu/speech/2008/s080403g.html.
21. Foreign Ministry of Finland, "Stubb Proposed Consideration of a New Negotiating Format in the South Ossetian Conflict" (press release), May 30, 2008, http://www. finland.org/Public/default.aspx?contentid=131152&nodeid=40958&contentlan=2&culture=en-US.
22. Zaur Alborov, *SShA provotsiruet voiny v Zakavkaz'e* [*The USA Is Provoking War in the Transcaucasus*], Osinform News Agency, July 14, 2008, http://osinform.ru/6920-ssha-provocirujut-vojjnu-v-zakavkaze.html.
23. "Saakashvili's Televised Address on S. Ossetia," *Civil Georgia,* August 7, 2008.
24. Amnesty International, *Civilians in the Line of Fire: The Georgia-Russia Conflict* (London: Amnesty International, November 2008), 2.
25. Adrian Bloomfield, "Georgia Conflict: Screams of the Injured Rise from Residential Streets," *Daily Telegraph,* August 10, 2008.
26. "Putin Says Georgia Seeking 'Bloody Adventures,' " Reuters, August 9, 2008.
27. Amnesty International, *Civilians in the Line of Fire,* 6.
28. Idrak Abbasov, "Gori: Russian Allies Triumphant as City Burns," IWPR Caucasus Reporting Service, August 14, 2008.

29. *Independent International Fact-finding Mission on the Conflict in Georgia*, Vol. I, 11, available at http://www.ceiig.ch/.

30. Confidential document seen by this author. The OSCE reports were kept secret at the time but were first cited in the article by C. J. Chivers and Ellen Barry, "Georgia Claims on Russia War Called into Question," *New York Times*, November 6, 2008.

31. *Independent International Fact-finding Mission on the Conflict in Georgia*, Vol. I, 20.

32. For the UN Security Council session, see "The Situation in Georgia," Friday August 8, http://www.securitycouncilreport.org/atf/cf/{65BFCF9B-6D27-4E9C-8CD3-CF6E4FF96FF9}/Georgia%20SPV%205952.pdf; Ossetian radio report mentioned in International Crisis Group, *Russia vs Georgia: The Fallout,* Europe report no. 195, August 22, 2008; on Ossetian witness, see Larisa Sotieva, "Eyewitness: Carnage in Tskhinvali," IWPR Caucasus Reporting Service, August 12, 2008.

33. Brian Rohan, "Saakashvili 'Planned S. Ossetia Invasion': Ex-Minister," Reuters, September 14, 2008.

34. Jan Cienski, "Tbilisi Admits Misjudging Russia," *Financial Times*, August 22, 2008.

35. Saakasvhili BBC interview, August 8, 2008, available at http://news.bbc.co.uk/2/hi/7548715.stm.

36. Helene Cooper and Thom Shanker, "After Mixed U.S. Messages, a War Erupted in Georgia," *New York Times,* August 13, 2008.

37. Vyacheslav Borisov, interview, "Voenny Sovet" [Military Advice], *Ekho Moskvy*, June 6, 2009, http://echo.msk.ru/programs/voensovet/596473-echo/.

38. Dmitry Rogozin, interview, *Zavtra*, http://www.zavtra.ru/cgi/veil/data/zavtra/08/770/31.html.

39. Mikheil Saakashvili, "Moscow Can't Be Trusted," *Guardian*, August 15, 2008.

Chapter 8

1. Audrey Altstadt, *Frustrated Democracy in Post-Soviet Azerbaijan* (Washington, D.C: Woodrow Wilson Center Press, 2017), 233.

2. Pew Research Center, *The World's Muslims: Unity and Diversity* (Washington, D.C.: Pew Research Center, 2012).

3. Altstadt, *Frustrated Democracy*, 196.

4. Shahin Abbasov, "Azerbaijan: Hijab Ban in Schools Fuels Debate in Baku on Role of Islam," Eurasianet, January 6, 2011; Altstadt, *Frustrated Democracy*, 213; Javid Zeynali, "Azerbaijan Strips 151 People of Citizenship for Fighting for Terrorist Organizations," APA News, September 12, 2017.

5. Grigor Atanesian, "Armenia's Revolutionary Government Steps Up Anti-corruption Purge," Eurasianet, June 19, 2018.

6. Berenice Magistretti, "Armenia: The Power of the Diaspora," *Repat Armenia*, June 6, 2015.

7. Thomas de Waal, "The Titan of Tbilisi," *Foreign Policy*, November 30, 2011.
8. Giorgi Lomsadze, "Georgia's Election Becomes Tom-and-Jerry Show," Eurasianet, October 7, 2016.
9. Ted Jonas, "Georgia: Time to Take Environmental Protection Seriously," *Civil Georgia*, February 14, 2018; Sopho Aptsiauri, "Practical or Destructive: Controversy Surrounds New Mountain Road in Georgia," OC Media, April 27, 2018.

Index